THE SECRET LIFE OF THE LAWMAN'S WIFE

THE SECRET LIFE OF THE LAWMAN'S WIFE

BJ Alderman

PRAEGER

Westport, Connecticut
London

Library of Congress Cataloging-in-Publication Data

Alderman, B. J., 1948–
The secret life of the lawman's wife / BJ Alderman.
p. cm.
Includes bibliographical references and index.
ISBN 0–275–99305–1 (alk. paper)
1. Sheriffs—Family relationships—United States—History. 2. Police spouses—Family relationships—United States—History. I. Title.
HV7979.A43 2007
363.28′20973—dc22 2006025926

British Library Cataloguing in Publication Data is available.

Library of Congress Catalog Card Number: 2006025926
ISBN: 0–275–99305–1

First published in 2007

Praeger Publishers, 88 Post Road West, Westport, CT 06881
An imprint of Greenwood Publishing Group, Inc.
www.praeger.com

Printed in the United States of America

The paper used in this book complies with the Permanent Paper Standard issued by the National Information Standards Organization (Z39.48–1984).

10 9 8 7 6 5 4 3 2 1

The author and publisher gratefully acknowledge permission to excerpt material from the following sources:

Rising correspondence. From the personal collection of Martha Chase Taylor, descendant of Josiah W. Kingsbury, brother of Sarah Kingsbury Rising.

Mary Richart Nelson Hall interview by Anne Dyni, 1988, OH 0400, Maria Rogers Oral History Program Collection, Carnegie Branch Library for Local History, Boulder, CO.

Excerpts from *The Poison Widow* by Linda S. Godfrey. Published by Big Earth Publishing. Reprinted with permission.

Excerpts from *The Texas Sheriff* by Thad Sitton. Copyright © 2000 by the University of Oklahoma Press, Norman, Publishing Division of the University. All rights reserved. Manufactured in the USA.

Excerpts from *Chief Justice Fred M. Vinson of Kentucky: A Political Biography* by James E. St. Clair and Linda C. Gugin. Published by University Press of Kentucky, 2002.

Mize Peters oral history conducted by James R. Fuchs, August 8 and 21, 1963 and March 3, 1964 at the Harry S. Truman Library, Independence, Missouri.

Roy Fling interview by Catherine Petito, 1990, OH 0485, Maria Rogers Oral History Program Collection, Carnegie Branch Library for Local History, Boulder, CO.

Dedicated to
Jim Alderman,
who first told me about the
Mrs. Sheriff in our own family tree

Contents

Preface		ix
Acknowledgments		xi
Introduction		xiii
1.	What's a Nice Girl Like You . . .?	1
2.	First Days on Duty	12
3.	Home Sweet Home	19
4.	Behind the Scenes	27
5.	Mrs. Sheriff's Hat Tree	39
6.	With a Little Help from My Trustees	53
7.	It Takes a County	62
8.	Wedding Bands and Badges	70
9.	With a Little Help from My Young'uns	76
10.	With a Pistol in Her (Apron) Pocket	84
11.	Here's the Grocery Bill, Honey	93

12. Loaves and Fishes 102

13. Bootlegging Babysitters, Straight Pins, and Whirligigs 107

14. Guests of the County 120

15. Pa, I Hear Them Sawing Again 132

16. Escape Encounters of the Fourth Kind 141

17. Nerves of Steel—or Not 153

18. An Unglamorous and Thankless Job 161

19. 'Til Death Do Us Part 172

20. The Final Chapter 184

Appendix 1. Jailhouse Family Members Who Provided Information 191

Appendix 2. Alphabetical Listing of Jailhouse Wives 194

Appendix 3. Jailhouse Wives by State and County 198

Notes 203

Bibliography and Recommended Reading 211

Index 215

Preface

During the Victorian era, on both sides of the Atlantic, etiquette dictated that a woman be addressed by the position of her husband, if he had "a position." Therefore, the wife of the doctor was formally addressed as Mrs. Doctor So-and-so. She who married a professor became Mrs. Professor So-and-so. In like manner, the wife of a sheriff became known by the title of Mrs. Sheriff.

Since the spring of 1998, on behalf of my family and then as an interesting research subject, I've been delving into the life of my great-great-grandparents, Sheriff James G. (JG) and Kate Weakley. Since 2002, I've been most fortunate in publishing articles about JG's life in various publications.

When it occurred to me to write something about Kate's life, I hit upon the idea of a piece about the four years she spent in the county seat, serving alongside JG as Mrs. Sheriff Weakley. What did a sheriff's wife do exactly? The results of my preliminary research, though sparse, proved so intriguing that it was used in an article published online in the *American Western Magazine*. The editor, Taylor Fogarty, generously agreed to forward responses to my request to hear from families with a Mrs. Sheriff in their past. I also directed to this site everyone I contacted during a nationwide search so they would understand the type of information in which I was interested.

Jailhouse wives represent almost every type of American woman. There were saints, long-suffering martyrs, and sinners; those who bore no children and those with as many as ten; those who were generous to a fault, or immensely practical; and even a few self-absorbed individuals who didn't really function as their husbands' helpmates. They were farmers, teachers, businesswomen, mothers, musicians, community-minded, and married to men who served as sheriff or jailor. All of them were educated women even during the earliest years after the founding of this nation. They had to be because it was these women who kept the records of incarceration and release plus their own boarding records used to collect payment from the county for feeding the inmates.

If you know similar stories about a Mrs. Sheriff in your family, please share them with me via my publisher. I confess that I've fallen in love with all of the women in this book. I'm very proud to be the one telling their long overdue story.

Ms. BJ Alderman
Kansas City, Missouri
April 10, 2006

Acknowledgments

I wish to thank the generous families who lived the life described in this book, and shared their history. Your enthusiasm for the project was the engine that kept it moving for three years.

Much appreciation also goes to all of the staff at the hundreds of county historical societies and old jail museums without whom this book would not have been possible. I hope that each and every reader will support his or her own local historical society with donations of money, time, family information and family pictures. Future historians may find your contributions invaluable.

I also wish to thank my dear friend, Mary Margaret Wisler, the cheerleader that every writer should have every step of the way. Thanks to Charlie Pinzino, who edits, with velvet gloves, everything I write for publication.

Speaking of editors, a most deeply felt thank-you to Elizabeth Demers, Praeger's editor for this project, who understood from the beginning that this was a fun project and an entertaining popular history instead of something stodgy.

Finally, a thank-you to my family for their enthusiasm and encouragement. This was a labor of love buoyed up by your love.

Introduction

In England, the county sheriff reported directly to the ruling monarch and was recognized as the highest-ranking individual for each county. The American colonies imported the British system of justice and, like so much else, adapted it to their own needs as they evolved into Americans. Prior to the Revolution, county jails were primarily used to house debtors and those awaiting trial. Convicted criminals suffered some form of public corporal punishment such as flogging, hanging, branding, time spent in the stocks or sometimes in a cage on the courthouse square.

In those days, justice was swift and a suspect stood before a judge hours after being caught. Juries could be rounded up in short order and jury trials did not take days, weeks or months. Punishment took place immediately after the sentence was read. My own ancestor who settled in the Pennsylvania Colony in the 1730s, the first of many James Weakleys in our family tree, is on record as having served on two juries who voted punishments of flogging and time in the stocks.

It wasn't long before the English system of corporal punishment lost favor. Even before the Revolution, the concept of punishment and justice had begun to change in the colonies. After the Revolution—as individual states had an opportunity to settle down to business—the highest-ranking county official remained the sheriff. Jails became mom-and-pop operations; were purposefully designed to be homey. Living quarters for the sheriff or jailor and his family were built near the courthouse, rooms were attached to house inmates, only some of which were cells. The cells held short-term convicted criminals, while debtors and those awaiting trial were confined in larger accommodations. If someone was found guilty of a lesser charge, he might serve thirty to sixty days in the county facility rather than be transferred to prison. Over time, the definition of "short-term" changed and prisoners who had a year or less to serve would sit out their sentences in the county jail. In some counties, prisoners had the choice of where to serve their time if their sentence involved a year or less.

Not all counties created such a system, but for the majority that did, the term "jailhouse" held a larger meaning. County jails were designed to provide an atmosphere of home: families moved in, family members cooked for the prisoners, cared for their needs, and kept them from escaping. Pets roamed freely between jail and house, children helped around the place and many befriended the inmates.

Until the twentieth century, the nation's population was not mobile for the most part, so most county prisoners were known to the sheriffing family. Those who could be trusted not to escape earned the position of trustee. Often housed in cells that were locked only at night, if at all, trustees were released from their cells to help with the wide variety of chores, often unsupervised. Some labored around the jail, in the courthouse, on county farms, or the children's home [orphanage].

Normal, everyday citizens of the county took on the burdens and joys of facilitating this system of punishment. In doing so, they presented a socially acceptable face to their communities while engaging in a secret life of caring for the insane, the drug addicts, hardened criminals, and men intent on gaining their freedom at any cost.

Entire extended families devoted themselves to running the jail for only the pay that came to the sheriff and jailor, plus food, and in many cases, a roof over their heads. Everyone, from the youngest to the oldest, kept what went on behind the jailhouse door to themselves. If they didn't, the sheriff might not be reelected. This concept carried over even decades after the family left the county facility. During the interview process for this book, some former jailhouse wives would not share stories of escape attempts that took place thirty or more years ago. Making the sheriff look good to his fellow citizens by keeping escape attempts to themselves and the jail functioning effectively was the goal of each family enterprise. That goal was impressed on even the youngest members of the family, many of whom found life behind steel doors endlessly fascinating.

Besides the county, others who used the jail for holding prisoners included federal district courts, federal officers transferring prisoners from place to place, and city law enforcement—especially with regard to housing female prisoners. Often there was a city jail and a county jail in a county seat, but female prisoners held by either agency were housed in the county facility. Not only could the women be segregated from the men in the often larger county jail but there was also a matron in residence . . . usually the wife of the sheriff or jailor.

The mom-and-pop jail was the norm after the founding of this country until the widespread transition to a "more professional" approach to jails in the second half of the twentieth century. For most counties, a period of transition took place as professional staff were hired to supply the labor that once was provided free of charge by the wives and children, the parents and siblings of the sitting sheriff.

The attitude of most women who viewed themselves as their husbands' helpmates was not one of subservience. In the words of my dear friend, Mary Margaret

Wisler: "I see myself as his helpmate, we work together well as a team. But I don't ever feel beneath him, subservient. Ha ha. Imagine me that . . . I dare you!"

The reader will find that this book is written with reference to county names. The modern reader, like the author, may need an atlas to identify the geographic location of the counties named. This would not have been so a century ago. Counties *were* the geographic location for most Americans living on their farms. Rural mailing addresses consisted of a name, a county, and a state: Mrs. John Doe, Labette County, Kansas. That was all it took.

As you read this book about the mom in the mom-and-pop county jail and her family, consider the context in which you find the anecdotes. This is not a collection of biographies nor an intellectual narrative that would make an academician proud. While the history is sound and the facts are accurate, the text is written with a general readership in mind.

This is an informative piece about the day-to-day lives of Any Jailor's Family. What if there was a hypothetical family, a normal everyday family like your own, who was mulling over the idea of serving their county as sheriff during the era of the mom-and-pop jails. What if that hypothetical family wanted to make an informed decision? Perhaps they would invite those who knew the life to a gathering to discuss one aspect of the life and then another. Our hypothetical family might ask, "what did you do to get elected?" or "what was it like the first day at the jail?" The experienced families might respond by sharing their own stories and memories until our hypothetical family built up a picture of what elections and first days might be like if they ran and won. That's what this book is, the answer to my own question about what might life have been like for Mrs. Sheriff Kate Weakley.

Contrary to convention, given names are used throughout the text for two reasons: so the lawman and his wife are not confused as they might be if each is known only by their surnames; and more importantly, to preserve the informality that comes with such an intimate exploration inside the heart of these families. Use of surnames inappropriately creates a distance when speaking of those who have so generously invited us, for the first time, for a look behind the scenes into their previously secret life.

In addition, quotes from family members are not footnoted. They answered a questionnaire, participated in telephone interviews, wrote letters and supplied memoirs. A table has been included in the Appendix denoting who provided information for specific families and by which method.

I sincerely hope that the families who lived the life will enjoy comparing their unique experiences with those of other sheriffing families, and that "civilian" readers will come away with an awareness of what any sheriffing family might have experienced in any county over the course of three centuries.

The historian Kathryn Hughes, stated that "women's experience, along with that of others who often go unheard—children, marginal men, people whom history placed at the scene quite by chance—are shown as being entirely integral to the story"[1] of recorded history. Kathryn was speaking about why history needs to

Prior to the American Revolution, Amherst became the county seat for Hillsborough County, New Hampshire. The village square contained the courthouse, jail, pillory and whipping post. Those judged as guilty of various crimes were bound to the steel ring in the center of this stone and publicly flogged for their transgressions against society. (Postcard from author's collection.)

diversify in its scope. Within these pages, you will hear from or about each of those groups—women, children, marginal men, people whom history placed at the scene quite by chance—as they educate our hypothetical family and you, the reader, about the secret life of the lawman's family. I hope you enjoy this journey into a family lifestyle to which most of us never gave thought.

1

What's a Nice Girl Like You . . . ?

> Follow recipes carefully. Measure accurately. Season carefully. Always taste food before sending it to the cell block.[1]
>
> —From the 1961 *Handbook of Jail Food Service*

> One day, after cooking and tasting food she'd prepared for inmates of the Oswego County, New York, jail, Eileen Chesbro took her meals to the women's jail. She unlocked the heavy steel door to their common area. Once she'd pushed the door open about an inch and a half, Eileen caught sight of a woman standing behind it, holding a chair over her head. It appeared that the prisoner was completely prepared to bring the chair down on Eileen's head as she cleared the threshold. Eileen stopped. In a firm voice she instructed the woman to put down the chair or she was going to lose all privileges. With the element of surprise gone, the inmate complied. During her interview for this book, Eileen laughed as she reported, "I closed the door again and leaned against the wall, panting heavily while my knees banged together for quite some time."
>
> —About Eileen Chesbro, who served alongside Sheriff Ray T. Chesbro from 1973 to 1977

On October 22, 1893, Mrs. Sheriff Jennie Krider sat down at her desk and penned a letter to her brother-in-law and his wife. A widow with two sons, Jennie had married Sheriff Charles A. Krider a few years earlier and they lived in the Stark County, Ohio, jail family quarters. By the time she wrote the following letter, Jennie and Charles had become the proud parents of a toddler named Ruth. While appearing extraordinary to the modern reader, Jennie's letter makes mention of facts that the reader will come to understand were typical in the life of a jailhouse wife during the long era of the mom-and-pop jail.

Brother and Sister,
We have just finished our dinner work. Charley has gone to Millport and as Baby is asleep, I am sitting here alone, thinking of you, I thought I would write! Charley received your letter some time ago. I do not know if he answered it or not, he is very busy now and so am I. We have thirty-nine in our Jail now. I have one large girl and one small one. With our own family we have forty-seven to cook, wash and mend for. So you see we have our hands full. We baked eighty large loaves of Bread last week and it will take the same this week. We quilted a small quilt last week for the crib. This week I want to make me a dress if we don't have too much company, had company every day last week. I made fifty-one yards of rag carpet. Just got it home last Monday. Sewed all the rags myself. It is nice. Wish you could see it. . . . Charley has sprained his back. He can't get around very good. He took Mrs. David Oberlin to the asylum and lifted too heavy. She was very bad. I tell you, there is a great many hard things to see here. . . . It is time to get supper and milk the cow. I churn over five pounds of butter a week besides what milk we use of our Jersey cow. Charley thinks it is the best butter he ever ate. . . . Write soon, Jennie Krider.

From this letter, now in the author's collection, we learn that Mrs. Krider lived in the family quarters with her husband, their daughter, and Jennie's two sons. She hired two helpers, both girls, one older than the other. As we will see later in this book, it would not have been unusual for the girls to live in the family quarters.

The letter also reveals that Jennie had been caring for an insane woman, Mrs. David Oberlin, between the time that she was legally declared insane and a bed was made available at the Insane Asylum. She mentions how Charles transferred Mrs. Oberlin to the other facility and strained his back in the process.

Nothing about this letter is remarkable except that it still exists. Once we understand the role of the sheriff's or jailor's wife and family in the care of inmates and the performance of his administrative duties, we will see how typical this letter of Jennie Krider's turns out to be.

HOW A JAILHOUSE TEAM WAS BORN

To understand the life of any given jailhouse wife, whether she be married to the sheriff or the jailor, we must start at the beginning. As noted in the Introduction, we will explore the myriad aspects of tending to inmates through the stories of the women and children. In this first chapter, the ways that women found themselves taking up the responsibilities of assisting their sheriffing husbands will be explored. How did they come to tie on the county apron when their husbands pinned on their star?

Like most of the families starting their terms of office after winning at the polls, we civilians have no idea about how to tend to prisoners or what the duties of the sheriff's office entailed. Some men took up the star as an extension of their careers in law enforcement, and were not so completely in the dark. Others, quite frankly, didn't have a clue where the decision would lead. But once this course was set, wives, children, and extended family members embarked upon a grand adventure and entered into a double life.

The sheriff, paid for his services by the county, hired a live-in deputy who became the jailor if the budget was sufficient. The families of both men served without pay, and without their fellow citizens becoming aware of all that was required to carry out the myriad responsibilities at the jailhouse. Many of the participants interviewed for this book emphasized the importance of everyone in the family learning discretion if the sheriff or jailor wanted to keep his job for more than one term.

The personalities that women brought to their jobs as helpmate to the lawman varied as widely as the tasks required of them. Some were gentle, refined women like Mae Brown of Pacific County, Washington, who'd come west from New England to teach during the second half of the nineteenth century. Mae was described by Rod Bunnell, her grandson, as "petite, dainty, reserved, and interested in things of beauty and of the intellect—what she would have called a 'person of refinement.' " Others were tough old birds like the unnamed Georgia sheriff's wife who reportedly argued with her husband until a fist fight broke out and the couple thrashed each other "all over the cotton field until both became too exhausted to continue. You bet she could run a tough jail in her husband's absence," reported former ATF agent John Guy.

As a teenager, Nadine Alexander thumbed through a movie magazine, stopped at a picture of Douglas Fairbanks, Sr., with Mary Pickford, and fell in love with another man in the photo. While traveling as a dancer a few years later, Nadine stepped off a ship in Hawaii, met the man in that photograph, and married him. In doing so, she became a sheriff's wife.

Nadine's husband, Duke Kahanamoku, is best known to the world as the father of modern surfing, a multimedaled Olympic champion and an actor in thirty movies during the 1920s. At the time they met, Duke was in the midst of serving thirteen consecutive terms as sheriff on the Big Island. He won election from 1934 until Hawaiian statehood, even when he didn't campaign. Nadine and Duke married in 1940 when Nadine discovered that Duke "was more wonderful than I had imagined."[2] They served the citizens of their island until 1962.

Sophie Alberding, unlike Nadine Alexander, did not take to the idea of marrying a sheriff. An 1882 visitor to Lincoln County, New Mexico, Sophie found herself central to a plot hatched by her host, Captain Lea, and the famous Pat Garrett. The men devised a plan to marry Sophie to their friend, John Poe, but proved rather inept at matchmaking. When presented with their proposition, Sophie exploded in anger, demanding to know if they thought she was "one of your prize short-horns?"[3] Sophie retreated to her guestroom "stunned that outsiders—even so good a friend as Captain Lea—should undertake to choose a husband for me. As a civilized woman, I felt that it was my affair, that I had the inalienable right to pick my own man."[4] Lea and Garrett proved better at the match than the matchmaking. Sophie married John the next year, right after he won his election as sheriff.

LEADING THE DOUBLE LIFE

In 1785, travel for county business took many hours or days by horse over rutted roads often mired in mud. Citizens coming to a county seat required a place to sleep and eat. The residents of Tolland, Connecticut, and other communities across the nation wisely built a county hotel. In Tolland, theirs was known as *The County House*. A courthouse, jail, and livery stable completed the county seat complex.

The sheriff could run the hotel and the jail, or hire a jailor and his family to do so. The wife of the chosen party ran the hotel, supervised meal preparation for inmates, "spent her days in the dining room, the milk room and the laundry, all without pay."[5]

By the 1880s, the Tolland County Jail had been rebuilt twice and finally attached to the hotel to facilitate simultaneous care of guests and inmates. A cell for female inmates had been added on the floor above the men's jail during the last build. That cell was reached by way of a staircase located in the men's bull pen.

One morning while court was in session, the sheriff's wife organized breakfast not only for her family and numerous prisoners but also the twelve men of the jury, several lawyers, and the judge. One of the prisoners, whose case was being heard at the time, had been incarcerated for fatally shooting her husband. Because the inmate was female, the jailhouse wife also tended to her needs as part of her duties as jail matron for women and juveniles. As a kindness, the matron unlocked the accused woman's cell door when she brought her breakfast every morning and left the door open during daylight hours to ease the burden of the woman's incarceration.

While those involved in deciding the woman's guilt or innocence fortified themselves with a hearty breakfast in The County House dining room, the accused woman sat in her cell quietly fashioning a noose from strips of her bedding. Believing that the case was going against her, the prisoner walked with her noose through the open cell door and made her way to the staircase that led to the bull pen. Once there, she proceeded to try to hang herself.

The suicide attempt failed. Male prisoners made a racket to attract someone in authority and the woman was cut down before she died. The jailhouse wife continued to tend to her dining room full of diners, her guests who were blissfully unaware of the suicidal prisoner. At the same time, she also ministered to her desperate female inmate.

While the last of the coffee was drunk and the last of the porridge and bread with butter was downed by those on their way to the courtroom, not one jury member, judge, or lawyer was allowed to become aware of the terrible scenario being played out on the other side of the dining room wall. The sheriff and his family successfully kept the entire event under wraps.

This story dramatically illustrates the double life lived by jailhouse families. Whether it be 1800 or 1960, to all outward appearances the sheriff's wife was a typical woman of her period. Her children attended school and played with their friends like any other kids. What the community didn't know is that she and her children performed chores like none dreamt of by their friends and neighbors.

YOU WANT TO DO WHAT, HONEY?

What set of circumstances led to a family standing at the jailhouse door? How did the women included in this book step across that threshold and come to work in and around the jail?

For a variety of reasons, men have sought the responsibilities that come with the star. Some husbands were appointed, some elected. The first sheriff in the American colonies, William Stone, was appointed by the king of England in 1634 in Accomac County in the Virginia Colony. Sheriff Stone didn't appear to function much as sheriff, and is often discounted by historians. Three years later, James Baldridge, also appointed by the king, took up his post in St. Mary's County, Massachusetts Colony. He is often credited as the first functioning sheriff in the American colonies.

James Baldridge's wife, Dorothy, appears to have been a feisty woman—a characteristic that served many a sheriff's wife well through the centuries. Long after she and James quit Massachusetts for Virginia, she is recorded to have sued one of her fellow citizens, a man. Unfortunately, no record exists that reports the outcome.

Law enforcement, like firefighting, tends to run in families. King George instituted that tradition early in America's history. James and Dorothy were replaced a year later by his brother, Thomas, and wife, Grace Beman Baldridge. Thomas served until 1641.

Many men began their careers when they accepted the sheriff's offer of a job as deputy. Other women's husbands started in law enforcement on the local level, winning the office of Constable or Town Marshal. Such was the case with August and Rose Singler. In 1903, August and Rose emigrated to Oregon. After selling sewing machines for a while, August served four years as Constable of Medford.

August decided to further his law enforcement career by running for sheriff of Jackson County, Oregon, in 1912. By this time, he and Rose had produced seven children. During his campaign for sheriff, Rose was pregnant with their eighth. He is remembered as being the first lawman in the area to use bloodhounds to search for criminals. Always progressive, he was the first Oregon lawman to learn the new art of fingerprinting, having picked it up while picking up a wanted man in Sacramento, California.

Unlike August Singler, John Poe required some persuasion to run for sheriff. While John courted Sophie Alberding, influential citizens of Lincoln County, New Mexico, courted John. They wanted him to put his name on the ballot because of his extensive law enforcement background. John had seen service as deputy in Wheeler County, Texas, during the roughest days in the panhandle. He'd also served as a deputy U.S. marshal. John worked for the Canadian River Cattlemen's Association where he proved instrumental in putting a stop to extensive cattle rustling that raged across the range. It was during that service that John hunted down the remnants of Billy the Kid's gang in 1881, after The Kid shot Sheriff Brady in Lincoln County, New Mexico, while breaking out of jail. It was no wonder that the folks of Lincoln County wanted John as badly as he wanted Sophie.

Some years earlier in Albany County, Wyoming, Malcolm Campbell took on the responsibilities of deputy at the request of the sheriff. All we know of his wife, Priscilla, at this point in his career is that they'd been married for three years and she moved their household to the county seat. In 1888, Malcolm won election to the top office in Converse County, Wyoming, and Priscilla took up her job of inmate care to go along with that of raising children and tending to the needs of her community.

On the other side of the nation, Alice Adkins Ketchum found herself in the same position as Priscilla Campbell. In 1894, Alice and her husband floated down a West Virginia river from Lincoln to Wayne County. John Ketchum, a farmer and timberman, eventually found that growing a family provided incentive to increase the family income. Shortly after 1900, John took up the position of deputy to help keep food on the table. He later added the title of Jailor to his resume and the family moved from farm to family quarters in the jail.

Economic pressure proved to be a strong motivator in the histories of many families included in this research. It drove young Ed and Mary Ann Darrow to Powell County, Montana, after he graduated college in the early 1950s. Staying with Mary Ann's cousin in Deer Lodge while looking for work, Ed was asked if he'd fill in as undersheriff for a couple of months. Sheriff Ellsworth expected a new deputy to report for work at the end of that time. The new guy never showed. Ed's two-month temp job ended thirty years later after serving as undersheriff, sheriff and U.S. deputy marshal.

The reasons for taking on the role of deputy were often economic, but economic incentive was sometimes motivated by matters of the heart. This was true for JB Ross, Tennessee farmer turned miner. Exploring out West with gold and silver in mind, JB became discouraged after several claims failed. He grudgingly surrendered to fate and turned his face to the east, resigned to returning to the family farm in Tennessee. Fate had something a little different in mind. In Independence, Missouri, JB met a local woman, Ella Thomas, and so ended his trek home.

JB wanted to marry Ella and fulfill his destiny as a Tennessee farmer. Ella refused to leave Independence. Her father's recent death left Ella as the sole support for her mother. A college graduate, Ella earned her own way by teaching piano lessons. So as not to lose the love of his life, JB found that "there was always a need, however, for a sturdy man who knew how to keep the peace. He was offered a job as deputy county marshal and accepted it."[6]

Eventually, the Ross family consisted of JB, Ella, son Charlie, and Ella's mother, Fannie Rogers Thomas. The four of them moved into the county jail in 1884 when JB won election to the office of county marshal. They lived there for ten years while the Ross family grew.

Once husbands found themselves suited to a badge and their wives discovered they could at least tolerate the life, a couple often sought advancement. In 1920s Greenwood County, South Carolina, Ella Mae White's husband, Cal, took on the responsibilities of serving as deputy sheriff and as the county's first motorcycle officer. Bundled up against the elements, Ella sat holding their two children in the sidecar while Cal drove eighteen miles to her "mother's home with the wind blowing in our faces." Cal's long service as deputy helped him win election to the top office twenty years later. By then, Ella and Cal were the proud parents of six children, including Clemson University's star quarterback, Harvey White.

Dedication to law enforcement and augmenting a family's income were common reasons to take up sheriffing. Another Greenwood County, South Carolina, family took on the role of jailor for a different reason. Vernice Yates Cooper's husband pursued that position in order to get off the night shift duty he'd drawn as deputy. Sonny succeeded in 1965, and the family moved into the jail family quarters.

A year later in McNairy County, Tennessee, another southern woman's husband pursued the position of sheriff after serving on a local police force. Pauline Mullins Pusser's husband, Buford, decided someone had to clean out the corrupt sheriff's office. Buford campaigned on the platform that "if you elect me, I will clean up the corruption and violence that has made the state line notorious."[7] We will see over the course of several chapters how his election took its toll on Pauline and changed the family forever. They were not unique.

JUMPING IN WITH BOTH FEET

While we are exploring how jailhouse wives found themselves stepping behind barred doors, it seems appropriate to look at families where pop donned the sheriff's badge without any previous training for anyone in the family. Francis Sinclair farmed and augmented their income by helping at the local grain elevator while Elma farmed and worked full time in a medical facility. "One day, during a discussion with friends, it came out that there was going to be an opening for sheriff. The friends tried to talk Francis into running. He said he didn't want to, and besides he couldn't afford to campaign. The friends all said they would put up the money for him to run. So he did, and won." Francis and Elma took office in 1960. Elma continued working full time at the nursing home while also cooking three meals a day for her family and inmates of the Hodgeman County, Kansas, Jail. She also functioned as the matron and janitor for the jail.

In 1827, Phebe Lindsley's husband decided to run for sheriff of Morris County, New Jersey, without the benefit of previous law enforcement experience. His career as a carpenter was no deterrent to success as Joe and Phebe took on the tasks of county administration and running the jail.

Like Joe Lindsley forty-five years earlier, another carpenter brought his family to live among farmers and Kansas pioneers after the Civil War. Taking up his free

Kansas homestead in 1872, JG Weakley became sheriff of Russell County three years later. With four young children at home and one on the way, Kate Weakley uprooted her household yet again in 1875 and moved into the county seat. There she tied the county apron over her expanding waistline and began her work for the community.

Kate Weakley's husband had earned his homestead in Kansas after serving in the 3rd Pennsylvania Cavalry during the Civil War. Veterans, used to discipline and firearms, returned from their wars and some ran for the office of sheriff. Marian Edinger, at the age of 25, donned the McHenry County, Illinois, apron in 1923, after the American Legion Post encouraged her husband to run. "The Company G boys sponsored his candidacy." Neither the Weakleys nor the Edingers had any experience with politics, public service, or law enforcement prior to running for the top office in their counties.

Amos Ward, a World War II veteran, "came home one day and said he wanted to run" and asked his wife, Irene, what she thought. She enthusiastically gave his idea a thumbs up. He'd returned from the war with the rank of staff sergeant and his friends thought he'd make a good sheriff "because of his expert shooting and ability to handle a gun." Ironically, when he took office, he didn't wear a gun. He had one handy just in case, but rarely had a need to use it in the thirty years that Amos and Irene served Rogers County, Oklahoma.

Like Saul on the road to Damascus, law enforcement can come like a bolt out of the blue. Some families had just embarked upon new business ventures when they "got the call." In 1956, Dolores Lee and her husband opened a motel, gas station, and store in Van Buren County, Iowa. Out of the blue, the sheriff asked Orville to come on board as his deputy. Life got a bit busy while building up the new business and also learning something about law enforcement. All of that paled in comparison to the next surprise. Orville's boss suddenly resigned just months into Orville's first year. Orville agreed to the appointment to fill out the unexpired term and then ran for the office at the next election. He won. The motel/gas station/store went by the wayside and Dolores turned her hand full time to inmate care and raising her sons.

Likewise, in 1930s Antrim County, Michigan, Maud Tanner worked alongside her father, helping with his responsibilities as postmaster. Maud's husband purchased a meat market and a new home despite the Great Depression. In the memoir written by Maud fifty years later, she noted that

> on the night of November 9, 1937, Howard and I were in Medalies Store picking out a new suit for him. During the transaction, Sid [store owner] said "I suppose we'll have a new Sheriff tomorrow." Howard pricked up his ears. He said "I'd be interested in that job." Sid and I encouraged him. The Judge of Probate, the Prosecuting Attorney and the County Clerk appoint a replacement when an office is vacated. Judge Severance and Prosecuting Attorney Wellman were in Wellman's Mancelona office that evening. Howard went up there and applied for the Sheriff's job. The next day he was appointed Sheriff of Antrim County. On November 11, 1937, he took office at the old jailhouse in Bellaire.

The Tanners went in to buy a suit for Howard to wear in his fledgling business and came home with a new life's work.

SOMETIMES A CAMPAIGN IS IN ORDER

When a man ran for county sheriff, he advertised in the newspaper and took advantage of any public event that came along to place his name before the voters. Like Geraldine Spielman of Dubuque County, Iowa, most candidates' wives in the late 1950s attended public functions with their husbands. Geraldine typified a sheriff candidate's spouse. Seen as supporting her husband by attending events with him, she never spoke in public for his election. She did not hostess teas nor in any way put herself forward. This experience was all about her husband and his ability to serve their county.

During the second decade of the twentieth century in Coleman County, Texas, Emma Banister's husband ran for office by attending box suppers, ice cream parties, "speakies," and rallies at all the county communities. John campaigned by buying from the women of the county anything that they were selling such as eggs, handwork, dairy products, or canned garden produce. He'd previously earned his living as a Texas Ranger and successfully pursued the office of sheriff in order to settle down with his growing family.

Bessie and Harry Kelly of Texas County, Missouri, began each campaign for his reelection during the Fourth of July picnic season. For four months, the couple attended barn dances and other social events so Harry could speak with their fellow citizens about voting for him. His first run for the office of sheriff took place in 1924.

Twenty years after the Kelly family proved successful in their first run for the sheriff's title, Dorothy Everson accompanied her husband to Boulder County, Colorado, dinners and meetings during the first year of World War II to campaign for sheriff. Dorothy's daughter, Shirley, reported that "they'd hand out personalized match book covers and dad usually gave out star pins with his name on it."

In 1912, between the beginning of the campaign and the primary in Jackson County, Oregon, August Singler mailed postcards to the voters that included a picture of himself with his entire family on one side and the announcement of his candidacy against a very popular Democrat incumbent on the other. Just after the primary, August assisted Rose in the birth of their eighth child. August updated the postcard by having a picture of the newest member of the family inserted into the existing photograph and he printed another batch when he won the primary. This must have warmed many a voter's heart. August surprised everyone by winning the election.

Shortly after taking on the position of undersheriff of Powell County, Montana, Ed Darrow found himself appointed sheriff when the position suddenly became vacant. He liked it. He and Mary Ann decided he'd run during the next election. Ed remembers that "as a family during the campaign we attended many church suppers and became quite well known throughout the county."

August Singler's revised campaign postcard sent after the birth of their last child. His attention to detail and devotion to family helped him win the office of sheriff from a popular incumbent in Jackson County, Oregon. (Courtesy of Diane Walker's family archives.)

Most sheriffing families believed that they campaigned every day of their tenure by effective performance of their responsibilities, so campaign season remained largely uneventful. This was true for Dolores Lee's family. Their son, Larry, recalled that his mother accompanied Orville to events all over Van Buren County, Iowa, but neither parent made speeches. The boys helped pass out combs, pencils, and other useful items imprinted with Orville's name when they attended parades.

Campaign workers of an unexpected nature cropped up in many elections. Those who found themselves incarcerated on a frequent basis for minor offenses campaigned on behalf of the candidate whose wife was the best cook. If the incumbent's wife made a tasty supper, those who were most likely to partake of her efforts took up the sheriff's reelection cause. If the candidate's wife was known to lack in culinary skill, that element of the population campaigned vigorously for the opponent in hopes of better meals when they found themselves with a county spoon in their hands.

Unless there was a controversy, electing a sheriff generally proved to be pretty straightforward. Controversy reared its ugly head in 1875 Kansas when Alexander Ramsey campaigned for sheriff of Ellis County. There was a hue and cry from his opponent due to the fact that Alex had taken to "living in sin" with Mary Walsh, wife of a Hays saloon keeper. For reasons unknown, Mary left her husband and took her son to Fort Hays. Having worked as a laundress while living with her husband, she took up the same position at the Fort to support herself and her son. While there, she began a relationship with Sheriff Ramsey. She and her son then moved into Ramsey's home. "A friendly justice of the peace backdated a marriage certificate for the couple but nothing could change the fact that Alex and Mary

Ramsey told the world that they were married before John D. Walsh secured his divorce from her in the District Court."[8] The voters forgave all and reelected the well-liked Alex as their sheriff and Mary became Ellis County's Mrs. Sheriff.

Now that we have seen how our hypothetical jailhouse family might find themselves about to cross the threshold to living a double life, in the next chapter we will investigate what transpired just after they took the next few steps through the jailhouse door. It was one thing to be married to a lawman and another to move your children into the jailhouse and live with prisoners on the other side of the kitchen wall.

—— 2 ——

First Days on Duty

All walls, floors, ceiling, windows, cabinets, etc., should be cleaned regularly and thoroughly. It is especially important to keep after corners and those places under or behind pieces of equipment.

—1961 *Handbook of Jail Food Service*

"My mother did her ironing in the room just outside the jail door. She overheard a plot to escape by attacking my father. There was a heated argument [among the inmates] and a near riot. She called the State Police, loaded the gun, and sat outside the door until the police came and Dad returned from wherever he was." This took place at the Tolland County [CT] Jail.

—About Mabel Cook who served alongside Deputy Jailor George Cook from 1943 to 1947, reported by their daughter, Barbara.

Few counties burdened their budgets by paying full-time deputies when there were able-bodied sheriffs with wives and children used to hard work on their farms. Once campaigns ended and ballots were counted, someone won the position of sheriff. For most families during this predominantly rural era in our nation's history, winning involved a move into town. For many, that meant moving into the county jail's family quarters.

It was normal in most counties to provide the one in charge of the jail with housing in or near the jail. This not only kept the lawman close to his charges but offset the low pay. Many families rented their farms or homes in town to another family for the duration of their service.

Even the relatively simple process of moving to take up a jail life could be fraught with difficulties. In Boulder County, Colorado, the Richart family prepared to move into the family quarters when George won his election in 1931. A week before the move, the courthouse burned. Unfortunately, the courthouse contained the jail and sheriff's quarters.

The county commissioners quickly found a building on Walnut Street for a temporary jail but it didn't come with space suitable for the family. Mildred unpacked everything and the Richart family stayed home.

Over the course of his first year in office, George battled bootleggers, illegal gamblers, and the county commissioners over new courthouse plans. The commissioners thought the new jail should not include quarters for the sheriff's family. They argued that a jail was no place for a family with six children. George insisted that housing was part of the compensation of any Boulder sheriff no matter how many children he had. In the end, George won. The Richarts moved into the new courthouse family quarters as soon as the building opened for business.

In Fillmore County, Minnesota, another sheriff's family suffered a temporary delay in moving. On December 30, 1958, Heidi Haugerud came into the world stillborn and her mother, Helen, required a hospital stay to recover. At the turn of the year, Sheriff Neil Haugerud took up his new position and divided his time among sheriff's office, county rounds, taking care of their children while continuing to pack, and visits to his wife in the hospital. The outgoing sheriff continued feeding prisoners and answering the phone. That helped. The Haugerud family was finally able to move to the jailhouse in late February.

HURRY UP AND PACK

In some counties, the newly elected sheriff took office as soon as the vote was certified, usually just days after voting took place. In Coleman County, Texas, John Banister brought his youngest children into town as soon as his position was certified in 1914. His wife, Emma, and their oldest daughter, Leona, stayed home to pack the household. They followed a couple of weeks later. Leona noted that "it was after dark and getting cold, that night in late November, 1914, when Mama and I reached the Coleman jail. We stopped at the iron fence on the east side of the courthouse, not knowing where to go."[1]

In 1937, when Antrim County, Michigan's Maud Tanner expressed her enthusiasm in the tailor shop over Howard's inspiration to take up sheriffing, she mistakenly assumed that Howard would commute the twelve miles from their new house. She'd envisioned that she'd continue helping at the post office, and young Howard would continue at his current school. "It didn't work out that way." Instead, Sheriff Tanner moved into the living quarters on November 11, 1937, a day after his appointment. "He slept on a cot" in otherwise bare rooms. Maud moved furniture and household belongings two days later. "Fortunately there were no prisoners in the jail. I hired a strong Bohemian girl, Florence Kratervelt, to help me in the house and cook for the prisoners" while Maud commuted for several weeks. By the time she'd hired and trained her replacement in the post office, her son's term at his Mancelona school ended. He started ninth grade the following year in Bellaire.

COLD ENOUGH FOR YA?

Winter weather often worked against families who made the move to town at the beginning of the year instead of at the end of the election. Betty Vinson recalled what conditions were like in Lyon County, Iowa. "It had been snowing off and on for two weeks in December 1968. We moved to the jail on January 2, 1969. The moving men were concerned they would get stuck at our front door, the snow was so heavy." With the first signs of spring, all of that snow melted, creating a disaster requiring Sheriff Vinson's attention. "We had flooding in our river. It was Easter Sunday when the calls from the farmers and truckers began, telling us of the areas that were in trouble. Of course, the Sheriff was out and he had no deputy at the time and I was the sole radio operator. Also, I had a prisoner to feed. It was nerve wracking for the entire day and I was brand new to this life style. At midnight, the sheriff came in to eat and get some rest—and we waited for the new day when the office secretary came in from the far end of the county to handle the telephone and radio for the office."

Sixty years earlier, four-year-old Lulu Knapp's father won the position of Griggs County sheriff in North Dakota. Lulu recalled that "one stormy day we were loaded into a sleigh: my mother, brother, Papa's sister and [her] husband, and their little girl, Grace, and Papa. Papa had nailed canvas over the top of a sleigh box and we had a lantern in there to keep us warm. We were moving to Cooperstown to live in the basement of the courthouse."[2]

Lulu's mother, Mamie, incapacitated by a fall some years earlier and unable to walk, utilized the talents of a housekeeper to take care of domestic chores. Amanda Russell moved with the family to the jailhouse and stood in for Mamie as needed. Mamie functioned as a capable administrator, while the housekeeper performed the physical tasks of running the home and the jail. Those tasks included cooking for and tending to the needs of the inmates.

Marjorie Price of Randolph County, Missouri, recalled that she was happy her husband won his election at the end of the 1960s "because he wanted the job so badly. But I hated to leave my nice home and rent it to people I did not know." She also hated the winter move "to the dreary house in front of the jail" but took comfort in the fact that the house "was attached by a steel door to the jail."

WE'RE HERE. WHAT DO WE DO NOW?

Not many new sheriffs were as lucky as Howard Tanner, sleeping in unfurnished family quarters yet with no prisoners on the other side of his steel door. When Emma Banister moved into the Coleman County jail, the family found three hardened criminals in their cells who had already served time for other offenses elsewhere. The trio assumed the new sheriff wouldn't know how to stop an escape, unaware that he'd served as a deputy U.S. marshal.

For other families, inexperience made first days difficult. No one provided novice Sheriff Francis Sinclair with helpful information when he moved Elma and the girls into the Hodgeman County, Kansas, jail in 1960: No helpful hints on how to keep the inmates from escaping, "no information about how to manage the jail or the job, or even how to operate the cells." Francis and daughter, Dot, spent their first evening in their new home figuring out the above through trial and error. The cell door mechanism was such that "there were a variety of ways to maneuver the bars to open one cell, a block of cells, etc."

On January 1, 1935, Edith Brand Weiss, husband Harry, their five sons and one daughter moved into the Holmes County jail in Millersburg, Ohio. Those children old enough to help joined their parents to learn the ways of the jailhouse. Evelyn, Edith's oldest, reported that "after Harry and Edith had lived on a farm all their lives, it was quite a change to live in town and have all of the modern conveniences. What a heyday the children had, flushing toilets and turning the lights on and off! They'd hardly ever seen [an indoor] bathroom."

Evelyn was a sophomore in high school when the family took up sheriffing. The only similarities between running a farm and tending to the incarcerated was that it involved a lot of chores and everyone had to pitch in. That was about where the similarities ended.

In the Fulton County, Indiana, jail, Bess Voorhees remembered her first days during the Great Depression:

> Our first prisoner brought in from out of county was Harry E, age 39. He said he had written a check for $4.00 in Winamac and dated it ahead and told the grocery man to hold it, but he turned it in anyway. Our eight year old daughter, Peggy, thought it was terrible to put an innocent man in jail. But we soon found out that although they all seemed innocent, they generally were guilty or they wouldn't end up here. Harry had been in several times before and several times since for bad checks, false picture, drunkenness and non-support. He was a regular clown. He auctioned off an old Ford sitting out in front of the jail one day and he had everybody going along the street looking. It wasn't his. We expected him back every few months. The last time he was here, he got eight months in jail.

FIRST NIGHTS ON THE JOB

When Essie Myers Bailey served as Mrs. Sheriff of Fulton County, Indiana, in 1902, her youngest was a year old. "The first night the Bailey family lived in the sheriff's quarters of the jail, they heard a thud outside. Upon investigation, Sheriff Bailey found a brick on the ground. Red Hayes had tried to escape from the second floor by removing bricks,"[3] a feat accomplished by scraping away the mortar.

Several families who lived in the Fulton County, Indiana, jailhouse are included in this book. Bess Voorhees reported that "we moved into the County Jail on Saturday evening, December 31, 1938. Russel's term as Fulton County Sheriff was to begin at midnight as the new year came in. The outgoing Sheriff gave Russel all the keys to the Jail and house and told him he could find out where they went. This was our first time inside the Jail so we had a lot to find out by ourselves." She went on to describe the six rooms downstairs in the house and the same upstairs. "A stairway led to the third floor attic which covered all of the house and jail cells. The Jail was eight cell blocks, some with double decked beds. The bull pen was in the middle with a long table and a small one with benches to sit on. Around the cells ran a runway between the cells and the windows. When we first came, we noticed a bar sawed off at a window and some bricks taken out of the wall."

Bess had one prisoner in the cells her first night on the job.

The first night kept us busy answering telephones (one upstairs and one downstairs), doorbells (one at jail entrance and one at living quarters entrance), and hearing the police radio come on unexpectedly. We were up almost all night as drunks called in and other calls that didn't amount to much had to be answered. The next morning, Russel slept in and I got up to feed the prisoner. All I knew about it was to put the tray through the hole in the kitchen [to the prisoner area] and call the prisoner and he would come and get it. I got it ready and called real low. I called twice and he didn't come. Upstairs I went as fast as I could and told Russel the prisoner was gone. He must have escaped! Russel jumped out of bed, grabbed his pants, and down he ran to the jail. The prisoner was laying back there reading. He said he had never heard anyone call him. I had called to him so quietly, I was afraid he would come, I guess.

Feeding inmates took some getting used to, as noted by Bess. She reported that "in preparing prisoner meals, I used the usual tin trays, but I put bowls in for cereal, glass in for dessert to keep it separate, and even knives for cutting meat. I soon found out though that no glass, knives, or forks were to be put on the trays. Just the tin tray, spoon, and tin cup were to go back to the prisoners. Didn't want them killing themselves or anybody else!"

Betty Swanson of Lucas County, Iowa, reported that her first night on the job in 1955 still stands out. "Not knowing and imagining everything was bad enough, but the jail was next to the Burlington railroad tracks and a crossing! It seems there were steam engines going through constantly—blowing their whistles for the crossing." Betty was 28 and her husband was 29. "His salary began at $3,750 per year—mine was zero. He had one deputy and one office clerk." The living quarters came furnished with a stove "but we had to furnish the rest of it, including the fridge." The house vibrated with each passing train. Added to the sounds of the steam engines in the winter were the noisy radiators in each room, heated by a coal-fired stoker. "Oftentimes the stoker would shear a pin and stop, resulting in no heat. Seems this always happened at night."

At the other extreme of the seasons, "the bedrooms were very hot in the summer as there was a flat roof. All we had was a fan. Later on we were allowed [by the County Commissioners] to have a window air conditioner, but we had to purchase that ourselves."

As was typical in many counties, Betty described that it was the sheriff who "had to mow the lawn and shovel snow, so again, we had to purchase the lawn mower and snowblower. By the way, the roof was leaking when we moved in. It took a windstorm to get a new roof. And we had bats—boy, did we have bats! Finally, we found where they were getting in and took care of that."

Marjorie Price recalled that when they first moved to the Randolph County, Missouri, jail in January 1969, "late one evening, my husband and the deputy took a prisoner out of town to a state hospital. A woman prisoner in the jail sort of went crazy, tore up her cell while screaming. The prisoners were all scared. I called the bailiff and he called in the highway patrol until my husband got there. It was a scary time for me."

When Helen Haugerud took up her position as chief cook and bottle washer at the Fillmore County jail in Minnesota, she found seventeen prisoners to be fed three times a day. Never again would she feed so many, but the first three weeks were her baptism by fire. Helen's husband, Neil, pondered the ramifications of the life into which he'd brought his family: "I thought of Helen alone there in the jail with two young children, cooking for [seventeen] prisoners, listening to the two-way radio, and answering the office phone. I wondered if this was the kind of life she wanted, if I was the kind of man she wanted. Maybe baby-sitting a jailhouse full of misfits at suppertime was too much to ask."[4]

Ed Darrow must have felt something akin to this their first morning on the new job in Powell County, Montana. Mary Ann recalled that she was "totally overwhelmed" with two small children under the age of four and eighteen prisoners for which to provide. "Everything for the kitchen was packed in boxes that were strewn all over the floor. The area in front of the stove was so narrow there wasn't room to stand in front of the oven door to open it. I had to stand at the side of the range to remove or place anything in the oven. Ed prepared breakfast for the prisoners as I stood at the window and cried."

Emotions of all sorts ran high the first days and nights on the job. The worst case scenario occurred in Tennessee when Pauline Pusser discovered that her husband had been shot his first night making rounds in McNairy County. When two men raced past Buford in their car, a high-speed chase ensued. The new sheriff pulled the men over, got out of his car and walked to the driver's side to question the occupants. In a heartbeat, he was shot—twice. As the car sped away, Buford struggled to his own vehicle and managed to drive to the hospital. "Pauline Pusser was never the same after the highway shooting of her husband."[5]

Just three weeks into the job, Florence Kratervelt—hired to feed prisoners in the Antrim County, Michigan, jail while Maud Tanner trained her replacement at the post office—found herself tripping over lawmen in her efforts to prepare meals. "The usually quiet county on the peninsula of Michigan experienced a murder investigation that involved lawmen of all branches. Howard knew he didn't have the experience to investigate a murder so he called in the State Police." Howard and his deputies, the state police and other law enforcement officers from the area turned Florence's kitchen into the hub of the investigation for several weeks. Maud's son, Howard A., a ninth grader at the time, remembers being fascinated by the crime scene photographs. Florence prepared meals as best she could and kept the coffee urn filled in a kitchen full of investigators.

This chapter has provided a glimpse into what might be the first experiences of our hypothetical jailor family if they win their election. The beginning of the next chapter provides a detailed view into what life might be like if they didn't live in the jail. The remainder deals with details of living arrangements in the jailhouse, if the county provided one. The family quarters proved to be anything but tranquil. As we will see, there was always something going on to keep a family busy.

—3—

Home Sweet Home

> You simply cannot sit back and think that because you give the place a good going over every Friday or every Saturday that your responsibilities are over. Of course, a thorough cleaning once a week is fine. But, germs are present every day and not just on Fridays or Saturdays. Your day's cleaning chores should begin with the moment you set foot into the kitchen in the morning. From that time, through the entire day, each time equipment or utensils are used they should be cleaned.
>
> —1961 *Handbook of Jail Food Service*

> "Many of the prisoners were infested with lice or crabs. The matron had to scrub down the female inmates as they were booked" at the Nassau County (FL) Jail.
>
> —By Annis Moore-Littles who served alongside Jailor Bobby Moore from 1969 to 1977.

When the Boulder County, Colorado, courthouse burned just before Mildred Richart's family moved in, county commissioners tried to get out of including quarters for the sheriff's family in the new structure. They argued that it wasn't a safe place to raise six children. Other counties had always felt the same. Some provided a separate residence close to the jail. Some expected the sheriff to continue at his own farm and commute to the office.

NOT ALWAYS SO SWEET

Before Sophie Alberding met and married John Poe, he'd been involved in the capture of Billy the Kid's gang members for stealing cattle. When citizens of Lincoln County, New Mexico, elected John as sheriff and the couple married,

Sophie moved into the sheriff's quarters above Murphy, Dolan & Riley's store. Sophie described their apartment in detail: the bedroom was "the room which had held Billy the Kid after the young outlaw's conviction and sentence for the murder of Sheriff Brady. It was from the east window of this room that Billy had shoved out a shotgun, in April of 1881, to murder Deputy Bob Ollinger"[1] during Billy's famous escape from Lincoln County.

Sophie also observed that "there was one feature of the new home which I did not enjoy. The back stairway, up and down which I had to travel many times during the day, was still stained with blood, a grim reminder of the day two years before, when Billy the Kid had shot and killed his guard, James W. Bell. Bell had been climbing those stairs and his body had fallen to the bottom of them."[2]

A decade later in neighboring Arizona, Jim and Linda Scott set up their household in St. Johns, trading places with the outgoing Apache County sheriff who agreed to manage the Scott's ranch while Jim served his term. Linda settled her family into the sheriff's living quarters.

The Scotts were people of substantial social standing in their Victorian Arizona community. Linda planned meals for prisoners as well as for those she entertained at her table who were in town on official business. She supervised her servants as those meals were prepared. During Linda's tenure as Mrs. Sheriff, she was responsible for feeding not only Apache County's prisoners but also those of neighboring Navajo County. Originally, this new county had been part of a larger Apache County but Navajo's citizens voted to form their own identity. They elected their own sheriff who hired deputies but had no jail, so he and his men set up shop in St. Johns and used Jim and Linda's jail. Both sheriffs held the dual title of Sheriff and Tax Assessor, one often seen across the United States. When they weren't tracking down criminals, much of their time was spent pouring over maps to identify property owners along the new boundaries between the two counties.

Linda may have been an upper-class Victorian woman, but she was no lady of leisure. She more than once proved that she was a real trooper. In 1895, just a short while after Linda settled her husband and family into their county-provided home sweet home in town, the commissioners decided that the sheriff's home would make the perfect place to house county offices while the courthouse was reroofed. Linda graciously gave up her home, found another, and moved her family yet again. She then decorated it, as she had the previous one, in a manner appropriate for a family of their station.

Having settled in, Linda felt comfortable taking her daughter to visit Jim's family in Show Low, Arizona. Their first night away from home, Jim discovered that someone had entered his house and stolen a riding bridle. Burglarizing the sheriff's home and taking a bridle was not only grand larceny, it was just plain rude.

During the Roaring Twenties, Bessie Kelly's Texas County, Missouri, home was also burglarized during their eight years in the sheriff's office. Bessie tended inmates and her five businesses plus worked the 204 acre farm where the family continued to reside. Despite her busy schedule, Bessie cooked for the inmates, and the sheriff took into town her meals when he went. He also took down stills in the Missouri Ozarks while raiding local bootleggers, confiscating whiskey for evidence. He stored that whiskey in their basement. While the Kelly's attended the Texas County Reunion [county fair] their home was broken into by someone in search of that whiskey. It was all they took except for some of the garden produce Bessie had canned. No sense getting drunk on an empty stomach.

The day of the Texas County Reunion was probably the only day that this burglary could have been committed. Usually, several deputies guarded prisoners who lived in the Kelly barn. The prisoners, known as trustees, were put to work on the sheriff's farm as this was viewed as a higher and better use of able-bodied men who needed to work for their meals instead of sitting idly in cells, dreaming up trouble.

Before she claimed the title of Mrs. Sheriff, Pauline Cushman decided she would spy for the Union cause during the Civil War. She signed up wherever one signed up for such things and trained to be useful. Her first foray below the Mason Dixon Line, however, found her in prison, captured by the Rebels—not very useful at all.

After the Civil War, adventurous Pauline trekked West and married Jere Fryer. The couple owned and operated a hotel and livery stable in Casa Grande, Arizona. This experience helped them to then take on inmate care at the Pinal County jail.

Emma, the couple's adopted daughter born in 1881, turned out to be sickly. "Emma suffered from a chronic nervous disease of some sort that left her with periods of paralysis and spasms," reported Bill Christen, Pauline's biographer. According to Bill, Pauline talked Jere into adopting Emma after Pauline convinced him that Emma was his daughter by another woman. She's definitely not one of your Mrs. Sheriffs to be listed in the "saints" category.

In 1886, Jere ran for sheriff of Pinal County and won. He moved Pauline and Emma to Florence, into a home a block from the jail. Six months later, to "escape the heat" Pauline took Emma to her family in Michigan. They did not return until 1888, with Emma dying on the way. "It is speculated that the natural mother came forward and disclosed to Jere that Emma had not been his daughter after all, but that Pauline had talked the mother into playing along with this ruse," Bill Christen continued. This disclosure put a strain on the marriage, needless to say. Pauline returned to Casa Grande to run their hotel, while Jere stayed on in Florence to win election for a second term.

For those women who remained at the hotel, on the farm or ranch while their husband served as sheriff, the existence could prove lonely. Viola White of Leelanau County, Michigan, found this to be so in 1948. Viola's daughter and family moved to the farm so that Viola could watch their children while Ruth and Ed worked. Sheriff Bob came by the house at least once a day while he was making his rounds of the county to check that all was well. When Leelanau County built a new jail ten years into Bob's tenure, the White's sold the farm. Viola moved into the family quarters and took up cooking for inmates. She saw more of Bob but never got used to him being called away in the middle of a meal. "Can't you tell them you're eating and you'll come as soon as you're finished?" she'd ask. Bob always said no.

Joyce, one of Viola's daughters, disclosed that her mother "found the life lonely even when surrounded by family. She rarely saw dad and that impacted her tremendously. She went a couple of times to the Sheriff's conventions but because she was basically a homebody and dad gave his all to work or to the convention, she did not find it to be a time for them to share."

By way of contrast, devoted family man August Singler not only moved Rose and the children immediately into their new living quarters in Jacksonville, Oregon, after election, he also brought those bloodhounds for which he was famous. "The neighbors said the Singler kids made music during the day and the Singler bloodhounds took turns serenading the moon and stars at night."[3]

SET ANOTHER PLACE AT THE TABLE

Like Bessie Kelly with her trustees in the barn, other sheriffs' wives found prisoners on their property, sometimes upstairs in their own home. Kate Weakley of Russell County, Kansas, fed and housed WJ Gaines who, in June 1876, sued a fellow citizen in District Court. When he lost, he could not pay court costs and Gaines found himself incarcerated. As he saw no way to provide for his wife and children if he sat in a cell, he appealed to the county commissioners and asked them to rectify the unfairness of the Court's decision.

Sheriff JG Weakley received instructions from the county commissioners to release his prisoner. That created a quandary as the commissioners had no jurisdiction. What was a sheriff to do? JG solved his dilemma by turning to his wife.

In response, Kate scurried around the house, removing children and their belongings from one bedroom, rearranging another bedroom to bunk kids together, and clearing a space for Gaines to sleep. She put another plate on the table and made do as best she could until the district judge could decide on the case. Her husband put the dilemma before the judge that Gaines had no material possessions to sell at Sheriff's Sale so he was never going to be able to pay his court costs. The judge agreed that they were incurring a needless expense by boarding a man who was better off earning a living for his family. The Sheriff submitted Kate's boarding bills and the couple were reimbursed for the food Gaines ate, but not for use of the bedroom nor for the inconvenience.

LIVING IN

"Living in" is a term used to describe the circumstances found by those who moved into the sheriff's quarters attached to the jail or who took up residence in the courthouse. Over the course of two hundred years, thousands of families lived in this manner across the United States.[4]

The concept of living in was greeted with a variety of reactions that ran the gamut of emotions. We have seen how farm kids who'd rarely seen modern conveniences found delight in flush toilets and electric lights early in the twentieth century. One of the daughters of Mary Weber Jahnel felt quite the opposite in

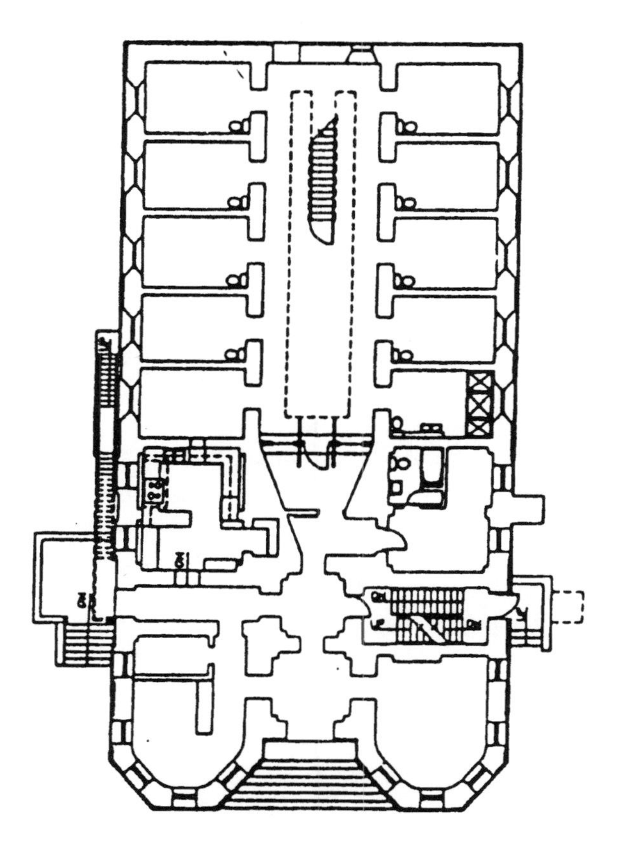

FIRST FLOOR PLAN

The old jail in Clarion County, Pennsylvania, typical of many "live in" jails, with the family living quarters at the front of the first floor. The basement was used for storage. Two additional bedrooms were located on the second floor (not shown) along with a second bath. The kitchen was used for both the family and preparing food for inmates. (Courtesy of the Clarion County Historical Society.)

1964. "We'd had a nice ranch home about seven blocks south of the Mitchell County Jail in Osage, Iowa and I didn't want our family to have to move to that old red brick house known as the 'Jail.' That would really take care of my social life! This was the month of my high school graduation. I didn't want to have my reception in the Jail!"

Lassie Baldree took up her duties as jailhouse wife during the 1940s in Sumter County, Florida. Louise Milton, who worked with eight Sumter sheriffs over a fifty-year period, described the arrangement this way: "Sheriff Baldree and his wife lived in the jail which was right across the street from the Sheriff's Department in Bushnell. The office was within the courthouse. There were private [family] quarters in front of the jail and the jail was in back of the building. It was a two-story red brick building and either the sheriff or the deputy/jailor was there at the jail during the night. The sheriff's wife served as matron."[5]

A GLIMPSE INSIDE

Maud Tanner described her 1937 Antrim County, Michigan, jail as "an old rambling affair. It was unhandy and hard to keep clean. But it was our home for seventeen years. We had [experience with] murders, suicides, fatal accidents and drownings with [prisoners in for] breaking and enterings, family fights and disorderly drunks. We averaged eight male prisoners at one time, fifteen at the most, very few women or juveniles. We also kept mental patients until we could get them into the State Hospital at Traverse City. Sometimes there would be a vagrant [who would] stop and ask to sleep in the jail. They came in off the freight trains." Maud's observations are typical and often reported by other jailhouse wives.

Madge Harris resided in her jail for seventeen years as well, in Wilson County, Kansas, from 1950 to 1967. She had "three big rooms and a long, wide hall downstairs and three big bedrooms and bathroom upstairs, also with a long, wide hall. There was also a big basement. The residence had a large front and back porch."

The old jail in Williamson County, Illinois, is described this way: "the Jail Section of the building is separated from the Sheriff's living area by 13-inch concrete walls. There are only two ways to get from the jail area to the Sheriff's quarters. One is through the door off of what was the kitchen into a hallway. There is a solid steel door separating the two areas. The other is from the parlor into the Sheriff's Office. There is a heavy steel door with see-through bars separating these two areas."[6]

The daughter of Leila Pederson of Chippewa County, Minnesota, recalled in a newspaper interview that "the sheriff's family quarters were attached [to the jail], separated only by a large solid steel door which was seldom locked."[7] Marge Pederson, only nine months old in 1927 when her mother brought her to the jailhouse, lived there for twenty years.

Florine Johnson Gooding provided details that help round out the picture of a typical jail family quarters: the "front door was on the street, across from the [Allegan County, Michigan] courthouse. The sheriff's office was entered via a side door. The jail cells were behind the family quarters.

Prisoners came in through the side door, went through the sheriff's office, and right into the cell area. There was a big front porch and a small utility porch off the back door to the family quarters so groceries could be delivered or laundry could be taken to the line." Florine's mother, Mildred Barrett Johnson, moved her family into the jailhouse in 1941. Florine noted that the "male prisoners were fed by lining up outside the kitchen door that had a 2½ by 2½ foot barred pass-through in the door between the family quarters and cells."

During the Great Depression, Edith Weiss moved her family into the Holmes County, Ohio, jail that "consisted of the Sheriff's office and main jail on the first floor, an upstairs jail that housed the dangerous criminals and a [separate] women's jail that consisted of one big room with several beds." Edith's daughter went on to describe the residence that "consisted of three bedrooms [upstairs] with walk-in closets and one bedroom with no closet, which my parents took. Downstairs there was a living room, a music room, a dining room and a small kitchen. There was a half bath downstairs and a full one upstairs."

Because most kitchens served as food preparation and meal staging areas for inmates as well as the family, most were described as large. Mary Ann Darrow described her Powell County, Montana, kitchen differently. "The apartment consisted of a living room, two large bedrooms, dining room and [a] tiny, very impractical kitchen. The entire apartment had twelve-foot ceilings. The windows were tall and narrow. Under each window was a steam radiator that kept the apartment comfortable in the winter."

Sid Edinger described the living quarters where his mother, Marian, brought her children during the 1920s as "a two story building with four large bedrooms, a large kitchen, dining room, living room, and what we would now call a family room. Only one bath." The Edingers moved in and out of this facility in McHenry County, Illinois, as dad was elected sheriff. Because the rules governing the sheriff's office decreed that the sheriff could not serve consecutive terms, the family moved back and forth from the large family quarters to their 1,200-foot bungalow between terms. Because the Twenties roared long before storage rental facilities had sprouted on every corner, Sid reported that "somehow my mother made the furniture fit both houses very nicely. She did say 'three moves are as good as a fire.'"

When the family was large, even the most spacious family quarters didn't always suffice. In Mitchell County, Iowa, in the 1960s, the seven Jahnel girls used the shower in the women's cell when there were no female inmates. The basement contained a darkroom and a shooting range but one of its several rooms also contained a bed. This came in handy when company stayed the night and the older girls got booted from their bedrooms.

In Van Buren County, Iowa, the Lee family moved into family quarters that, like many others, shared a floor with the cell reserved for women and juvenile offenders. Dolores Lee's boys were six and eight in 1956 when they moved in. Her son, Larry, reported that both he and his brother, Gary, "hated to go past the steel door to that cell on our way to the bathroom at the end of the hall. Both of us hated to do that when someone was in there. Even though we couldn't see in or be seen because of the solid steel door, we disliked walking past to go to the john."

Larry Lee recalled that "the first time we went upstairs to the family quarters and saw the old 6-inch key in the big steel door to that cell, for some reason it scared the crap out of both of us." As time went by, the boys got used to living in such a place and often had sleepovers with their friends in the rarely used cell.

BRINGING HIS WORK HOME WITH HIM

It was noted by several participants in this research that one of the main benefits of having a live-in sheriff was that he then had time to interact with inmates. This helped him to identify problems before they blossomed into escapes or attacks. This practice was not universal. In some places, the sheriff maintained his office in the courthouse while the family lived in the jail building across the street.

Betty Vinson of Lyon County, Iowa, reported that after her husband took office in 1969, he wisely moved his office from the courthouse to the basement of the jail. Not only did that place him nearer the inmates but also freed prime space in the courthouse for other county functions. Betty noted that the move provided her with "many contacts with jail visitors and state law enforcement men. They ate with us—often."

ALWAYS SOMETHING GOING ON

When a courthouse occupied a large plot of land, there was often room to build the jail as an attachment to the official building. In 1955, Lily Serles moved into quarters attached to the courthouse in Adams County, Wisconsin. Not only was there a jail and family quarters, the attachment also included rooms for the offices of probation officers and driver's license exams.

But what about those counties where the jail and family quarters were located in the courthouse itself? How did families go about their lives after regular business hours? The jailhouse family worked around the clock even when the building had been locked after business hours. Therefore everyone, including the children, was provided with a key to the outside door.

Dorothy Everson moved her children into the courthouse in 1943 where they lived on the fifth and sixth floors overlooking Boulder, Colorado. Once inside the public building, the family used a private elevator to "get home." Dorothy's daughter, Shirley, recalled that the family was provided with rooms not originally meant for housing a family. "My mother made it real homey."[8] Young Shirley and her brother, Bob, had a playroom on the sixth floor directly under the clock tower. They could, and often did, climb out their window to play on the flat roof "that was walled like a castle." Shirley noted that this was also the space devoted to the clothesline. The only special care that they took was to "make sure that the laundry didn't show from the street below. We didn't want to detract from the dignity of the Courthouse."

In this chapter we learned what could take place once our hypothetical family gets a foot in the door. We've gathered first impressions about how donning the county apron affects families who either lived apart from or directly in the jail. The chapter that follows takes us deeper behind the scenes for a more in-depth look at a variety of aspects of jailhouse life and how they affected family members.

—— 4 ——

Behind the Scenes

Thorough cleaning is the best means of keeping down roaches and rodents. Pest poison use may be necessary, but it should be done carefully. Never allow the poison to touch any equipment or utensils which will be used in handling food.

—1961 *Handbook of Jail Food Service*

During Prohibition, Marian Edinger coped with an overflowing jail full of Chicago bootleggers and several small children underfoot in the family quarters. Marian's efforts to provide meals for everyone were hampered by the fact that the stove with two large ovens was not properly vented, "but she could not persuade the County Supervisors to have the problem fixed. Finally one of the ovens exploded. Mother had all of her hair burned off. Her hair did grow back, but it was white. After that incident, the Supervisors did have fans installed."

—About Marian Edinger who served alongside Sheriff Lester "Doc" Edinger between 1923 and 1942, reported by son, Richard.

The threshold between the dual lives of jailhouse families has been crossed and first impressions have been gathered. In this and subsequent chapters we investigate how everything functioned, how tasks were accomplished, and how thousands of jailhouse families lived during the mom-and-pop jail era.

In the beginning, there were no bathrooms in homes, courthouses, or jails. Family members and inmates used chamber pots placed under their beds at night. Someone had to empty them each morning. During the Depression, Pearl Hobbs, jail matron and wife of the sheriff of Moore County, Tennessee, assigned her young daughter, Nell, the chore of emptying chamber pots, or as they were called in the South, "slop jars." At the farthest corner of the backyard "a big steel drum connected to an underground pipe that drained into the creek about 100 yards behind the jail and all of the slop jars were emptied into the steel drum. The jail did have city water at this time, the source being the Jack Daniels Distillery spring." An outhouse was built in the jail garden, put in about the same time that Pearl took up her duties in 1928. Outhouses weren't for inmates though so slop jars remained in the inmates' chambers.

During the mid-1890s in Arizona, Apache County sheriff and tax assessor Jim Scott found enough revenue in the county budget to put an end to the cesspool that held the human waste behind his jail. A trench was dug on a decline and lined with a pipe. Linda's husband also found tax money for the purchase of water rights sufficient to keep the line flushed all the way to the river. "This improvement to the overall atmosphere of that section of town in the heat of the summer has been vastly appreciated by those who live and work there, but none more so than the staff at the jail,"[1] reported the editor of the St. Johns Times.

Before the days of automobiles, there was a need for stables to house the sheriff's horses and those of visiting judges, lawyers, and jury members who stayed with the family during court sessions. Behind the Schuyler County, Illinois, jail, a "stray pen" as well as a stables was located. Wandering cows, horses, chickens and pigs were kept in the pen until the sheriff identified their owners. The animals were locked up "when found wandering up and down Rushville streets until their owners came to reclaim them."[2] One of the chores for the sheriff's children was to care for the strays.

Ella Ross produced twin daughters who were born while the family lived in the Jackson County, Missouri, jailhouse. Many years later, the twins, Helen and Louise, recalled that on the north side of the jail stood a vacant lot with hitching posts for those who'd come in from the farm to shop. The girls had been instructed that this lot was "off limits" to them because they were girls—not because of the horses but because one never knew what manner of salty talk might emanate from the jail cell windows. Prisoners would "lower a small bag or just a string and beg for tobacco or money"[3] from the farmers in the vacant lot. Charlie, the twins' older brother, was asked to buy tobacco with whatever coins had made their way through the bars, and he did so.

The building that replaced the vacant lot next to the Jackson County, Missouri, jailhouse originally served as a bank and is now a National Park Service museum. The museum staff directs visitors to various Harry S. Truman sites in Independence, the county seat. Ella's son, Charlie Ross, remained friends with Harry from third grade until Charlie's death in 1951 at his desk in the White House, serving as President Truman's press secretary.

Leila Pederson's daughter, Marge, lived in the Chippewa County, Minnesota, jail family quarters for over twenty years. Marge later recalled "the good smells of food cooking for about 15 prisoners plus the members of her family, and she remembers the sounds of the motorcycles which the highway patrolmen and FBI agents from St. Paul parked outside the jail. These were Depression days of bank

Former Sheriff Sanford Buster of Boulder County, Colorado, stands to the left of his preschool grandson, Louden (on top of barrel), at the disposal site for bootleg whisky after a raid on May 16, 1928. (Courtesy of Joy Buster.)

robberies and Prohibition, which meant bringing in the 'big guns' from the cities occasionally to help local law enforcement officers."[4]

Wildcat whiskey stills during Prohibition were confiscated in Moore County, Tennessee, as well as many other places across the nation. But in Moore County, Pearl Hobbs' husband waited until the stills were vacated before he'd swoop in to remove them. Her grandsons grew up hearing about grandpa waiting until the bootleggers scattered into the woods and how he never pursued them. Sheriff Hobbs took the stills to the jail in Lynchburg. At night, the sheriff or one of his deputies deposited the stills on the front lawn. "The next morning the stills would be missing. It was the height of the Depression and this was how families were being fed and clothed."

Farther north, the McHenry County, Illinois, jail had a basement filled with confiscated property: slot machines, equipment from stills, liquor. When Marion Edinger's four children were raised in the jail, they were not allowed in the basement. However, they found living in the middle of town adventuresome enough to satisfy them.

Marian's son, Sid, described the situation this way: "The courthouse and the sheriff's residence/jail were adjacent to each other on the west side of the square in Woodstock. At the time we lived there, the square was the business center of the town. Therefore, our front yard was right where everyone in town might come by on any given day. When I was a boy, the carnival would set up right outside our front door and cover the west side of the square."

HONEY, I NEED THE CAR

Sid Edinger also reported that despite the tremendous number of inmates during Prohibition, his dad's entire department consisted of five people: the sheriff, the chief deputy, a clerk, a janitor/jailor, and the cook (Marian Edinger). "The mobile units were our family car and the chief deputy's family car for which the county paid half the cost." There came a time when Sid rode with his mom through town and, somehow, Marian managed to activate the siren switch installed on the floor. When she heard a siren, like any good citizen, she dutifully pulled to the curb and then "looked to see what emergency vehicle was coming." She was so embarrassed when she discovered that she and Sid were the "emergency."

Richard Edinger, another of Marian's four children who spent their childhoods in the jail, wrote "not every boy went on a date in a car that had a twelve gauge shotgun fastened to the ceiling over the driver's side and a thirty-eight revolver in the glove compartment. Additionally, the car was equipped with a large, flashing red light mounted on the front bumper and a siren. Of course, these were untouchables; and except for a couple of occasions with the red light, I never did violate his trust."

Dode Jahnel, Mary's daughter, was one of seven daughters who lived in the Mitchell County, Iowa, jail during the 1960s. Dode recalled that "two things stand out most in my mind, the family car became the patrol car and the family phone became a business/emergency phone. Our family car was equipped with a two-way radio and a single round, revolving red light mounted on the top of the roof. I learned to drive and parallel park in that car. I took my driver's license test in that car."

The family car also doubled as a patrol car in 1971 Kossuth County, Iowa. Deputy Tom Fitzpatrick used it to bring Nancy to the jail family quarters from the hospital with new baby, Sara. Tom "got permission to drive with the red lights going, but no siren, of course. The whole courthouse turned out to welcome our new baby home." Sara's older sister, four-year old Laura, "was so proud!"

Tom and Nancy Fitzpatrick's jail had been condemned for years prior to their twelve months as jailors. They were only allowed to keep male prisoners overnight before transferring them to Fort Dodge. Nancy described their facility as an old Victorian home built in the 1860s that the Fitzpatricks moved to 110 years later. They'd agreed to take on the job of jailor after the sheriff's family moved out. The winter of 1971, Nancy discovered why the sheriff and his wife hadn't stayed. When three weeks of minus thirty degree weather struck Kossuth County, the home became a refrigerator. The Fitzpatricks moved their dining room table and television into the large spare bedroom upstairs to escape the cold downstairs

Interior of a cell area of a jail in Tompkins County, New York, showing iron cages that formed the cells and the area called the "bull pen" where prisoners gathered to eat or socialize when the jail was not locked down. (Postcard from author's collection.)

where they could see their breath at all hours of the day. The top floor stayed a bit warmer from the small amount of heat sent upwards from the ancient boiler. Nancy descended to the main floor only to cook. "I turned on all of the burners and the oven. I'd keep the oven door open to warm the kitchen and then prepare meals."

THE SOUNDS OF THE JAIL

Ella White's daughter described her mother and conditions at the Greenwood County, South Carolina, jail in 1941 this way: "she was a very patient and capable mother and wife. She endured the sounds from the jail that was connected to the living quarters. Constantly there was yelling, banging on the walls or the cells, etc. but she rarely complained."

Kathy gahnel noted that "mother wasn't used to opening drawers and seeing mouse tails scurrying!!" The Mitchell County, Iowa, jail, a vintage Victorian two-story Italianate, housed the sheriff's office next to the living room wall. The male inmates were held in "one large cell but inside of that, their bunks were surrounded by iron walls. If there were no prisoners and a tornado threatened, we girls were sent to that iron room until the storm blew over."

On June 22, 1919, a pair of tornados leveled forty-four city blocks of Fergus Falls, Minnesota, including this damage to the Otter Tail County Jail and Courthouse. Note the bedroom furniture left intact on the second floor despite the absence of walls. (Postcard from author's collection.)

OFFICIAL VISITORS

Over time, the function of the county jail changed from a temporary holding facility for those awaiting trial and those serving short sentences to a place for housing prisoners with longer sentences for more serious crimes. Lack of prison space and the need not to spend more money to build additional prisons forced states to look at their mom-and-pop jails with a new eye. Considering the costly and unpopular alternative, these looked like an attractive option.

County jails, however, had not been built for long-term incarceration. Extra effort was required to jerry-rig what was meant to function only as a temporary holding facility into a prison.

Eventually around the nation, county jails were inspected by either grand jury members or county commissioners once a year. When inspection time rolled around, the jailhouse wife was required to show her kitchen, equipment, and utensils. Current inmates were asked whether they were getting enough to eat, what they ate, if they were warm and clean in their cells. Betty Vinson remarked that when the grand jury came to inspect the Lyon County, Iowa, jail during the 1970s, she "would provide coffee and cookies and conversation."

Visitors of all sorts seem to have been in abundant supply around both jails and family quarters. In the 1960s, the Harvey County, Kansas, jail provided the setting for a constant flow of people. Families were allowed to see their incarcerated kin in the evenings. After clearing away the supper dishes for family and trays for inmates, Lorna Werner cleaned her kitchen and then released prisoners for their family visits. Local churches provided prayer meetings. In some locations, one church group or another came every night of the week.

During the Great Depression, when Olive Rosenkranz served as Mrs. Sheriff of Washington County, Kansas, visitors who came to see her prisoners were escorted into the family's living room. Olive then released the prisoner from his cell and escorted him to the living room where he was allowed to visit with his kin in a comfortable, homey environment. Olive's ten-year-old daughter, Helen, recalled that "if prisoners were brought in [following an arrest] while I was home, I was required to get into one of the rooms and close the door. Most people came peacefully, but I was to be out of the way regardless."

During the same era in Allegan County, Michigan, Bertha Miller gave over her den for use as an interrogation room when necessary. The sheriff held lineups there also. Bertha's family "peeked around the corners to see if we recognized anyone in the line-up." Bertha allowed mothers to visit their incarcerated sons in the den, so the women didn't have to go into the cell block.

Further west, in Saguache County, Colorado, Irene Gray reported that in the 1950s she was married to Undersheriff Jack Gray and they lived with their two children in the jailhouse. Irene cooked, washed bedding and the day always started with the same visitors gathered around her table for a cup of coffee. Irene recounted that "there was Town Marshal Ollie Wilson, the Wildlife Conservation Officer Phil Hawker, and the local mortician whom we called 'Digger' O'Dell. There were always several friends who joined us because they liked to catch up on what was happening."

Many of the jailhouse kitchens became a favorite room for visiting lawmen. The grandson of Viola White of Leelanau County, Michigan, recalled that "many of the State Police drank coffee and ate at her table as well as sheriffs of neighboring counties" after Viola moved into town from the farm. He recalled how Viola and Bob provided a home for two girls unrelated to them simply because the girls were in need of a home. More intimately ensconced in the family quarters than visitors, the girls became like daughters to the Whites.

Viola White may have warmly welcomed her foster daughters into the family quarters, but Marian Edinger never quite lived down the visitor she flatly turned away. Her son, Richard, told the tale this way:

> Federal marshals were in the habit of bringing their prisoners to the front door of the sheriff's residence which meant they had to go all the way through the house to reach the jail where they would wait for the jailor to admit the prisoners. Mother got tired of this, so she started having them go around the house to the back door in order to be admitted. One day, a man came to the front door whom she assumed to be a federal marshal, so she asked him to go to the backdoor, which he did. After he came into the house, she learned that he was a Congressman who had come to see dad. Later on they became good friends, but he never let her forget the time she made him use the back door.

UNOFFICIAL VISITORS

Communities often used the jailhouse for functions as well as for housing the sitting sheriff and his family. It might be the family home but it was also a public building. The family moved out of the way and their fellow citizens conducted business or enjoyed themselves in the parlor, the dining room, the kitchen.

The dungeon of the jail in Clarion County, Pennsylvania, made a wonderful setting for Halloween parties when it was no longer in use for inmates. "People would dress up as ghosts and hide in the cells. When the party guests entered the dungeon, the lights were turned out, and the ghosts would 'float' out of the cells to scare them."[5]

Of course, living in the jail did not stop the normal, everyday life of a sheriff's family. Children still went to school. Wives still had their friends and social obligations. In 1970s Lyon County, Iowa, Betty Vinson and a friend decided to host the wedding shower for the daughter of a dear friend. Betty's cohost experienced a family emergency a few days before the shower. One thing led to another and the location of the shower had to be changed to the jailhouse at the last minute.

While the bridal shower was taking place with appropriate "decorations, lovely food to eat, and piles of wedding presents," Sheriff Vinson came down the hallway next to the living room with three alleged cattle thieves who were not entirely delighted to be on the premises. The men created a terrible ruckus while protesting their innocence and resisting their impending incarceration. "I was a nervous wreck by the end of the day," Betty confessed.

Weddings as well as showers took place in the family quarters. Several daughters wed in their homes. Several prisoners did likewise. Madge Harris and her son, Randy, recalled one such event during the 1950s in Wilson County, Kansas. Madge was told that a prisoner wished to marry while he was incarcerated in her jail. "We asked them if they would like to be married in our living room. They said, 'you mean you'd do that for us?' 'Of course,' we said. 'We'd be glad to.' Their guests were their families from Kansas City and our son's girlfriend. The sheriff stood up for him and myself for her. We had a beautiful wedding cake. It was a very enjoyable day. [The inmate] went from here to the prison for a short time."

During Randy Harris' interview later, he vividly remembered the wedding day and serving as photographer. He reported that "one of the bride's relatives didn't care to be included in the pictures I was taking. The guy stuck out in my mind because he would have fit in as a character on *The Sopranos*."

At about the same time in Chickasaw County, Iowa, Pauline Folkers put together two weddings at her jail. Daughter Paulette recalled that the first time a prisoner planned with the sheriff to get married while he was incarcerated, the men decided it would take place in the back office. "When mom heard about this, she said that was no place for a wedding. Why not in our living room? The ceremony took place in front of the bay window, with momma as witness. She set up the dining room table, complete with flowers, punch and even made a cake for them. Needless to say, the bride and groom were really surprised and grateful. There were two weddings and mom did the same for both."

REMODEL? REBUILD?

Expanding the family quarters proved to be a rarity. As the responsibilities of the sheriff's department grew, space in the family quarters was often converted for official use. The few small rooms reserved for the county marshal's family in the Jackson County, Missouri, jail already included a room set aside for the judge when court was in session. In the basement, trustees prepared meals and fed prisoners who sat at trestle tables. Mrs. Marshal made do for her family with a tiny winter kitchen out back and a summer kitchen in the basement to prepare meals. In 1918, it was decided by the county court that one room in Mrs. Jesse Allen's cozy quarters was to be dedicated to housing juries overnight. Juries at that time were made up solely of men so one room proved sufficient. As things worked out, Mrs. Allen didn't have to figure out which of her precious rooms she had to give up as Jesse died the following month, leaving her with four children to raise elsewhere.

In 1900 Moore County, Tennessee, space just off the dining room in Sheriff Woodard's family quarters was taken over to install two cells, one for female prisoners and the other for juveniles. They also installed the evidence safe in an alcove off the same dining room.

When the Sinclair family moved to the top floor of the Hodgeman County, Kansas, jailhouse in 1960, space was tight. As previously mentioned, the family was provided with three rooms for parents and two daughters. To alleviate the pressure, Elma's oldest daughter, Dot, converted the rarely used women's cell into her bedroom. Sister Betty reported that Dot thought "it was so cool to have a toilet and sink in her room!"

Getting those tightfisted county commissioners to spend any money for anything to do with the jail or family quarters was tough work for both the sheriff and his wife. Modernizing and updating the premises was most often accomplished by the labor of the sheriff and his wife. Betty Swanson of Lucas County, Iowa, recalled that husband Wayne and her father installed the new downstairs bathroom in 1968. With the new bathroom and a washer and dryer installed just off the kitchen, Betty reported, "I was very comfortable."

THEY DECIDED TO BUILD ANEW

It too more than a remodel to make Mary Agnes Buckler comfortable when she was married to the county jailor in St. Mary's County, Maryland. It took more than a remodel to make her comfortable. Mary Agnes served as jail matron and cook before, during, and after World War II, a time of tremendous change in the county. The building they lived in prior to the War had been built in 1858 as a temporary holding facility. When the jail population swelled well beyond its official capacity after the Navy came to St. Mary's County, the inefficiencies of the old jail and jailhouse kitchen became abundantly evident. Out-of-date and ill-functioning appliances made meal preparation for so many prisoners a nightmare. There was nothing to be done but build a new and larger facility behind the courthouse. Only then was Mary Agnes content.

To illustrate what happened to jailhouse life in a county after any branch of the armed services moved in, take the example of Brown County, Texas, during World War II. When Camp Bowie was in full swing, there came a Saturday night in which fifty-six were arrested and jailed. The jailhouse wife went to bed with a handful of prisoners to feed the next morning and overnight, she was faced with a mob—many who were not hungry but hungover and had been sick in their cells.

In New Jersey, when Phebe Lindsley's husband, Joe, became one of the architects for the new Morris County jail in 1827, she must have felt most fortunate. Joe was not only an experienced carpenter used to building construction but also the sheriff. He helped design the new courthouse that also contained the jail and family quarters. Being so intimately aware of the needs of the family in such a setting, Joe provided Phebe with a facility that functioned well. What more could Phebe ask?

A hundred years later, in Allamakee County, Iowa, Martha Barthell Bulmans's husband lost his bid for reelection and they moved away from the old jail. In 1939, the Bulmans ran again and won. Martha found things a lot nicer during that stint as jail matron when the family moved into the new courthouse. Her daughter, Charlotte, noted that while "there still was no dishwasher or clothes dryer, we did have an electric washing machine and a bathtub with a shower in it. We lived on the third floor, so that meant mom had to go down the elevator to the back door and out to hang clothes to dry." Charlotte recalled that "Dad hung a cowbell outside the dining room window with a string that ran the three floors to the back door, so people could pull the cord and ring the cowbell by the window if the back door was locked after hours."

Also in Iowa, Pauline Folkers experienced tremendous excitement when the builders started her new jail during the 1950s. Daughter Paulette revealed just how much excitement there was as the crew for the new Chickasaw County Jail broke ground. "She couldn't wait until I got home from school to show me that they had started digging. She was like a kid at Christmas time when we were able to move in. She had the biggest smile when they held an open house. She enjoyed giving people the grand tour."

Schulyer County, Illinois, probably wasn't the only county to build its jail and sheriff's quarters while forgetting about the need for a kitchen, but it is the only one that shared that fact during this research. The new jail was "designed by men and built by men"[6] in 1858, none of whom had ever had to feed prisoners apparently. By the time Sarah Barbee Edmondson moved into the family quarters two years later, a kitchen had been provided. It cost all of $75 and was built onto the stone building as a wooden attachment.

Maud Tanner's son, Howard A., provided the following information about the first jail his parents called home in Antrim County, Michigan: "The old jail was built in 1872 of white pine lumber, a sprawling combination of Sheriff's residence, office, men's jail, women's jail, laundry and garage. The hub of everything was the kitchen." Seven doorways entered the kitchen from various parts of the building. "In 1937, the kitchen came complete with walk-in pantry, wood stove, wood box, electric stove and table where our meals were served except for special occasions." Young Howard made his way through high school while his parents served their community, and then left home for college and military service during World War II.

Maud made note in her family memoir that "the old jail got more and more decrepit. The furnace gave out. Stoves were installed in the living quarters. The jail part was condemned in 1949. Prisoners had to be transported to Charlevoix, 32 miles away. Howard kept the roads hot. One day, he made three round trips." When the new jail came under construction, Maud recalled "I 'inspected' it at the end of every day after the workmen left, slipping over the wet Taraza floors and stumbling over plaster pails and lumber. The miserable old fire trap of a jail we had lived in for 17 years caught fire from Clara Zook's trash fire in the alley. The fire didn't amount to very much but the water and smoke made it unlivable. The new jail was about finished and we moved in willy-nilly in April 1955."

Maud described the changes brought about by having "a beautiful building with large pleasant offices and attractive living quarters beside a modern wing of jail cells. We were delighted with it. Howard got the Antrim County prisoners back from Charlevoix and we were in business again." She noted that she "always had trustees to help. They kept the place shining. The new jail was designed to hold 14 prisoners but we had as many as 20 at times. I did the cooking in the stainless steel kitchen. Edith Severance helped out when the load was heaviest."

WE NEED SOME CHANGES AROUND HERE

When Anne Werth set up housekeeping in 1960 at the Ellis County, Kansas, jail and family quarters, they were located on the north side of the courthouse. For decades prior to 1960, citizens accessed county offices by walking from the parking lot to the north door, and traipsing through the family kitchen. Anne recalled that "it disturbed them all when I refused them that entrance, but I stuck to my guns." Anne put her foot down on other matters as well. She "insisted on draperies that would divide the ten foot windows in half and paint that lowered the ceiling. I insisted on a shower, residential style toilet seat, floor covering and garbage disposer. All these we had in our own home. I constantly defended my attempts to make it a home."

As many families found, a little paint worked wonders. Helen Haugerud discovered that the water pipes that ran overhead through her kitchen would virtually disappear with a coat of paint. She recalled that "once the entire room and pipes were painted white, it didn't look too bad." Even paint has its limits though. When the Haugeruds moved into the Fillmore County, Minnesota, jailhouse in 1959, "one of the five bedrooms upstairs was covered in old linoleum that had been painted over as a quick fix. The problem was that it stuck to our feet instead of to the linoleum, no matter how carefully we walked. As elsewhere, any changes to the family quarters had to be approved by the County Commissioners. They did approve replacing that floor."

Sarah and Enoch Edmondson of Schulyer County, Illinois, brought their three boys to live in the jailhouse that had been constructed of stone quarried not very far from the site. They discovered, like those who resided in the building afterwards, that the stone caused the building to feel forever "clammy."

Clammy might have been an endurable option when one is faced instead with fire. Larry Lee, one of two boys living in the 1956 Van Buren County, Iowa, jailhouse, earned his spending money by boxing groceries after school. He took a phone call from his mother one afternoon. Dolores asked him if there was anything in particular he wished to save from his room. Upon inquiry, Larry learned that a juvenile prisoner had set fire to the cell between Larry's room and the bathroom in an attempt to get free. Yes, Dolores was sure the entire building would go up soon so he'd better decide quick.

Firefighters extinguished the blaze in time to save the jailhouse. The Lee family cleaned up as best they could and got into their beds quite late that night. They were awakened again at 2:30 a.m. by Larry who was sleeping lightly because he felt anxious. He smelled smoke coming from the cell before much of a blaze took hold. The fire crew returned, put out the new blaze that had flared up in the wall, and that visit did the trick.

Our hypothetical family has grown comfortable after their efforts at making a jailhouse a home. Everyone eventually knew where everything was located, how equipment operated, and how records were to be kept. With experience, various duties and responsibilities could be streamlined. In the following chapter we will explore the wide variety of tasks that a sheriff's wife was required to take upon herself.

5

Mrs. Sheriff's Hat Tree

Keep yourself and your clothing clean. Wear a cap or keep hair tied up. Wash hands frequently, especially after using the toilet, and keep fingernails clean. If you have any contagious disease, or if you have any open cuts, sores, or boils, stay away from food and areas where food is prepared and stored.

—1961 *Handbook of Jail Food Service*

One night about midnight, my husband was called to a shooting in a neighboring town. At two a.m., our back doorbell started ringing. On the back step stood a tall, wild looking man. His hair was standing in all directions. He was quite bloody. He was in shock and shaking violently. He said 'I think I just killed a man.' He asked if he could come in and would I make him a cup of coffee. I grabbed a jail blanket that he wrapped around himself. He asked me to locate the sheriff but not tell anyone else where he was. I learned that Harley was driving the victim to the hospital. I asked the dispatcher to tell my husband 'that he was needed at home.' Harley immediately came home, knowing that something was wrong. He was very upset that I had opened the door to a suspected murderer. He arrested him immediately and placed him in jail.

—By Martha Kinkade who served
alongside Sheriff Harley Kinkade
from 1959 to 1973.

The Hollywood image of the old-time sheriff sitting around just cleaning his gun and chewing the fat with his cronies until gunfire broke out at the saloon doesn't stand up to closer investigation. The sheriff's role as county administrator took up far more of his time than rounding up bad guys. What exactly was required of a sheriff during the era of the mom-and-pop jail that he needed so much help from his wife and family? The array of administrative duties assigned to the office of sheriff through the centuries turns out to be rather mind-boggling: bailiff

Mildred Barrett Johnson sitting at the desk she shared with Sheriff Louis Johnson from 1941 to 1954 in Allegan County, Michigan. This picture was taken shortly after the couple assumed office. Note the stacks of ledgers behind Mildred. (Courtesy of Florine Johnson Gooding from the family archives.)

at county and district court, probation officer, supervisor of the jail, and county farm; tax assessor, tax collector, auctioneer for the sale of property confiscated for delinquent taxes; census taker, social worker, and driver's license examiner. The record keeping required just to maintain information on the prisoners filled various types of large and small ledgers.

In addition, many counties didn't pay their sheriff a set salary but reimbursed him for his expenses such as boarding prisoners and travel, paid him so much for individual services that he performed such as serving subpoenas, selecting juries, and notifying jury members when they were required to hear a case, for collecting delinquent taxes, and auctioning property. Many times, the calculations for how an arrest could be billed to the county practically required an advanced degree in mathematics. Old court records are covered in handwritten notations that the sheriff had been paid twenty cents to serve the subpoena, a dollar for travel, ten cents each for rounding up the jurors, etc. In those counties, the sheriff was paid virtually on "piece work" so every transaction that could be billed at the end of the quarter had to be accounted for in order to be reimbursed by the county commissioners.

Jan Jahnel Wepler, who grew up in the Mitchell County, Iowa, jail, observed that when she feels overwhelmed with all she has to do to provide a home for her family today, she thinks "of the day-to-day work mom did for her family while wearing the many hats of a sheriff's wife."

This chapter highlights the various roles taken on by the wives of sheriffs and jailors. These duties were the norm, requiring attention no matter what else might be happening with family members or inmates.

DEPUTY AND BAILIFF

In Washington County, Rhode Island, as elsewhere during the years just after the American Revolution, wealthy sheriffs turned their jails over to the jailor and his family. The jailors' wives "did the cooking, made clothing for prisoners, emptied tubs, and when necessary, served as guards to prevent escapes."[1] Jailhouse wives serving as unofficial deputies continued in most U.S. counties until the middle of the twentieth century.

As in most counties, the Chippewa County, Minnesota, sheriff's sales to foreclose on property of all kinds were traditionally conducted from the steps of the courthouse. During the Great Depression, there came a time when Sheriff Pedersen required a long stay in the hospital. Leila took over the functions of the office as well as those of the kitchen and became "the CEO of the jail and residence."[2] Marge remembered how her mother carried a small chalkboard with her and on it she wrote everything that needed attention.

While we were still an English colony, in what is now Bristol County, Rhode Island, a sheriff's wife also had a role to play: as bailiff. Courtrooms were not considered an appropriate place for a lady but there were occasions when a lady was required to be present. In 1722, Sheriff Charles Church summoned the unnamed wife of Christopher Green to appear before the grand jury to testify against one of her neighbors.[3] It was alleged that Israel Sabin did not attend religious services as required by the laws of the Massachusetts Bay Colony, the governing body for that county. It would have been appropriate for Mrs. Sheriff Church to accompany Mrs. Green to the hearing and wait with her until Mrs. Green was required to testify. Two hundred years later, Leila Pederson, like most of her sheriffing sisters across the nation, served this same function as bailiff in the court room when a woman or juvenile was on trial.

There were many times when the sheriff's wife found herself alone with prisoners. She might not put herself forward on our side of the jailhouse door, but she had to take charge should the times dictate. Dolores Lee of Van Buren County, Iowa, in the late 1950s, was such a woman. When it came to inmates, Dolores Lee's son reported that "she stood up to them!"

In 1960s Ellis County, Kansas, Anne Werth sat alone all night in the jail at the top of the courthouse as the building rocked and creaked from hundred-mile-per-hour winds. When the wind broke the television tower from the roof over her head, the situation appeared a bit bleak. Anne "stayed on alert and ready to spring into action if things worsened" so she could release the prisoners from their cells and herd them to safety. Fortunately, the falling tower was the worst of it, and she did not have to organize an evacuation single-handedly.

Of all the sheriff's wives included in this book, fewer than a dozen became official deputies while their husbands served as sheriff or jailor. For the majority of those few who did, becoming an official deputy did not change one's pay status. Just like all of the days when the sheriff's wife acted as unofficial deputy, the majority of official deputy wives didn't receive compensation for their time and service to the county.

Dorothy Rumbaugh of 1960s Jefferson County, Kansas, noted that she became an official but unpaid deputy the last few months of their term, and as such, she "served papers" for her husband. Another Kansan, Christina Peterka, was officially deputized for one specific occasion during the 1950s in Republic County. A woman had been brought in for stealing and the sheriff wanted the doctor to perform a cavity search on the suspect. As a deputy was required in the exam room during this procedure, and since the prisoner was a woman, the job fell to Christina.

In 1923, Violet Joss of Niobrara County, Wyoming, was sworn in as a deputy by her husband, Chris. He, like all sheriffs, had to be gone from the jail every day and many nights and this was his solution to that problem. Most sheriffs never thought to make it official. Other sheriffs turned down their wives' request to make it official. Because Chris Joss proved he had good sense, Violet is reported to be the first female deputy sheriff in Wyoming.

In the decade following, Martha Terrell's husband deputized her to serve as jail matron in Garfield County, Colorado. Martha and Roy's son, Hal, described his mother as standing over six feet tall, a former basketball player. She was a woman who brooked no nonsense from prisoners or from family.

Hal described Martha as a loving mother, but firm. This phrase cropped up often during interviews with jailhouse kids from across the nation. According to Hal, Sheriff Terrell was Martha's opposite in many ways. His strong suit was his ability to talk to people until they saw the error of their ways. This sheriffing pair, no-nonsense Martha and eloquent Roy, formed an effective team.

Evelyn Smith, a Victorian citizen of 1880 Kent County, Rhode Island, has come down through history because of her determination. It served her well as the wife of the county jailor, and upon his death, as jailor herself. During the twenty-five years that Evelyn served her county as deputy and jailor, her determined manner allowed for only two successful escapes.

Another deputized wife took up her duties when Arthur Brosenne took up the Howard County, Maryland, star in the early 1920s. Three days later, he appointed his wife, Katherine, as his deputy. Al Hafner of the Howard County Police Department informed the author that Katherine is reported to have said "I expect to fulfill the duties of a Deputy Sheriff just as a man would do. I ask nor do I desire any quarter because of my being a woman." The Brosennes served their two-year term and then retired from law enforcement. Apparently, Katherine didn't care for life on that side of the law. A few years later Katherine returned to the public eye "when she was charged with trying to bribe the county sheriff during a raid on her business establishment. She was charged with 'keeping a disorderly house.' "

In 1913, Olive Belle Field Chambers, at the age of fifty-four, pinned her official deputy sheriff badge on the bodice of the dress covering her corseted figure and began her career as San Diego County, California's "first petticoat turnkey"[4] (jailor). In 1913, Olive lived across the street from the jail and carried food from her kitchen to the inmates. "For a third of a century—and much of the time with no pay whatsoever— Mother Chambers devoted her life to the health and welfare of prisoners, particularly women prisoners."[5]

MAMA RODE SHOTGUN

Every once in a while, even the most dedicated sheriff's wife had to get out of the kitchen, out of the office, and out of the jail. "Mama rode shotgun for dad a lot," reported Deb Gebers Wood about her parents, Sheriff Don and Dell Gebers of Ida County, Iowa. "Many times she was his only back-up. She helped on booze busts before [the] liquor-by-the-drink [law was enacted], later in drug raids acting as matron for all female arrests."

The Gebers served Ida County before and after that elusive date in the last half of the twentieth century "when drugs became a problem." That date varied from county to county, but became the low-water mark that changed everything as it struck each county. Deb noted that once drugs came on the scene, the family members were threatened by a drug dealer and his gang members. Unfortunately, this was not a rare occurrence.

Loretta Fenton recalled that in Coleman County, Texas, she functioned as "secretary, the jailor, a deputy. We did the whole office, we did it. I went on calls with him to keep him from being by himself, an extra precaution, I thought, for me. I went on calls with him for four years, always, before we had any kids. Every call he went on, I went. I'd get in the back, and he'd get in the front, and I'd hold my shoe over their [the prisoner's] head!"[6]

In other counties, wives accompanied sheriffs on night patrol with their children asleep in the back seat. At other times, sheriff's drove the county on patrol with their children beside them, as young as four or five; grandchildren just as young.

Besides riding patrol, transferring prisoners was the most usual way for jailhouse wives to get away from those four walls. Transferring women and juveniles proved to be one of the major responsibilities for wives, daughters, mothers, and daughters-in-law, depending on the county and who was able to travel at the time.

Irene Ward of Rogers County, Oklahoma, noted that after World War II—"It was customary for an officer to take his wife because it was almost impossible to find another man who could take off work for several days as the County only paid for their motel and meals." Irene provided us with a glimpse into what a transfer was like. "For the first decade of our thirty years, there were no fast-food drive-in diners so we stopped at small diners and took the prisoner in with us. Some who were not trustworthy were kept handcuffed until they were in the booth. The prisoner went into the booth, Amos sat down next to him, and then the cuffs came off. I sat across from them."[7]

Transfer trips were planned so that each night was spent at a county seat along the route. This arrangement ensured that prisoners could be locked in jail. "The County Commissioners liked for the officer to take his wife to 'ride shotgun' because they didn't have to pay for another room. There weren't many motels and all had small rooms with one size bed, a double." Irene "collected receipts as they traveled, putting gasoline tickets in one envelope and food and motel tickets in another, making it more convenient for the commissioners when Amos turned in his mileage after we returned with the prisoner."[8]

ADMINISTRATIVE ASSISTANT

Early in our nation's history, Nabby Lillibridge "frequently filled out the required forms"[9] as part of her husband's job. This included collecting taxes for the town of South Kingstown in Washington County, Rhode Island, and filling out paperwork associated with keeping inmates such as arrest records, boarding records, expense reports, travel reports. Nathan Lillibridge served as the local jailor under a sheriff who delegated many of his responsibilities. Nabby also cooked for and tended to the inmates as long as they were incarcerated.

Because they had no children at the time, Mattie Campbell joined her husband in his office on a full-time basis while he served in Logan and, later, Ada County, Idaho, at the end of the nineteenth century. Mattie was placed in charge of administering the tax collection department. Mattie was listed as "Under Sheriff" in the Boise City Directory in 1899. By then the couple had two sons. The family was listed in the 1900 Census as living in the jail with six prisoners and their maid named Lodema Bates.

Maybel Simpson of Lincoln County, Oregon, became the deputy in charge of the tax collection department for her sheriffing husband in 1919. Because tax collection involved other people's money, it was a job of a sensitive nature. It required a great deal of attention to detail and considerable organizational ability. It appears to have been a job delegated to many a Mrs. Sheriff. It was noted by a local historian that Maybel was "thoroughly capable of handling the administrative affairs of the office."[10] When her husband died while still in office, county officials thought nothing of asking Maybel to serve out his term.

Emma Banister of Coleman County, Texas, in 1914 was reported to have possessed an "innate ability to manage everything"[11] as was true of most jailhouse wives who had to juggle family, home, and work that not only involved long hours in the kitchen but also pouring over paperwork and danger to kith and kin if one let her guard down.

In addition to assisting her husband with regular administrative duties when they took up the star and the apron in 1950, Essie Riddell of Burnet County, Texas, prepared and presented periodic reports to the county commissioners on

Maud Allen Tanner at her desk in the Antrim County, Michigan, Sheriff's Office in 1954. Her routine included distributing license plates, giving road tests, and writing driver's licenses. (Courtesy of H.A. Tanner family archives.)

the state of the jail finances. In most counties, the records might have been kept by "the little woman," but the official presentation was carried out by the sheriff.

In 1930s Holmes County, Ohio, Edith Weiss raised her seven children and worked alongside her sheriffing husband, with the help of their oldest daughter, Evelyn. In addition to most of the tasks discussed in this chapter, Evelyn also helped with one other: "In those days, license tag numbers were kept in a box and if anyone called to inquire as to whose tag was on a car, for any reason whatsoever, mom or I would look it up for them."

Not only was tax collecting and paperwork part of the administrative responsibilities assigned to a county sheriff, the responsibility for conducting driving tests fell to the sheriff and, more often, his wife. In Antrim County, Michigan, Maud Tanner noted that "I often had to shed my apron to write a driver's license or give a road test when Howard was out of the office" during much of her long tenure as sheriff's wife between 1937 and 1960. All paperwork, incoming and outgoing, was processed by Maud. Any records that had to do with the prisoners or the running of the office was her bailiwick.

MAMA SHERIFF

The sheriff's wife put her hand to anything and everything, with the majority of her time going toward cooking and serving as administrative assistant. In addition, she was required to function as the jail matron. For Betty Vinson of Lyon County, Iowa, that earned her the nickname in her community of "Mama Sheriff."

In counties across the nation, eventually paid professional matrons were hired to tend to inmates. This became commonplace after the 1960s. The San Diego County Sheriff's Museum Web site lists the responsibilities of professional matrons. Until then, all of these activities were performed by the sheriff's or jailor's wife and children in thousands of county jails since the American Revolution:

Booking prisoners
Searching prisoners
Fingerprinting
Accompanying them to cells
Report writing
Accompany juries to lunch during deliberations
Stay overnight with juries when sequestered
"Going on psycho pick-ups"
Making runs to State Hospital once a week,
Any out-of-county runs requiring a female
Sitting in on DA interviews involving juveniles.[12]

Annis Moore, her jailor husband, and daughter lived in the Nassau County, Florida, Jail in the 1970s. At the local historical society in 1999, Annis Moore-Littles and Cindy sat down to tape an oral history of their experiences. Because the synopsis to that oral history describes so well what went on in many county jails, it is included here verbatim:

Both Mrs. Moore-Littles and her daughter spoke of their years at the jail with warmth and humor. They indicated that "times were different back then" and that for the most part the prisoners were good people who had just done something foolish—like getting drunk on a Saturday night. There were many "repeat customers." Cindy felt that the inmates looked out for her and protected her. She played on the grounds and had friends visit her, just like other children. Mrs. Moore-Littles was cook for the inmates on Sundays and holidays, and was matron presiding over the female prisoners. As matron, Mrs. Moore-Littles was required to deal with women of limited mental ability who possessed little knowledge of hygiene. This was a time before social workers, and the jail staff tried to fulfill that role in addition to seeing that prisoners completed their jail sentences.

Annis noted that the jail held 75 to 80 inmates and on one Sunday morning after a poker party raid, Annis found 150 inmates waiting for their breakfast. While both the county and the city had their own jails, all female and juvenile offenders were housed in the county facility. This was not unique, many county jails entered into the same arrangement across the nation.

Annis also commented on a startling situation that resulted in a change in the law. "[Male] deputies were not allowed to touch females in the process of arresting them. On one occasion, as the matron was preparing an arriving female for booking, a gun was found in the woman's bra. The woman had ridden to the jail in the back of a patrol car with a gun on her body. After that happened, deputies were allowed to touch the center of a female's chest between her breasts to make sure that she was not concealing a weapon in her bra. It was not unusual when booking a female prisoner to find a straight razor taped to the woman's upper thigh.

"Juveniles were housed along with female inmates on the first floor and cared for by the matron. A young boy hanged himself while he was being held, and was found by my husband, Bobby. He never quite got over it." She made no comment about her own response to the suicide.[13]

COMMUNICATIONS OFFICER

Edith Weiss and many others developed a communications method before there were two-way radios for law enforcement. In Holmes County, Ohio, during the 1930s, Edith turned on the front porch light if the sheriff was required at the jail. As the sheriff made his rounds, he'd spot the porch light and know she needed him. Edith's grandson, David, wrote about the night that the porch light came on while the sheriff and his deputy ate supper at a local restaurant. The sheriff looked up from his plate, noticed the porch light, and "excused himself saying he had to go over and see what the trouble was. The next thing the deputy knew, the sheriff raced off with his red light flashing and the siren blaring . . . a very rare occurrence. He'd just gotten word that one of the Amish farmers had been shot and robbed."[14]

Counties did not have two-way radios until well after World War II had ended. This was true in Rogers County, Oklahoma, when Amos Ward started his thirty-year stint as sheriff. Irene recalled that if Amos or the deputy were out and needed to call in, they found a pay phone.

When another Irene, Irene Gray of Saguache County, Colorado, worked alongside her undersheriff [and jailor] husband, Jack, she turned to Ma Bell for help. She reported that she had to "enlist the aid of the local telephone operator to help me find either Jack or Charlie [Sheriff McCormick] when a call came through for them."

By 1954, Mary Ann Darrow's sheriff's office had a radio but no transmitter. The transmitter was located in Ed's car in Powell County, Montana. "I was able to hear the calls from the Butte and Anaconda sheriff, the police departments, and any Highway Patrol cars in the vicinity. The city police had a transmitter in their car." The city police used the sheriff's office as their headquarters, they were in and out of the office often. "In the event the sheriff was out of the office, and I needed to contact him, I would have to wait until a city policeman stopped by and ask the officer to relay a message to the sheriff." The officer then let Ed know Mary Ann needed to talk to him and he'd either call from a phone or come by the office.

Eventually, everyone had the ability to speak directly with sheriffs and deputies in their cars. That added to the number of ways in which citizens contacted their local sheriff. Dell Gebers' daughter, Deb, recalled how the Ida County, Iowa, family quarters included her dad's after-hours office and how her mom ran the radios, answered the phone, and "people came to our house at all hours." This appears to have been the status quo for most jailhouses.

The family quarters usually functioned as the after-hours office of the sheriff, if his office was not located in the jailhouse. Glenda Camelin of Boone County, Iowa, noted that their sheriff's office was located in the courthouse. The family lived in the jail nearby. "At night and on weekends, when the sheriff's office was closed, the jail office served as the booking room, communications center, etc. I answered phones, took radio calls and served as matron as necessary."

Serving as communications officer became a constant responsibility when the sheriff's office was in the jail. Mary Jahnel's daughter, Dode, wrote: "My mother was a soft spoken, hard working lady who went about her duties without fanfare and very little recognition. There was only the Sheriff and one deputy, so when they were out of the office, everything was left for my mother to do. She prepared meals for the prisoners, answered the phone, radios and the door. She was never given an official call number to use when responding on the radios; everyone referred to her by '22-1W.' The 22 was our county number, 1 was my dad's official number and W meant 'wife.' There were radios in the kitchen, my parent's bedroom and the office so the sheriff could be on call 24-hours a day."

While Mary Jahnel might represent the norm for sheriffs' wives in the 1960s, a few were more fortunate and did not endure the constant distraction of the sheriff's radio. Anne Werth in Ellis County, Kansas, recalled the one occasion in which she monitored the radio for the sheriff's office. It was the "night of a big blizzard. A farmer with a bad heart needed to go to the hospital so they called the Undertaker to come out to get him in his big car, but the Undertaker got trapped out at the farm." The sheriff was then called to bring in the Undertaker and the sick farmer. "Clarence got trapped. The Undersheriff thought he might be able to get them all back to town but he got trapped . . . they were all taken in by a nearby farmer who put them up for the night. The sick farmer and everyone else survived the ordeal." Anne took charge of the office until they all returned.

Not everyone got their license before using the radio. Neva Allen of Poweshiek County, Iowa, filled in on the radio when needed but she didn't know the official military-based clarification words to keep things clear (A = alpha, R = roger, W = wilco) so made up her own as she went. That must have been a hoot for the men at the other end of the transmission, but it got the job done.

Up in Door County, Wisconsin, during the 1960s, Gloria Bridenhagen, the sheriff, and their four children did not live in the jail but Gloria served as dispatcher and receptionist for her husband. The family home was situated thirty miles from the county seat, yet Gloria performed her duties from home. "Citizens knew that if they needed the sheriff they would do best to call at his home where Gloria could relay calls."[15]

Not every Mrs. Sheriff served as communications officer for her husband, but most did. In some locations, the requirements did not stop there. Evelyn Robinson of 1950s Windham County, Vermont, not only lived in the jail family quarters and raised her family there during this time of expanding communications equipment, "but she also answered the 'fire phone' for the Volunteer Fire Department." She managed to stay on top of all that plus cook, wash jail bedding, matron, and do all of the things that a Mrs. Sheriff needed to do.

LAUNDRESS

Just as Evelyn Robinson washed jail bedding, so too did many sheriffs' wives through the ages. Irene Gray, who lived in the Saguache County, Colorado, jail with husband, Jack, noted that she served as jail laundress between 1951 and 1959. Maureen Elston reported that "for thirteen years we lived in the Wright County, Iowa, jail apartment (really nice living quarters, by the way)—a two-story brick apartment with three bedrooms, living room, dining room, 1½ baths and finished basement. I cooked lots of meals there and washed lots and lots of bedding in the laundry room in the basement."

Before the modern age of electronic displays and washers that can handle a variety of fabrics with the push of a button, washing clothes and jail bedding was a physically demanding ordeal. Zita Singler Maddox recalled during an oral history interview late in her life what it was like to wash clothes prior to the use of wringer washing machines. The Singlers sheriffed in 1913. "We washed by hand then, see. You know they used to boil clothes in those old copper boilers? Well, we had that. I remember I used to take the big sheets, you know, get a stick to lift them up to get them out of there."[16]

Nothing had improved very much by 1928, when Martha Bulman of Allamakee County, Iowa "had to do laundry for inmates as well as her family and it was done on a washboard and several tubs and dried outdoors." Martha raised daughter Charlotte in two jails during the Depression, the old one with the washboard and tubs, and the new facility with "a wringer washing machine but no clothes dryer so we carried wet washed clothes down three floors to hang them outside on the line."

Laundry was handled differently in the 1960s for Elma Sinclair, but the trips were the same. The family lived at the top of the Hodgeman County, Kansas, courthouse. She too served as jail laundress and was required to tote dirty clothes and bedding down three flights of stairs, out to the local laundromat, and back up three flights of stairs. Groceries were handled in the same manner.

As amazing as it seems, even as late as 1971 at the Kossuth County Jail in Iowa, Nancy Fitzpatrick was provided with only a wringer-style washer to use for bedding and clothes. Tom and Nancy purchased an electric dryer to make life a little more modern since the couple were expecting their second child during the year they spent as jailors.

When Christina Peterka moved into the Republic County, Kansas, jail in 1950, she cleaned it and the family quarters from top to bottom. After that, she helped the janitor they hired to keep it clean. "She put herself in charge of washing the mattress ticking," her daughter reported. "Sheets were not allowed due to them being used in escape and suicide attempts."

Not every sheriff's wife attended to laundry. It was noted that the trustees who worked at the Jackson County, Missouri, jail during the day boiled the blankets for the beds every two weeks, washed the cement floors daily, and cooked for the thirty-eight prisoners. The trustees bathed twice a week while those on the chain gang-bathed daily.

MOTHER, NURSE, AND TEACHER

For ten months, Bernice (Bennie) Mills Cooksey watched over her husband as he recuperated after being shot in the line of duty. In 1965 Terrell County, Texas, Bill Cooksey went looking for the "Mexican bandito" wanted for robbery. The hombre raided across the border in the tradition of a century earlier, making life miserable in the county. Bennie, who was noted for having "served beautifully in her role as Bill's 'straight woman' to his quips and joke set-ups watched her husband and a Texas Ranger drive away at the end of those ten months, determined to track down the bandit." Another shoot-out ensued near the old general store at Dryden, and this time, Bill brought the fellow in and locked him in a cell for Bennie to feed.

Pauline Folkers in the Chickasaw County, Iowa, jail during the 1950s "sat up with sick prisoners," noted her daughter, Paulette. In Mitchell County, Iowa, a decade later, Mary Jahnel's daughter observed her mother functioning "as a medical aide as she doled out prescription drugs at their appropriate times and determining whether a headache warranted an aspirin."

On top of everything else going on in and around the jailhouse, care of the insane fell to jailhouse wives everywhere. When families were no longer able to care for the member whose mental health continued to deteriorate, the judge held a hearing. The judge then turned the insane family member over to the sheriff until a bed could be found in the appropriate institution. Often, this wait for a bed took months. Usually, the sheriff and his wife would then transfer their charge to a state insane asylum.

When Marge Pedersen Bovee was growing up in the Chippewa County, Minnesota, jail in the 1920s and 1930s, she noted how her mother, Leila, took on the role of teacher for inmates, in addition to all of her other responsibilities. Marge recalled how her mother "saw young men coming in for public drunkenness, being jailed for not knowing when to stop drinking. And many were so poorly educated. After I started school, mother would take her blackboard and ask 'who wants to learn to read and write?' "[17] Leila had been a school teacher in her younger years.

Providing reading materials and games for the prisoners was a common task taken on by a jailhouse wife. In the 1950s, Essie Riddell of Burnet County, Texas, "took books and magazines to male and female prisoners, ran the jail library (which soon became the first Burnet municipal library), and escorted prisoners to church on Sundays."[18]

AND THEN SHE WAS SHERIFF

In some counties there were laws on the books forbidding a sheriff to succeed himself or legislating that he couldn't serve for more than two consecutive terms. This protected citizens from someone taking hold of the office and abusing the enormous power, especially when the sheriff also served as tax assessor, which many did. The law provided protection from abuse, but it ensured that a neophyte held office too much of the time, especially as times became more complicated after drugs and gangs became a problem.

For the majority of the era of the mom-and-pop jail, it was relatively common for an incoming sheriff to hire the outgoing sheriff as his deputy, if the county budget allowed. This kept at least one knowledgeable man with a badge in the county while the new sheriff "learned the ropes." Anne Werth's husband, Clarence, also hired the outgoing sheriff as his undersheriff when he took office in Ellis County, Kansas, in 1960. In Hodgeman County, Kansas, that same year, the elderly former sheriff was hired on as Francis Sinclair's deputy. He spent most of his time walking around town, talking to folks, reporting to Francis if he heard of any shenanigans taking place. This proved extremely useful when Francis made his rounds. He knew what to look for as he drove the county roads.

One of the results of term limits was that the jailhouse family moved a lot as they came in and out of office. Sometimes the leapfrogging pair consisted of the sheriff and his wife during the twentieth century. Who knew better than the jail matron and sheriff's helpmate how to administer the county jail? By keeping the job between husband and wife, the family could remain in the family quarters term after term.

Mary Jacobson of Barron County, Wisconsin, served as her husband's paid deputy in the late 1920s and then won the top spot when her husband couldn't succeed himself. At some point between the November elections and January 1 when she took office, something about a visitor to the jail attracted Mary's attention. Deputy Mary arrested the visitor for possession of moonshine. She pinned on the star come New Year's Day and she kept a close eye on that moonshine smuggling jail visitor while he served out his sentence.

For the first two terms of Francis Sinclair's tenure as Hodgeman County, Kansas, sheriff during the 1960s, Elma continued working outside the home. When Francis, a Republican, was not able to run for office again due to term limits, the county fathers asked Elma, a Democrat, to run. She took a leave of absence from her job, ran for sheriff, and won. The Sinclair's are one of many sheriffing couples who leapfrogged each other for several elections, but this is the only one the author heard of where the individuals belonged to opposing political parties.

Elma recalled that the most disturbing thing that she encountered while sheriffing was being required to retrieve body parts. There was a law on the books that stated that only the sheriff could perform this function. Elma remembered one ghastly night in which she had to collect the dismembered foot of a woman after an auto accident.

When her two years as sheriff were over, Elma did not return to her former full-time job. Instead she stayed on as her husband's undersheriff, taking care of the office work, record keeping, and cooking—traditional work for a Mrs. Sheriff, but one that came with a modern title in this case. Speaking of titles, Elma had a nickname bestowed upon her by a friend when she donned the star. The Highway Patrolman always called Elma "Dickless Tracy" which to this day makes her blush.

Delores Lein of Sawyer County, Wisconsin, ran on the platform of "two for the price of one"[19] and won. Because she, like almost every other sheriff's wife, was already handling so much of the administrative responsibility, it took no imagination to see that she could continue doing so. Delores declared that she would continue in the many non-policing aspects of the job and Ernie would continue "tussling with the bad guys." When Sheriff Delores took office, Ernie took up his position as unpaid deputy.

In the following chapters, we discover who in the county helped Mrs. Sheriff perform all of her functions. She had to become adept at supervising the work of assistants who ranged from inmates to family members, from father-in-law to her youngest children.

6

With a Little Help from My Trustees

If asked the question as to whether you would rather see a movie in black and white or Technicolor, it is a safe choice that your answer would be Technicolor. The Technicolor movie, in addition to having its stars and a story to tell, has color which emphasizes the entire picture. Need it be said that the same thing is true with salads? Take cole slaw, for example. What crossed strips of pimento or a dash of paprika won't do for its appearance! Or lettuce or tomato—doesn't a dash of French dressing make all the difference? Follow your cook book suggestions as to color combinations and do not be afraid to let your artistic ability be shown.

—1961 *Handbook of Jail Food Service*

The Kossuth County, Iowa, jail "was horrible inside, all steel panels and peeling paint, rancid smelling mattresses on small cots. Each cell had a toilet with no seat and a tiny sink, all horribly stained and impossible to clean. I refused! However, about once a week, I did a quick once over, and again after a prisoner was transferred. We cleaned the cell as well as we could. Usually the prisoner had been a drunk and had vomited in the cell, so we had to scrub it down."

—By Nancy Fitzpatrick Layton, who served alongside Deputy Tom Fitzpatrick in 1971.

Now that the breadth of responsibilities assigned to each sheriffing family has been revealed, the next logical question is "How did they get it all done?" The following four chapters explore who helped make it so. This chapter is devoted to inmates, known as "trustees," who helped with the chores.

Lulu Knapp, four years old when her family moved into the basement of the Griggs County, North Dakota, courthouse in 1907, recalled the time that her dad heard about two safecrackers in the area. He informed his fellow citizens and someone let him know when they'd seen two "suspicious characters get off the train"[1] and go into a restaurant. Mason and his deputy found the strangers eating at the counter. Mason took out his sidearm and covered the men while he questioned them. They turned out to be the safecrackers and, although they were armed, they came peacefully. The deputy jailed the men while Mason went through their bags. He found appropriate tools for breaking into safes and a bottle of nitroglycerin, which he buried.

One of the men was sent to the penitentiary. His sidekick, sentenced to just one year, served his time in Lulu's jail. After being a good inmate for eleven months, Mason "let him out of his cell and gave him work to do around the house or down at the livery barn. He ate at the table with the family and was so good to Mama [who had been left an invalid after a fall]. He pushed her wheelchair around wherever she wanted to go. I remember the day he was to leave. All morning, he played our phonograph and visited with Mama. When he said goodbye, he cried."[2]

The sidekick safecracker in Lulu's jail was an exception rather than the rule. Generally, trustees were citizens of the county in which they were incarcerated. They were well known by the sheriff, as were their families. Once an inmate proved that he was capable of serving his sentence in a responsible manner, he might be selected to function as a jail trustee. This privilege allowed an inmate to break the boredom of his incarceration with activities that were beneficial to the running of the jail and the family quarters. Some also cleaned the courthouse or worked on the county farm.

In some jails, all inmates were expected to do the work required to keep the facility clean. Irene Gray of Saguache County, Colorado, noted that while she and husband, Jack, served as jailors in the 1950s, their facility was heated with wood and coal. "The men would get their own from the back yard once a day." That was about it as far as finding a legitimate way out of one's cell in Saguache County.

Anne Werth recalled how, a decade later, the Ellis County, Kansas, prisoners kept their own cells clean along with the bull pen. Because of this, Anne never had specific "trustees" to help her.

Anne's jail had been declared fit to hold federal prisoners as well as county inmates. As a result, Bobby Seal of the Black Panthers spent a night with the Werths on his way to Chicago for the trial of the "Chicago Seven." Bobby became a knowledgeable commentator on the state of local jails during this long journey from Los Angeles. In his book, *Seize the Time*, he noted that Anne's jail had been painted by the prisoners. He also wrote that hers was the best jail he'd ever been in:

> The jail was a large building. They put us in a cell with three other prisoners.... [The Sheriff] lived in the jail and his wife cooked the food. He was an older cat who didn't like hippies and long hair at all, but he seemed to be a nice person. In that jail they had TV in the tanks [cells] for the prisoners, and there were razor blades and after-shave lotion, magazines, cards, checkers. You name it, they had it. The guards wore civilian clothes. There were four tanks with four bunks in each tank and a large day room. It was a clean jail because the prisoners had painted it. You went out across the hall after you came out

of the tank, into the day room. Close behind the bars was a telephone. The sheriff said, "if you need anything just pick the telephone up and let me know." You could stay up as long as you wanted. It was the best jail I've been in, in my life. But I still hate jails.[3]

Ironically, the next night, somewhere in Missouri, Bobby came across the worst jail he'd ever visited. "This was the dirtiest, filthiest jail I'd ever been in. The sheriff was an old cat with an old gun slung off his hip. I had never seen such a filthy place. When I say filthy, you have to imagine what I'm describing, and I'm not exaggerating one pound."[4] He elaborated on the details: "The cells had crud in all the corners, an inch and two inches thick. It smelled like it'd been there for years. The bunks were only two feet wide with little mattresses that were ripped open and filthy, with bugs crawling all over them. You could knock some bugs off, you'd look down at your hand, and there were some more bugs."[5] When writing about the food that was served, he noted that "it looks like slop. It was just a rundown, filthy, no-good, dirty jail, a place that almost made me vomit."[6] All of the prisoners in this jail slept in the clothes they came in wearing and "there weren't any blankets, no blankets at all . . . the next morning I noticed I was scratching and itching. Bugs were all over my body and I had to shake my shirt out. Later on at the Cook County [IL jail], I found out I had caught the crabs in that filthy jail."[7]

Anne Werth recalled that she had one inmate so intent on cleanliness that he had to be stopped. Anne's jail sat on the top of the Ellis County, Kansas, courthouse. An old man being held who was not used to life in a jail cell got carried away. "When he washed floors he used so much water, it ran down into the ceiling of the Clerk's Office below so we had to stop him from being quite so clean."

Mary Ann Darrow in Powell County, Montana, during the early 1950s had a baby in diapers when they took up tending to the jail. It being January in Montana, hanging diapers out on the line wasn't an option. Mary Ann set up drying racks in the living quarters to hold the diapers she washed three times a week. That is, until one of the inmates "offered to hang the diapers in the cell block to get them dry. He would hang the diapers and return them neatly tri-folded ready for use."

When Mildred Johnson presided as Mrs. Sheriff of Allegan County, Michigan, her son-in-law, Kirby, served as chief deputy. Mildred's daughter, Florine, recalled that in the 1940s she had babies in diapers and Kirby impressed her by volunteering to "take our new baby's laundry to the jail to do when not busy. Eventually, I discovered that the rascal had offered a pack of cigarettes to a trustee to do the job!"

The work of the trustees extended beyond the cell block. Florine Gooding also recalled that "one important duty of the trustees was to stoke the coal furnace which provided steam heat for the entire building. Clearing the walks and driveway during snow days was also a trustee task. Summer demanded lawn mowing by a prisoner. Depending on a prisoner's ability, laundry also provided work for some."

Who decided which inmates were reliable and trustworthy enough to be called a trustee? In many cases, the lawman had that responsibility. In other cases, the district attorney told Mrs. Sheriff who might leave their cells to help around the living quarters or the courthouse. Lily Serles of Adams County, Wisconsin, during the latter half of the 1950s gained her helpers that way. She said they "did the usual, and occasionally came into the kitchen for coffee, cake or pie when invited."

Some Mrs. Sheriffs decided themselves whom they trusted. This was the case for Martha Terrell in Garfield County, Colorado, during the Depression. Her kitchen housed a coal-fired stove for cooking and the trustees kept the coal bucket filled, cut kindling, and helped wash dishes and clean up after meals. In return, the trustees were allowed out of the cell area and ate meals with the family at the kitchen table. Her son, Hal, reported that Martha "never had any problems with any that she chose."

In 1970s Nassau County, Florida, "there were large sinks in the laundry area where the trustees washed the meal dishes and trays, and also did up the jail laundry in the washers and dryers."[8] The old jail has been turned into the Jail Museum and Annis Moore-Littles pointed out that the room now designated as the Victorian Room used to house two cells for trustees. One of those cells was not often used so had been turned into a repository for larger evidence. It was there that young Cindy's Christmas presents were hidden. "The trustees were not locked into their cells at night and could move around at will, but that sometimes led to them spying on female inmates from the windows of the one room that overlooked the female area on the first floor."[9]

Because Madge Harris is small of stature, standing only five feet tall, when she needed light bulbs changed in the twelve-foot ceilings in the 1950s Wilson County, Kansas, family quarters, she called in a trustee to help. They also cleared cobwebs from corners for her.

The same was true of Edith Weiss in Holmes County, Ohio, in the 1930s. Window washing was such a chore when the glass continues for ten feet. Trustees helped with that chore, with scrubbing floors and any of the heavy work there was to do around the place. When they first moved in, Edith took on the daunting task of sewing curtains for those windows and asked the trustees to hang them for her. Her daughter, Evelyn, remembered that one trustee fell off his ladder while helping to clean one day.

Several jails hosted the same people every winter. It seems to have been rather common throughout the country for older men to "gently break the law" in order to spend ninety days in the county jail when the weather turned cold. In this way, Viola White gained the help of Earl, an elderly man who stayed several winters in the Leelanau County, Michigan, jail. "He served meals, helped with cooking and washing up, washed the patrol cars, helped with laundry, yard work, snow shoveling" along with other trustees in residence the years that Viola lived in the family quarters. She also fed two or three elderly men from the nearby Reservation each winter. They helped put up the storm windows, raked the yard and helped Viola around the house "in exchange for a heated room and food."

Mary Jahnel's daughters remembered that in Mitchell County, Iowa, between 1964 and 1984, a retired painter spent many winters with them. During his stay, he always painted or wallpapered a room or two. "This got to be an annual occurrence, but he got a warm place to stay, good food, and eventually the whole house was re-decorated" at a considerable savings to the county taxpayers.

Mary Jahnel matroned for female prisoners and when one was with them for a long time and could be trusted, she was allowed out of her cell to iron. Mary's daughter recalled how much the women "appreciated the diversion from boredom and mom appreciated the help." Other women inmates "baked and cleaned with mom just to break the boredom of the four gray walls and barred window."

Lorna Werner's daughter, Karen, reported that one Harvey County, Kansas, woman was often arrested for being drunk and naked in public during the 1960s. "After she dried out, which usually took about a week, she'd get all cleaned up and mom would let her out to help with cooking and cleaning. She especially loved to iron. She could get stains out of clothes better than a dry cleaner's."

Fifty years earlier, John Banister and his wife, Emma, utilized trustees at the Coleman County, Texas, jail. "The whole jail was heated by big coal stoves, and usually one [trustee] or another was allowed to carry the scuttles of coal upstairs and down."[10] She also recorded that they "swept the halls and stairs if they volunteered, but Papa never left them unsupervised for a moment."[11]

In the same state, local historian Mary Kate Durham found something altogether different. She reported about her visit to the Hood County jail "only to find everyone gone except for one inmate who was in the kitchen, doing dishes. He explained that when he was finished with his chores he'd go back to his cell."[12]

Martha Bulman's daughter, Charlotte, told the Depression-era story of "the last year we were in the courthouse, three young men were in for stealing a sack of chickens. They were each sentenced to a year in jail. They were so thankful if mom would ask them to come into our quarters to do dishes or wash windows or scrub and wax floors because it was a chance to get out from behind the bars. They often shoveled snow in the winter" in Alamakee County, Iowa.

Those who knew her, remember Bertha Punches Miller as a pleasant, hardworking woman. She served her community as Mrs. Sheriff during the Depression, in Allegan County, Michigan. Like so many in her position, she paid a hired girl to help her around the jail and also supervised the work of one or two trustees. They'd peel potatoes, wash the dishes, mop the floors. Her family recalls that "she treated [the trustees] kindly and was very highly respected by all the inmates."

In nearby Chippewa County, Minnesota, during the same time period, Leila Pedersen often served as matron for a hairdresser. Leila's daughter, Marge, told a local reporter that "mom always had a permanent" when the beautician served her time. Marge added that "at mom and dad's 50th wedding anniversary celebration, so many people came who had been put in [their] jail at some time."

Lucky Leila took off her kitchen apron at one point and stepped aside when one of the inmates volunteered to cook while he was incarcerated. "It so happened he was a former chef on the Great Northern Railroad and a Number One cook!"

In the 1970s, Eileen Chesbro did not have to cook during their service in the Oswego County, New York, jail. She turned that job over not to an inmate, but to a local cook who came in to prepare meals in the jail's kitchen. The cook, the owner of a local restaurant, prepared jail meals when his own establishment was not experiencing its lunch and dinner rush. The basement served as the jail mess and inmates ate at tables down there after being served by trustees. "A section of the basement was used by trustees to butcher and freeze meat for meals. The jail was associated with the county farm where trustees worked" and errant juveniles lived. Eileen reported that the trustees "worked on the jail farm tending to livestock and even raised a couple of deer."

In Clarion County, Pennsylvania, trustees made an annual trek to the courthouse tower each autumn to "clear away the pigeon droppings that had gathered up there during the year. They would shovel the pigeon droppings and what not out the front and into the bed of a waiting pick-up truck. The droppings were taken to a local farm to be spread as fertilizer."[13]

In 1965, in Greenwood County, South Carolina, Vernice Cooper's children, Jeanne and Sam, were in their early teens when dad took up sheriffing. In a reversal of the scenario whereby a compassionate Mrs. Sheriff provides for her inmates, the Cooper siblings came under the care of two trustees.

Already incarcerated in jail when the Coopers took up residence, three trustees named Dot, Fox, and Junior were serving time for murders. It is not clear why the trio were allowed to serve their time in the county jail, but they did. Dot killed her husband's girlfriend. Fox shot someone in a drunken fight. And Junior, described by Sam as "a somewhat murkier figure," had a story not known by the children. Sam reported that Junior was an older man and more solitary in his ways. He performed his trustee duties "but didn't socialize with anyone, kept to himself so he was not as well known to the family."

Vernice taught developmentally disabled children at a local institution on a full-time basis before her husband won his election, and because of this trio of trustees, was able to continue doing so during her stint in the jailhouse. The sheriff spent his time in the courthouse or out in the county on official business. Dot took young Jeanne under her wing and Fox did the same with Sam. Jeanne found herself totally miserable over living in the jail. Just at the age when most teens want to fit in and be "normal," Jeanne withdrew from socializing because she didn't want to ask friends to visit her or have boys pick her up for dates at "the jail!" She spent all of her free time with Dot, either in the house or in Dot's cell. Dot had decorated her cell rather nicely, with her own television. Jeanne poured out her woes to Dot "as well as sharing the discovery of how interesting boys could be, and events that took place at school. Dot impacted my life in a very positive way."

Even the family dog, a Chihuahua named Pudgy, loved to visit Dot in her homey cell. Jeanne remembered how Pudgy "would scurry past the iron door to Dot's cell. I think Dot loved and cared for that dog more than the family did."

Sam found much more with which to entertain himself by hanging around with Fox, a young trustee in his early twenties. The two formed a strong friendship. During the day, the trustees worked around the house, cooking for inmates and preparing separate meals for the family. They cleaned both the house and the jail. Fox was given a bicycle to run errands. And it was while running errands that Fox and Sam had some of their best fun. While out and about on jail business, Fox stopped to visit with his own family from time to time. If Sam was along, he'd visit too. Fox washed patrol cars and let underage Sam drive them. Fox occasionally abused his privileged status and went out drinking. Then he brought beer back to the jail to bribe Sam to keep him from reporting the violation to Sheriff Cooper. Fox and Sam visited the "more interesting" cell-bound inmates incarcerated upstairs. They played cards with them to pass the time. Sam recalled that everyone bet toothbrushes because that was "the only currency they had."

Sam describes the relationship he shared with Fox as "a well-rounded relationship, with a lot of trust and a little deviltry tossed in. Fox helped me to understand that life is not black and white; that there is good in everyone." Sam looks back at those years as significant because a young man shared a friendship with him just as he was starting his teens. "It may have strained the bounds of jail ethics, but it was important to me." Sam grew up to become a Presbyterian minister.

As noted above, some trustees went beyond the jailhouse doors and into the broader community on jail business. Madge Harris had trustees who not only waxed her floors and shook the heavy rugs, but they swept the big porches in the front and back of the family quarters, cleaned the steps and sidewalks. "One was gone so long at this that another prisoner commented on it, and speculated that he was sweeping the walk all around the Courthouse just so he could stay out!"

Larry, one of the Wilson County, Kansas, trustees who helped with things like heavy rugs, still made Madge chuckle years later. "I had a garden in front of the residence, so I had one of the prisoner trustees (Larry) dig it up for a flower bed. Unknown to me, he went to the feed store close by and got a seed potato and planted it in my flower bed. Once the flowers came up, I went out to weed every evening. Eventually I spotted a tall weed, or so I thought, and I pulled it up. Of course, then I saw that it was a potato plant. I knew right away who had put it there. We all had a big laugh out of that."

In the 1950s, Essie Riddell of Burnet County, Texas, with the help of inmates, "landscaped the jail grounds, which included 'many rare plants' and the bamboo grove"[14] that supplied the local kids with fishing poles. Martha Bulman in Allamakee County, Iowa released her trustees "to shovel snow, cut grass or weed the garden and they appreciated a chance to work and get some fresh air."

During the 1920s in Texas County, Missouri, as noted earlier, trustees lived in the barn at the farm of Sheriff Kelly and got their fair share of fresh air also. They helped run the farm, tending to all of the work required to keep the farm producing. In addition, the trustees helped out in other ways, such as when the state police brought their blood hounds for practice. A trustee would be turned loose and the dogs tracked him.

Typically, an escape prompted the sheriff and his staff to hightail it in hot pursuit. The running shoe was on the other foot one warm afternoon in modern-day Clarion County, Pennsylvania, when a juvenile inmate escaped from his cell.

One of the trustees reported that he'd seen the direction the boy took. As the inmate was wearing running shoes and shorts, the deputy asked if he'd like to capture the escapee. The sheriff's office was called when a citizen discovered two men fighting in a parking lot. When "the deputies responded to investigate, they found the trustee still wrestling with the escaped prisoner. They broke up the fight and took both men back into custody."[15]

Betty Swanson and her mother lived in the Lucas County, Iowa, jail during the late 1950s. One of the prisoners kept the jail spotlessly clean, saving the family a lot of tedious work. He took care of the garden: weeding, harvesting, etc. The trustee confessed that he loved cherry pie. A cherry tree grew in the jailhouse yard. To maximize the harvest, this trustee bound the tree with cheesecloth to keep birds from the cherries. As his reward for the bumper crop of cherries, Betty wrote that "my mom and I baked cherry pies everyday. That tree was loaded!" Everyone reaped the reward of the trustee's hard work to save those cherries.

During that overwhelming period of overburdened jails and sheriff's wives during Prohibition in the counties around Chicago, Marian Edinger's children recalled that most of the inmates at the McHenry County, Illinois, jail tried to do things that helped Marian, "and please her. Two talented young trustees carved snow statues, including an almost life-size one of a man riding a horse. They made sure that mother came out to see them."

Annis Moore-Littles informed her interviewers, Suanne Thamm and Marlene Schang, that the prisoners at the Nassau County, Florida, jail during the 1970s were given what was called "good time" for performing helpful tasks. They could cut their time served by helping. The jailor reported to the local judge which inmate had "good time" and the judge reduced the sentences accordingly. Some "trustees went out on work-release during the week and served their time on the weekends. If they earned money, they had to reimburse the County $3/day for their keep."[16]

Dode, daughter of Mary Jahnel who served as jailhouse wife in Mitchell County, Iowa, during the 1960s, grew up to marry Sheriff Bill Westendorf of Bremer County in the 1970s. Mary and Dode are the only mother/daughter jailhouse wives found for this book. Dode reported that work-release was extended to include attending college classes for one young man who had to serve a year. "He went to and from his classes and spent the rest of his time in jail."

The oddest task assigned to trustees came out of Boulder County, Colorado, in the 1970s. The jailor was married to Goldie Fling who also served as a deputy. The mountainous forest outside of Boulder housed an ever-growing "hippie village" where young people not only communed with nature but bought and sold drugs. Goldie Fling's husband was given the task of cleaning out the village. The first thing Roy did was take twenty-five inmates from the jail. Then he talked the Game Warden into bringing along a black bear he'd recently caged for removal to a more remote spot. The Warden backed the cage to the edge of the hippie village while Roy and his twenty-five inmates stood waiting. The Warden "opened the bear cage and the bear came out but didn't show any sign of going into the village so the fellow from the State shot at the bear's rear, singeing its fur. That caused the bear to bellow and squall and run through the village, and hippies flew in every direction. The prisoners followed along behind and finished the job. Then the hippie camp was no more."[17]

If our hypothetical jailhouse family live in a county that allowed such activity, the sheriff-wanna-be's wife might find life less hectic because of the help of a few trustees. Few jailhouse wives found life leisurely. The responsibilities were too numerous and the work too arduous for anything approaching "leisurely." Because of that, despite the help of trustees, other citizens were asked to come to the jail to work. The following chapter deals with those citizens and how they contributed to the smooth running of the jailhouse.

7

It Takes a County

> This is where most salad makers fall down on the job. The vegetables should be cut or shredded in nice looking pieces that are neither too fine nor too coarse. The pieces should be such that they can be handled easily with a fork. And, above all, the pieces should be a size that can easily be chewed. If you are not too happy with the results you get when using a knife, invest the few dollars necessary in a good shredder. It will do a great deal in improving your reputation as a salad maker.
>
> —1961 *Handbook of Jail Food Service*

> In 1856, the good people of San Diego County, California, depleted their treasury while building a jail and then replacing it immediately. The first building was found not to be habitable. This building frenzy left no money in the budget with which to feed prisoners. Going into debt was not an option at that time. Who better to turn to than the women of their community? The women of leading families took on as one of their charities the task of providing meals for the prisoners. This charity continued for sixteen years.
>
> —From the *San Diego Sheriff's Museum Web site.*

A wide variety of people were required to help lawmen tend to inmates. Ministers tended to the souls of the inmates on Sundays and during evening prayer services. Repairmen tended to the physical structure of the facility. Doctors came as requested to address the needs of the physical body, as did dentists, who pulled rotten teeth but didn't perform any other type of dental work.

Leona Banister recalled that in Coleman County, Texas, a female inmate proved more than even her mother could handle. Sheriff Banister deputized a local practical nurse to care for a homeless woman he held in the women's jail. The inmate had been living under bridges, begging for food, and prostituting herself.

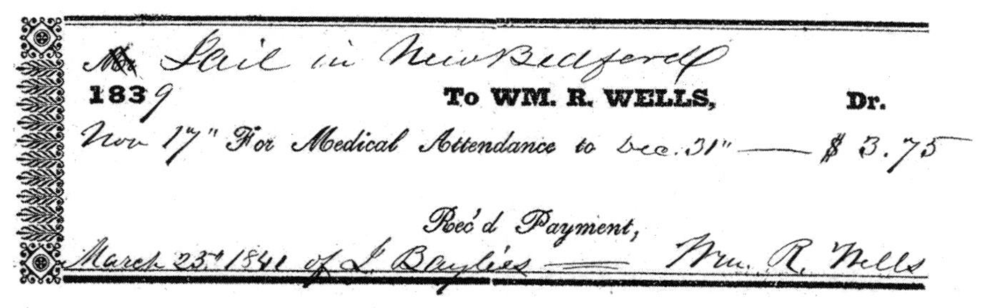

Jail in New Bedford
1839 To WM. R. WELLS, Dr.
Nov 17" For Medical Attendance to Dec. 31" — $3.75
Rec'd Payment,
March 25th 1841 of L. Bayliss — Wm. R. Wells

At the end of 1839, Dr. William Wells billed Bristol County, Massachusetts, for his services at the New Bedford jail between November 17 and December 31. His bill totaled $3.75. He finally received payment on March 25, 1841. (From author's collection.)

"Her face and neck were caked with dirt, her hair had not felt comb nor brush for weeks, her clothes were in rags."[1] The nurse bathed the inmate, trimmed her hair, cut her fingernails, and dressed her in new clothes provided by Emma Banister. It was reported that the inmate looked "rather pretty" by the time she appeared before the judge.

Leona also recalled that the inmate never said a word to anyone the entire time she remained incarcerated. But when the judge asked her where she wanted to go upon leaving Coleman County, she said, "Fort Worth." The men in the courtroom took up a collection among themselves and bought her a train ticket. "Momma gave her a purse, and Papa saw her up the steps into the chair car."[2]

Some law enforcement staff lived in with the Sheriff's family. In Wilson County, Texas, at the beginning of the twentieth century, Will Wright became sheriff and his family lived in four rooms. Young Dogie shared his bedroom with Chief Deputy Wade Lawrence who became almost a member of the family, living in and eating at the family table.

When Eileen Chesbro moved her family into the Oswego County, New York, sheriff's living quarters during the 1970s, they became acquainted with the two residents who already lived there: the day and night matrons. Both matrons had worked most of their adult lives and each was a widow. "Both women were mature and energetic so they were always looking for other things to do." The night matron, who worked from 11:00 p.m. to 7:00 a.m., took on the task of keeping up with the jail laundry. The day matron, on duty from 3:00 p.m. to 11:00 p.m., helped Eileen with the domestic tasks required to keep the family and inmates comfortable.

In a small jail where the wife of the sheriff served as both day and night matron, what happened if there was no wife, or the wife died? After Marion Alvis Bean took over the office of sheriff in Moore County, Tennessee, at the start of the Roaring Twenties, he moved his wife and nine children into the living quarters. During their term of office, Mrs. Bean, whose given name is lost to history, died. Her mother moved in to care for her grandchildren and the sheriff, and to serve as jail matron. She is remembered for watching the Bean children as they played behind the jail. It was there that the prisoners tossed down coins to the kids, who'd then run to the store to buy tobacco for those in the cells.

Mothers often helped their daughters or daughters-in-law with the tremendous task of running a jail. During World War II and into the mid-1950s, Maud Tanner's mother, Donnie Allen, lived with the family in the Antrim County, Michigan, jail to help with the many jobs needing to be done.

During the war, the nation experienced a shortage of teachers so Maud put aside her county apron for two years to teach. Donnie filled in for her. Donnie had the help of Helen Tanner, the bride of young Howard, who came to stay with the family while Howard was in the service. Maud noted that "often there would be a farm girl who wanted to come into town to go to high school. There was no bus service at the time" so living in town while attending school made all the difference. Maud hired some of those girls to live in and help with chores around the house and jail. "They helped in the garden, with meals, cleaning up, laundry," canning vegetables and fruit used by family and prisoners, alongside Maud and Donnie.

Maud reported in her memoirs that her brother, Kenneth, lived in Florida. To take a break from life at the jail was much appreciated by those who actually lived and worked there. Maud's brothers Jack and Bud rented an apartment in Florida for three months and usually took Donnie with them during the worst of the Antrim County winters. "Joan Dunson took over the cooking" so that Maud could fly down to join her siblings for two weeks. "It was a treat for me to be with the family and enjoy the warm weather."

Helen and Neil Haugerud of Fillmore County, Minnesota, enjoyed a two-week vacation away from the jail every year. Their deputies stayed at the family quarters while they were gone. The deputies prepared breakfast and lunch for the inmates, but to take the burden off of those unused to cooking jailhouse meals, supper was brought in from uptown.

Going on vacation could be fraught with adventures involving other lawmen if the family ventured out of state. When the family car served as the sheriff's mobile unit, a vacationing sheriff and his family was often stopped in another state, held for questioning until a call was put through to verify the veracity of their claim that he was truly the officially elected sheriff. Then the family could be on their way. Everyone seemed to take it good-naturedly.

Like the Haugeruds, the Vinsons of Lyon County, Iowa, were also able to take an occasional vacation. All of their deputies were older retired men, Betty reported. One of the deputies and his wife took on the cooking and cleaning chores while the Vinsons took a respite from jail life.

Meanwhile, back at the jailhouse, Loretta Fenton of post-World War II Coleman County, Texas, also reported that her eighty-year-old mother lived with them to help with the work. Loretta recalled one memorable day when she came in from running errands to find six inches of water standing in her bathroom.

> This old drunk lady had shoved a roll of toilet paper down that commode up there. I called the police to circle by and [to] help me go up and check so I wouldn't be by myself, and my mother stayed down there mopping. We went up there and that old girl was laying here, says, "I didn't intend to do that." Here I got my mop, just a-mopping, and she's sitting over

there smoking her cigarette. I looks around, and I'm tired and I'm mad, and I said, "Here, you mop that up!"[3] The inmate said it wasn't her job, she was a prisoner. But in the end, the inmate did the mopping.

Parents were often hired to help at the jail even when they were not compensated with a room in the living quarters. In the mid-1950s, Max Allen's parents had both retired in Poweshiek County, Iowa, so Max hired them to serve as his on-call day jailor and matron. "This gave him the dependable help he needed."

Down in Coleman County, Texas, fifty years earlier, Emma Banister received help from a nonfamily member, Mr. Culpepper, the cook. Her daughter, Leona, came to the conclusion that Culpepper never liked or trusted her after the day she accidentally swept a .45 shell from under the bed while doing her chores. She emptied the debris into the kitchen fire, realizing a second too late that the live round had not been removed. Emma, Leona and Culpepper hurried from the kitchen and waited. Finally the shell exploded, spraying ashes over everything, leaving Culpepper even more morose and irritated than usual.

Helen Haugerud felt fortunate to have "the help of Rose Connolly" one day a week. Rose came to lend a hand with housework and food preparation for the prisoners. On the other end of the spectrum, Florine Johnson Gooding reported that her mother's perfectionism led to having to break in "many new housekeepers."

When Mildred and Louis Johnson transferred prisoners from the Allegan County, Michigan, jail during the 1940s, the housekeeper *du jour* inevitably quit or, keeping in the spirit of this book, made her escape. "Mother was a good woman, but tough on help." Florine would find someone else to take the job and attempt to have the new woman "broken in a bit" by the time her mother returned to the family quarters.

During the last quarter of the nineteenth century, Mollie Latty labored alongside two live-in servants, Emma Subering and Augusta Johnston, both from Sweden. On June 14, 1880 when the census was taken in Des Moines County, Iowa, Mollie lived in the jail with her sheriffing husband, two children (Corinne and Matthew aged two and one), six boarders and a dozen inmates.

At the same time and south of Des Moines, the Sisters of Mercy established a motherhouse, a novitiate, and an academy in Independence, Missouri. The conditions at the Jackson County jail deteriorated terribly during the period prior to 1890 due to poor economic conditions after the Civil War and county marshals resigning after only one year in service. Mother Mary Jerome is remembered as "a pioneer in ministering to prisoners"[4] by her religious order.

"Locally, Mother Jerome became well known for her personal visitations and ministrations to prisoners and jail inmates. Besides supplying these unfortunates with food and reading matter, she and her Sisters often wrote letters for the prisoners to their families and friends, and assisted in preparing the condemned to meet their Creator."[5]

During her work in Jackson County, Mother Jerome was allowed a key to prison quarters in the county jail and could come and go as she pleased. She stood with the chaplain during hangings. On one occasion, she is said to have arranged for the burial of the unclaimed body of a murderer. Mother Jerome chose a spot in a corner of the Sister's plot at the local cemetery. "He had died repentant, she claimed, and deserved something better than Potter's Field."[6]

Mother Jerome died in 1894, during the term of County Marshal JB and Ella Ross. This was the same year that Ella's mother died in her room in the family quarters. In rapid succession, Ella lost two helpers who were good to the inmates and who made her life easier as Mrs. Marshal.

WHAT GOES AROUND COMES AROUND

Being good to your inmates during incarceration can sometimes reap reward later. In the late 1950s, Sheriff Orville Lee answered a call for help from a local tavern in Van Buren County, Iowa, because construction workers were raising hell. Delores Lee's husband tried to talk the ring leader of the unruly bunch into calming things down a bit. By way of reply, the giant of a man "broke the pool stick on the edge of the table and fully intended to use it as a club." Watching all of this from a table near the wall was a man named Jim, a frequent recipient of Delores Lee's cooking when he served time in a county cell. As the pool stick broke and tensions rose, "Jim sauntered over, tapped the ring leader on the shoulder and calmly advised him to go peacefully because Orville would make mince meat out of him. That was all it took. The improvised club was dropped and the fellow sobered up in jail without further ado."

Dolores patrolled with Orville, "often with the little boys asleep in the back seat. On school nights, the couple went alone. Their deputy, who had a room in the family quarters next to Larry's, would watch the kids."

It wasn't always human helpers who made jail life easier. Martha Terrell's son, Hal, had the good fortune to share his life with a big dog named Pooch, which the family considered to be their best trustee. Pooch went everywhere with Hal in Garfield County, Colorado, at the end of the Depression. Martha had an account at the grocery store and when she needed a few items, she sent Pooch. He'd accompanied Hal and Martha so often he knew just what to do when Martha gave him his big canvas bag. She'd put a note in it for the grocer and off he'd run. When the clerk noticed Pooch outside, he came out, took the bag and read the note.

To occupy Pooch while someone shopped for Martha, the clerk brought him a bone from the butcher. Shopping completed, the clerk brought the bag out to Pooch. Hal reported that "they usually wrapped up a little tidbit of meat scraps and stuck that in the bag, so Pooch would have a treat when he got home again."

Pooch and Hal were once separated when Hal experienced complications from a tonsillectomy. Pooch followed Martha to the hospital but stayed behind when she returned home. He found his way into the hospital and to Hal. "The next thing I knew, Pooch the giant dog, had leapt into the bed with me. When the hospital staff tried to eject Pooch, they were deterred by loud growling and menacing looks. They finally had to call mom to come down and take the dog away."

THE COUNTY AS HER COMMUNITY

When it was only mom and pop running a jail, social activities required adjustment when inmates sat in their cells. Many of the participants in this research commented on the "sixth sense that inmates have for who is on the premises." When both mom and pop left the facility, all manner of mischief could be gotten into by those behind bars. In 1878 Ellis County, Kansas, the jailor and his wife took a break from their responsibilities to enjoy the hot air balloon and attendant entertainment that came through town on the Kansas Pacific Railroad. The couple left their children at the jail in case the inmates required anything or someone showed up at the door. They paid a heavy price for such selfishness. The inmates had a need and the helpful children satisfied it. Later that night, the inmates dug their way out of the jail using the spoons and knives they'd talked the kids into giving them.

When there was no deputy to tend to prisoners, a couple could not attend family or community functions together. That included weddings, funerals, and parties. However, when there was a deputy or family member to help, Mrs. Sheriff managed to volunteer her time just like any other good wife and citizen of the community. They entered their handwork for judging at the county fair. Kate Weakley of Russell County, Kansas, won top honors for a quilted coverlet in 1878. In 1893, Jennie Krider of Stark County, Ohio, came home from the fair with mixed results. "I took some things to the fair. Got first Premium on [a] fancy apron and on [a] hand bag and on two rugs but got left on butter and [a] tidy" [a crocheted or tatted piece draped on the arms and backrest of a chair to keep them clean].

For more modern sheriffs' wives, the situation didn't change. While some were not able to find time for more than the work around the jail and helping their husbands campaign for re-election, many like Martha Bulman of Allamakee County, Iowa, were able to contribute on a broader scale. During World War II, Martha took charge of the Red Cross bandages committee. Martha remained active in Eastern Star, the Farm Bureau, and participated in various church circles. Several other Mrs. Sheriffs were reported to have done likewise.

In the 1970s, Dode Jahnel Westendorf, the sheriff's wife who had been raised in her parent's mom-and-pop jail, used her own jail to its full potential when it was empty. She held Boy Scout meetings in it and found it was the ideal place to paint scenery for school plays. "The big empty space [bull pen] was perfect for such activity."

Irene Gray of Saguache County, Colorado, reported that in the 1950s they entertained a poker group who met in their home occasionally. "Cub Scouts met once a week. Our daughter was in 4-H so we ran a taxi service for them as well as the Cub Scouts."

McHenry County, Illinois' Marian Edinger was devoted to politics. Her son, Lester, described it as "a very important part of her life that involved entertaining, attending various social events and regular campaigning. She knew a lot of local people, met people easily and had a great ability to remember people's names, sometimes better than my dad." A favorite story told about Marian was about the time she sat with the governor to watch a Rose Bowl game. Richard provided the details: "My mom and dad had attended the Rose Parade; and, after the parade, dad had a chance to buy a single ticket for the game. He was a big football fan who had never seen a bowl game, so mom told him to get the ticket. They went to the game together and dad went on in. Just after he'd done so, mother noticed that the governor of Michigan and his party had arrived. She wanted to meet him so she walked up and greeted him like an old friend. Of course, he pretended to know her and proceeded to talk with her. As they were talking, the usher came over and said that they were ready for the governor's party to go in to the game. The friendly governor put his arm around mother's shoulders and said, 'Come on. It's time for us to go in.' Mother just followed his instructions and ended up with a very nice seat for the game."

For many women between 1800 and 1960, their sense of community included family and church. Others embraced those and added their village or township. One of Marian Edinger's sons, Sid, noted that for his mother, "the community she embraced was the entire county." It was a rare Mrs. Sheriff for whom the same could not be said.

While Linda Scott served Apache County, Arizona, beside her sheriffing husband, Jim, from 1895 to 1899, she served as hostess to many local events. From organizing grand balls to entertaining officers from the 7th Cavalry and 11th Infantry stationed at the nearby fort, Linda Scott worked hard to bring Victorian civilization to their corner of the frontier. Linda and some of her peers organized an "Apron and Tie" party held on Thanksgiving night in 1895. The local paper described it this way: "Some natty aprons were worn by the ladies and their attendant cavaliers blossomed gorgeously in neckties to match."[7] The article went on to describe how the dancing was interrupted for a midnight supper after which more dancing continued until 2:00 a.m.

Jim and Linda also attended the gala costume ball held to celebrate New Year's Eve that year. He went as Blue Boy and Linda dressed as Santa Claus. As St. Johns, Arizona, did not sport any costume shops at the time, all of the finery that appeared at the ball was homemade.

In Colfax County, New Mexico, Sheriff Pete Burleson and his wife, Mary, embraced not only their county, but a sense of history as well. This couple knew they were living in historical times and took every opportunity to avail themselves of it. When the first railroad crossed the border into New Mexico in November 1879, Pete was there to drive the second spike (the first having been driven by one of the survey engineers). The railway line made its way to the county seat. The striking of the sledge hammer on the steel spikes there sounded the death knell for the stagecoach. Mary honored the passing of eras by buying a ticket "to Trinidad, Colorado, on the last stage coach that ran, for the next day the mail came in on the train."[8] The couple sheriffed until the end of 1881.

As noted, most jailhouse wives embraced the entire county as their responsibility when their husbands won election. Nadine Kahanamoku added to her hat tree the chapeau worn by tour guides and wore it often for visiting celebrities. During the twenty years that Duke and Nadine served his terms as sheriff on the Big Island of Hawaii, much of their time was spent playing host and hostess for famous visitors. Friends of Duke's in Hollywood would let the couple know that this person or that was coming from Tinseltown or from some European spa. Duke and Nadine were asked to show the visitors the sights. The pair met many a boat at the dock and hobnobbed with the rich and famous despite living what Nadine called "their simple life."

Sheriffs' wives weren't all saints and Lady Bountifuls. Take Mary Flynn Irvine in Custer and Ravalli counties in Montana. Not one but two communities had to put up with her. When she married Thomas H. Irvine in 1882, Mary was a twenty-year-old widow with a baby daughter, Maisy. Thomas built the family a home in the county seat of Custer County and over the years the couple produced five sons.[9] During their tenure in Custer County, a skating rink was built. Mary fell in love— with roller skating and, perhaps, a young man who skated with her. Thomas worried that his wife had become addicted to roller skating as she thought of nothing else, certainly not her prisoners. She did not function as a legitimate Mrs. Sheriff in any fashion. She indulged herself with more than money could buy and instead of a county apron, she tied on roller skates to go 'round and 'round and 'round.

Thomas sheriffed and invested their money in one failed business after another. Eventually, his widowed sister came from Deer Lodge to move in and take care of the family, leaving Mary free to skate even more.

By the time the Irvine family left Custer County, Thomas was being hounded by creditors. He took up sheriffing in Ravalli County and stayed there for several terms. He may not have made a success of things in Custer County, but at least he got his wife out of those roller skates and he got the creditors off his back by paying them as sheriff's fees and rewards allowed.

To run a county jail smoothly, it took a variety of people from the county. Just as parents were called upon to help, so too were the grown children of the jailhouse wife as well as their spouses. In the following chapter, we will see how sons- and daughters-in law became involved in law enforcement.

8

Wedding Bands and Badges

Drying dishes with a towel is not a good practice. Let them stand and air-dry. Never touch the inside of bowls, cups, or dishes, or anything but the handles of knives, forks, and spoons.

—1961 *Handbook of Jail Food Service*

Viola White's son, Glen, became his father's deputy on special occasions like helping with a town activity . . . parades, fairs, the circus . . . in Leelanau County, Michigan. "On one other occasion, Glen was pressed to help dad when a report came in of a man who had what appeared to be a nervous breakdown, had a gun [in the downtown section of the county seat] and Glen went with dad to help take the fellow in."

—About Glen White who served
alongside Sheriff Bob White between
1948 and 1964, reported by his sister,
Joyce White LeLonde.

Unlike most young men and women who marry into a family, the new members of a sheriffing family often found themselves being sworn in as deputies and learning to operate a two-way radio. With exposure to the ways of the inmates, they quickly picked up on what was normal and what was "not quite right" and to report it immediately. Their help, both in the office and the kitchen, was gratefully accepted by the always busy jailhouse mom and pop.

Many sheriffs hired their grown sons as deputies. In some counties, the son's families moved into the jail alongside his parents. This proved to be the case in Depression-era Moore County, Tennessee, when Oliver and Pearl Hobbs welcomed son, Lacy, and his family. "The house had ample living quarters for all eight people: four adults and four children" reported two of Pearl's grandsons seventy-five years later.

In Dubuque County, Iowa, during the 1960s, Geraldine Spielman's daughter, Shirley McGovern, son-in-law and eight-year-old grandson moved into the family quarters to help. While, in general, the situation worked out well, Shirley reported that soon after they settled in, "the inmates got in an uproar about something and a fracas broke out. Mom and I armed ourselves with brooms and took up positions on the landing of the staircase determined to hold our own if the prisoners got out." Fortunately, the deputies quieted the inmates before things got that far.

Another type of excitement occurred during Shirley's stay at the jail. The ornate Victorian family quarters were quite beautiful, she remembers. The tall ceilings had been decorated with fancy plasterwork. Wide woodwork added to the elegance. The bedroom the McGoverns chose as their own was especially fine. "One morning after breakfast, we heard a huge crashing sound and found that the entire plaster ceiling in our bedroom had fallen. Had we been in bed, we would have been killed."

Many sons-in-law found themselves involved in law enforcement on a part-time basis during special occasions. In Hodgeman County, Kansas, in the 1960s, Francis Sinclair needed help trying to figure out who'd been vandalizing microwave towers. Was it kids? Ecoterrorists? So Francis roped daughter Bettie's hubby, Lester, into sitting watch all night.

Lester worked full time at the local lumberyard and pinned on his badge only when asked to help. He'd gotten his radio license just like his wife and her sister, Dot, so he could fill in when needed. He did accompany his father-in-law on speed checks, setting up speed traps with Francis when the Highway Patrol needed help in their county. But that hadn't really prepared him for field work.

Lester agreed to sit in a field in his car near a microwave tower to keep watch. Francis "issued him a gun, just in case, and Lester took up his position. He did not fall asleep, he swears to this day," recalled Dot. "He claims he drifted into a relaxed state at some point during the long night of watching. Suddenly, a storm blew in and thunder jarred Lester out of his relaxed state. When he jumped, his gun went off and shot the window out of his car. That scared him to death. The next day he turned in his gun, never to take it up again." He continued as on-call deputy, but insisted that he'd be an unarmed one.

At about the same time in Van Buren County, Iowa, Dolores Lee's husband, Orville, took son-in-law, Cecil, out on patrol with him. Dolores and Orville's son, Larry, rode along and recounted the following story: "All of the little towns in the county had a night watchman who kept an eye on things, looked out for fires, and reported anything unusual to the sheriff as he made his rounds. About 1 or 1:30 in the morning, as we drove into one town, the night watchman came on the radio and said 'get that guy.' We saw a car speeding away in front of us. Dad gave chase and we soon were out of town, flying down gravel roads. We watched as the car we were chasing missed a curve and ended up in a muddy field. Dad pulled up, left the red lights running and asked Cecil to bring in the man stuck in the field. Cecil walked over to the car while dad called mom to let her know we were bringing in someone. He also radioed the night watchman to let him know the chase had ended and to ask what had started the whole thing."

As considerable time had been taken with the details of these radio calls, Larry and Orville were surprised "that Cecil was still standing next to the car in the field and didn't appear to be making any moves to bring the driver to the road. Dad yelled 'bring him over, Cecil' only to hear that Cecil couldn't. The driver had a gun on him. Both dad and I imagined that 'gun' meant shotgun or rifle. Cecil worked as a prison guard, so we assumed Cecil could handle that situation. We sat in the car and waited for Cecil to take the gun away from the drunk. Nothing happened. Cecil kept standing there. The drunk began yelling at dad to stay off the radio and cut the lights, and fired a shot to emphasize his demands."

"When we heard the pistol shot, both dad and I bolted from the car and hid behind it. Eventually, dad and Cecil talked the guy out of the car before he shot someone, and got him in the jail." Larry reported that he was too full of adrenaline to be scared.

On another night, when Larry was in college and old enough to be deputized, "dad got a call that the Highway Patrol were in pursuit of a stolen car so dad and I went out to join the posse of local citizens who had come out to help. The thief drove the car to a corn field and ran into the field to hide. The Highway Patrol, the posse members, dad and I began a search of the field in hopes that we would be able to capture the guy. During the search, some of the posse discovered the body of one of their members in the field, killed by the thief. When the posse eventually rounded up the guy an hour or two later and brought him back to the road, they showed great restraint in handling him professionally." Larry described what he saw as the irate posse members bending over backwards to stay within the law so the culprit wouldn't be turned loose on a technicality. As for himself, Larry reported "I had trouble sleeping that night as a result of the volunteer posse member losing his life. It really affected me."

One pleasant variation on the son-in-law theme involved Gloria Bridenhagen's daughter, Holly. While the Bridenhagens sheriffed for Door County, Wisconsin, in the 1980s, Holly's father hired a young deputy. Shortly afterward, the deputy met Holly. The sheriff gained a deputy and Gloria gained a son-in-law.

HOME GROWN HELP

Florine Gooding's husband became her father's chief deputy in Allegan County, Michigan, during the 1940s. As noted earlier, Florine's parents were Sheriff Louis and Mildred Johnson. The Goodings did not live in the family quarters but when Florine's children were born, mother and infant always stayed a few days in the family quarters under Mildred's care. Florine recalls that on one occasion it proved to be a full house as Mildred tended to inmates and nursed two relatives just out of the hospital.

In addition to everything else there was for her to do, Mildred Johnson also filled in for the staff involved with issuing driver's licenses when needed. Florine was the first staff member to be hired when the office opened as part of the sheriff's department, but was fired by her father "when I developed a problematic pregnancy, for my own good," she reported.

Mildred Johnson's oldest son, Crosby, served as a deputy when his dad needed to go out on an arrest. Crosby continued to live at home while attending college, so was available when needed. After he married, Crosby and his wife accompanied his dad to Canada to extradite a prisoner. "Dad was totally disconcerted when he was not allowed to bring his gun into Canada. No matter what he said or what proof of identification he showed, they would not allow it," recalled Florine. The trio then proceeded to the jail, and "with great trepidation, dad brought his prisoner out, and his gun was waiting for him when they reached the border."

In Holmes County, Ohio, Darrell Weiss served as deputy for his father and eventually replaced him when Harry retired. When younger, the Weiss boys worked to bring in more income by boxing groceries at the store. All of the children took on jailhouse chores: shoveling coal, tending the large garden on the farm that the family owned, laundry washed in an old wringer machine and hung out to dry. The family made their own root beer and canned hundreds of jars of apple sauce from their own fruit trees. Teenager Evelyn helped by answering phones, operating the radio and serving as matron. She never clerked in the sheriff's office although she helped her mother, Edith, with car tag inquiries. The role of young children, like those in the family above, will be discussed at length in the following chapter.

Leila Pedersen's son, Bob, became his father's deputy when he turned 21. His sister Marge recalled that he took on that job so he could help the other Chippewa County, Minnesota, deputies staff the jail while the rest of the Pedersens "went on our first vacation trip to the western states"[1] during the 1930s.

Howard Tanner became his father's deputy at the age of eighteen in nearby Antrim County, Michigan. Prior to that, for the first four years he lived in the family quarters, Howard A. kept the coal shoveled and the wood box filled for his mother, Maud. He reported that "I cut wood and stacked it in the basement. Every year, we got a carload (50 tons) of coal and it had to be shoveled into the furnace. Partway through the winter, we got another 25 tons of coal to finish out the cold spell. I shoveled ashes from the furnace, or dad did, or even mom. . . or the trustees. I shoveled snow, and there is a lot of snow on the Peninsula of Michigan. When my folks went out on rare occasions, I would 'babysit' the office and jail. I carried food to the prisoners."

When home from college or on leave from the service during World War II, Howard A. assumed the role of deputy again. He accompanied prisoners to their court appearances and took the night runs to investigate car accidents so his dad could get some sleep. "I went with dad when a farmer came in to report that a group of farmers had trapped a robber in a house. We went into the house with the farmers right behind us, armed with their weapons of choice: pitchforks. We searched it from top to bottom, and finally found the guy in a sub-basement that was accessed by a trap door in the basement."

Mary Richart, the grown daughter of the sheriff of Boulder County, Colorado, made a living by playing piano at local dances. This happened to be the era when the "Denver Mafia" brought slot machines into the back rooms of various dancing establishments. Mary noted how she'd be playing the latest songs on the piano at the same time her father was raiding the joint and confiscating slot machines. When Mary got married, her dad made the newlyweds a kitchen table from the wood salvaged from those slot machines.

A few years later in Boulder County, Dorothy Everson's daughter, Shirley, met her future husband, Clyde. While they were dating, Clyde came to the jail to help Shirley wash the inmates' sheets and blankets in the wringer washing machine. Both Shirley and Clyde were paid for their services. This in-house service came about when Dorothy found that she was not getting the jail sheets back from the laundry service, even after many complaints and after she'd put ID markers on them. Dorothy went to the county commissioners and showed them how it would be cheaper for her to pay Shirley, Clyde and her son, Bob, to do the wash rather than send it out. The commissioners approved the change.

Dorothy had been paying Shirley to do chores around the jail since Shirley came home from high school one day and announced she was going to get a paying job like her friends. Without skipping a beat, Dorothy offered to pay Shirley for the work she needed help with around the jail. Dorothy and Art paid for these services out of their own pocket. One of the jobs that Shirley was assigned was to take food to the female prisoners. "I slid the trays through a door, just like it's done on television,"[2] but Shirley was never allowed to enter any of the cells.

Both Shirley and her brother, Bob, helped their father transfer prisoners when the kids were older. Bob also helped with unruly inmates who resisted going into their cells. He covered the sheriff's office on Sundays, answering phones so his parents could have some time away from the jail. Once Shirley began dating Clyde, her parents were willing to allow the couple to watch the jail while the Everson's went out on Sundays. Shirley and Clyde often prepared Sunday dinner and baby-sat the inmates. Art said he wouldn't have allowed Shirley to stay alone in the family quarters since Bob was downstairs in the sheriff's office, but with Clyde there, he knew everything would be okay for a few hours.

In the twenty years after 1964, Mary Jahnel served the Mitchell County, Iowa, citizens as their Mrs. Sheriff. The Jahnels served as jailors for two years prior so knew what they were getting into when they ran for sheriff. Their oldest daughter, Dode, helped with everything around the jail and then married William Westendorf. Bill won election as sheriff of Bremer County, Iowa. Dode served her new county from 1973 onward. Several of those years ran concurrent with the end of her mother's tenure.

Dode and her sisters, Kathy and Jan, contributed many of their memories for this book through correspondence, interviews, and family photographs. As mentioned, the family included a bevy of daughters. When Mary asked if they couldn't purchase a dishwasher for the jail kitchen, Richard retorted, "What do you need a dishwasher for? You've got seven of them!"

In Republic County, Kansas, at about the same time, Charlie and Christina Peterka cared for the inmates while serving as the sheriffing couple. Their daughters, although grown and living in their own homes, helped Christina with the cooking and cleaning from time to time. Daughter Gloria also helped in the office, typing the list of license tag owners and similar clerical tasks.

Gloria and her husband Orville found themselves with an opportunity to help her dad one year at the County Fair. The couple stood talking with a group of family and friends, deciding what to see first, when Gloria "noticed a tall stranger moving into their crowd in what she considered an unusual manner." Her time spent around inmates had educated her as to what "unusual" might mean. Gloria pointed out the man to her husband and they then kept an eye on the fellow. "It was later that evening that Orville and another man in our crowd captured the man when he attempted to pick the pocket of one of the locals. The stranger fought so hard to get away that when he kicked, his shoe came off. But the men held on and got him to the sheriff's office. While being booked, the man tried to escape but dad subdued him and got him into his cell."

While Betty Vinson's daughter attended high school and then college, she clerked in the Lyon County, Iowa sheriff's office. "Peggy knew all of the radio jargon and she was her father's best dispatcher" during the 1970s, according to a totally unbiased Betty who also reported that Peggy was never allowed to go into the jail itself when she was young, not even in the women's jail. However, Peggy followed in her father's footsteps and currently serves as a deputy sheriff in South Dakota. Betty reported that when grandchildren began coming along, they too enjoyed coming to visit at the jail. "We had many wonderful holidays there," Betty recalled.

Sons, daughters and their spouses either lived in or came to the jailhouse to help with the large number of tasks required even in a relatively quiet county. As with any family business, everyone pitched in as they could. Children much younger than those discussed here had their chores while growing up, as we will see in the next chapter.

—9—

With a Little Help from My Young'uns

> Pots and pan should be thoroughly scrubbed in hot water and rinsed in the hottest water available. Store them in a dry place away from dust and dirt. NEVER place or keep pots and pans on the floor.
>
> —1961 *Handbook of Jail Food Service*

> Sam Cooper was asked to serve as bait. As a teen, he'd run into the Greenwood County, South Carolina woods and try every trick in the book to elude the bloodhounds on his trail. "I'd do my best to keep from being tracked. I'd run in a stream far enough so they lost the scent between where I went in and where I came out." Most of the time, the dogs caught him. Then "they would mill around me, barking like crazy or at worst, knock me down."
>
> —Reported by Sam Cooper, son of Vernice Cooper of Greenwood County, SC.

Youngsters from infancy onward interacted with inmates in most county jails across the nation. As each child was old enough, they took on one and then more of the many chores waiting to be done. When grandchildren grew to an age where they could be helpful, they too pitched in to lend a hand.

Sometimes, there was a dual purpose in making an assignment. Harry and Edith Weiss served Holmes County, Ohio, long enough to marry off their children and watch their grandkids grow up. During his freshman year in high school, one grandson took on the responsibility of staffing the jail office. David took the evening shift, answering phones and the radio. David recalled "Here was a freshman in high school who was responsible for the handful of prisoners and all radio and telephone traffic."[1] David lost his leg in an accident just prior to taking this job. The duties he performed were helpful to his grandparents and to David who declared "it was the most exciting period of my life!"[2]

When not serving as bait for the bloodhounds, Sam Cooper attended to more mundane activities. On the day he helped the trustees paint the jail walls, they took supplies upstairs and the sheriff locked them in to do their work. The sheriff then left the building on business. "I got a taste of what it was like to be incarcerated because dad was gone most of the day and all I could do was sit around and wait after the painting was finished."

Marian Edinger's son, Richard, reported how the family returned one night from an outing when he was in his teens during the Depression. The family sheriffed in McHenry County, Illinois. "We found a drunk sleeping on the steps leading to the jail. He was a former businessman who had lost his business and become a drunk. Whenever he'd been drinking, he usually would be picked up and put in jail until sobered up. Then, he would be released without any charges. Apparently, this night, he'd gotten drunk and decided that the jail was where he should be. So I got the keys, took him inside and put him to bed. The next morning, he went home."

In Clarion County, Pennsylvania, one sheriff's teenage son served as jailor for his father. It was reported that "on his first date with his future wife, they danced in the hallways of the jail."[3]

As we have seen, teens were left in charge of the jail, and provided assistance to the sheriff when unruly prisoners got out of hand. They also rode shotgun during the transfer of prisoners to or from other institutions. In the twenty years after 1964, Mary Jahnel's daughters helped transfer prisoners, rode along with their father to pick up blood and deliver samples to the lab in Mitchell County, Iowa. While dad drove the county roads on his regular rounds, Dode staffed the office to look up information as he needed it.

One day a week, the Mitchell County driver's license testers worked at the sheriff's office and their information was kept in a drawer. Kathy Jahnel confessed that when the girls were in high school and began dating, they and their friends used the information in the driver's license drawer to determine how tall a new date was so they'd know if they could wear heels.

When Neva Allen donned her county apron in 1955, daughter Debby was a teen who served as jail matron after school. Like the Jahnel girls, she accompanied female prisoners to other institutions when they were transferred. In doing so, she was required to accompany the women into restrooms along the way. In the Poweshiek County Sheriff's Office in Iowa, Debby functioned as dispatcher on the radio and answered phones. To help her mom, she washed laundry and fed prisoners.

At the turn of the nineteenth century in Jackson County, Missouri, Alice Stewart came to live with her grandparents at the jail so she could attend high school. Mel Hulse was the county marshal and his wife was known by everyone as Mama Hulse. Alice recalled that she had one special job: locking the hall door each night, the one between the cell area and the family quarters.[4]

Ten years earlier in Union County, Oregon, Sheriff Hamilton's daughter, Dolin, took an interest not only in the jail but in her neighbors. Like many of the children in sheriffing families devoted to service in their community, Dolin reached out and touched the lives of those around her. Ninety years later, Dolin was remembered by one of the neighbors in a written personal account. Dolin colored Easter eggs and hid them in a nest for little Alice and Ollie Balter to find. It was the very first Easter that Alice remembered because of finding that nest of colorful eggs. She also recalled that Dolin crocheted her a cap to wear. Alice recalled that it was "adorned with colorful pom poms and it sure was pretty."[5]

Leona Banister was another well-regarded daughter of a sheriff who recalled how she and her siblings helped around the jail as their ages allowed. All of them came home from school each day, eager to see what they had missed while they were gone. Among Leona's jobs was to drive for her dad. Deputies often drove until World War I and then Leona took on the task. Leona had finished school by that time.

On Easter Sunday, 1916, Leona donned her new taffeta dress, high heels, and silk stockings to attend church and Sunday School. But when a report came of a horse and buggy being stolen, she was called away from church to drive for her dad. Off came the Easter finery and on went the uniform: khaki corduroy dress and white blouse worn with her brown Stetson and high-top lace up shoes. John Banister and Leona trailed the horse and buggy to a quarry. John arrested the men and told Leona to head back to town, he was coming in the buggy with the prisoners. She got the car turned around and started down the lane only to see another car coming toward her. In it was "a notorious bootlegger who had had many run-ins with the sheriff, and three other men. I knew that meant no good. The lane was too narrow for me to turn around, and I could not risk backing so far. Then I heard a pistol shot, Papa's signal to me."[6] She somehow managed to turn the car around without getting stuck and "flew back down the lane."[7] What she found was her father out of the buggy with the two prisoners, and four bootleggers standing in a semicircle facing the trio. The only gun she saw belonged to her father. Because of the presence of his daughter, the bootleggers refrained from attacking the sheriff. Everyone returned to town without further incident.

During 1917, Leona fed prisoners, served as her father's office deputy, kept logs and records "of Papa's appointments of deputies, of the prisoners and of their offenses, of their fines and their days in jail,"[8] served as prisoner escort, and drove for the sheriff. John bought a new Overland car that year. Leona carried a .38 revolver for the many times she sat alone in the car while waiting for arrests to be made. The revolver was put in a "small pocket inside the left front door, right at my knee."[9] John told Leona that she had no right to carry a pistol and she was not to tell anyone about it. "Never put your hand on it unless you need to defend yourself,"[10] John instructed her.

Leona recounted the circumstances surrounding the time that her father had a murder warrant to arrest a man in another county. The father–daughter team drove out to the man's farm only to find him plowing a field. John noted that the man's wife had spotted the sheriff's car but the wanted man had not. The wife emerged from the house with a shotgun and started to run toward her husband who remained unaware of the drama being played out behind him. Leona described how she drove across the deeply furrowed fields to get her father to the farmer before the wife could get to him with the shotgun. As Leona bumped the car across the furrows, John yelled instructions about how she was to get down in the car if the wife got to her husband before they got there. Leona managed to win the race. Fortunately, the wife did not shoot at them herself. John arrested the man and Leona drove them back to the Coleman County, Texas, jail. With a prisoner in custody, John always sat in the back seat on the right so the prisoner could not reach his gun while those about to be incarcerated always sat behind Leona.

Not all children quite got into the spirit of the family work. Down in Brown County, Texas, the jail was run by Ivan Ellis and his wife. Son, BW, and cousin Marvin heard inmates yelling for attention so dashed upstairs to see about it. The prisoners requested two rolls of toilet paper. The ornery boys made a beeline to the dumpster, picked out two buckets of corncobs, and brought them upstairs. When the boys set the cobs where the prisoners could reach them, the inmates failed to find humor in the situation. They threw the cobs at BW and Marvin. The cobs, still wet from being processed in the kitchen, splattered cornstarch everywhere as they hit the floor or wall. Ivan Ellis came up to see what all of the ruckus was about only to find irate inmates and a hellacious mess. The inmates reported what the boys had done. "BW and Marvin had to get the toilet paper, buckets of water and mops and they spent several hours getting the dried cornstarch off the floor and walls"[11] closely supervised by the men they'd insulted.

This type of behavior was rarely reported during the research for this book and it was not found in what little literature is available on the subject. Many children reported that they were instructed to treat the inmates as they would anyone else, with politeness. Some recalled that inmates were like part of the family. Others noted that inmates were fellow citizens who'd fallen on hard times. There was little room for rudeness in those approaches. In the 1950s, Pat and Modina Riddell lived in the Burnet County, Texas, jail with their parents. Modina recalled that they were taught to respect prisoners as fellow human beings who happened to be in trouble. "They really all became our friends."[12]

One youngster, untrained in the finer points of prisoner treatment, refused $5 offered by a man brought in by his dad. David Norris, Marguerite's four-year-old son, understood that his father brought men to the Fulton County, Indiana, jail for drinking too much. When a man handed David a $5 bill, David "disdainfully threw the bill in the trash as he informed the man, 'I don't take money from drunk people!' "[13] As his father's mouth fell open, the man burst out laughing. He wasn't a drunk. He was "Arnold Palmer, brought in because he couldn't produce his drivers license when the sheriff stopped him for a minor infraction on US 31."[14] Once Palmer's license was forwarded to him, he was let go after paying his fine.

EVEN THE WEE ONES

In Kansas, when the *Russell Record* came out on Valentine's Day in 1878, right after Mrs. Sheriff Kate Weakley gave birth to her sixth child, the notice read only that "the big smile on Jim Weakley's face is due to the new deputy." New arrivals at any sheriff's home were often announced to the community in a similar fashion. In March of 1930, Martha Bulman gave birth to "a new inmate at the county jail" in allamakee County, Iowa. The authentic inmates enjoyed wheeling baby in her buggy up and down the sidewalks in front of the jail and courthouse.

Just like the big kids, youngsters had their work to help out around the jail. Jinny, Agnes Schumaker's daughter, was given the task of tending to a runaway brought to their Ellis County, Kansas, jail in the mid-1960s. "Dad brought in a young girl who had run away from home and hidden in an outhouse to keep warm. The girl was kept more in the family quarters than in the women's cell. I was put in charge of her" until she was taken away.

Annis Moore found herself caring for a runaway during the 1970s in Nassau County, Florida. Annis asked the girl why she'd run away and was told that her "mother liked her sister better than her and said things like 'why can't you be more like Judy?' When the mother arrived to take the girl home again, Annis looked at [the woman] and said 'why can't she be more like Judy?' "[15] and watched the proverbial light bulb go on over the mother's head. "Years later the mother wrote a letter thanking me for making her see what she had been doing."[16]

Even small children helped. When Howard A. and Helen Tanner brought their three sons to visit the jail run by his parents in Antrim County, Michigan, they accompanied Maud on her rounds of the cells to feed prisoners. In the new jail built in 1955, prisoners remained in their cells while Maud "took a cart around with their trays on it, and passed them through the slot in the cell door." One particular Sunday, Maud's meal for the prisoners included individual rolls of bologna along with vegetables and dessert. "They looked like the biggest hot dog that [grandson] Carl had ever seen." The boys helped her push the cart from cell to cell, and Carl watched everything through big eyes. When Maud and her grandsons rolled the cart back to the family quarters, the family then sat down for their own Sunday dinner of chicken, mashed potatoes with gravy, biscuits and apple pie. To everyone's dismay, Carl burst into tears. Howard A. was finally able to calm his son enough to ask why he was crying. The four-year-old sobbed "I want what the piznays had!" Carl didn't want chicken, he wanted a big bologna roll like the prisoners were enjoying.

There seemed to be no end to the chores needing to be performed to keep the jail and family quarters running. Children carried messages between the jail and courthouse or lawyers before the advent of telephones. By the time they were nine or ten, they were old enough to take meals to the prisoners. Little ones picked up the mail from the post office and went to the grocery store for mom. Even the small ones could help with meal preparation by buttering bread and putting dessert on the trays, and help clear up afterward. In Lee County, Texas, all of Sheriff Goodson's family looked after their trio of large gardens and put up food for everyone they had to feed.

Before the age of the automobile, children rode the county on horseback to deliver messages to other lawmen, and delivered subpoenas to grand jury members.

After 1910, Dogie Wright of Wilson County, Texas, carted ballot boxes around the county to various polling places. He drove their Model T before many of the adults could do so. Children caught on to the workings of that newfangled contraption just like so many of today's children can use a computer before their parents can. Dogie made pocket money by picking up "beer bottles after lawyers' gambling parties at court time, shined shoes in the courthouse, collected 'message fees' after people received long distance calls and were summoned to the sheriff's phone, distributed circus fliers, and guided generous [salesmen] to remote country stores."[17]

Once the telephone was widely distributed, it seems never to have stopped ringing at the sheriff's office or in the family quarters. Dode Jahnel recalled that all seven of the girls were trained to answer the phone properly. "If someone called about an accident, we had to find out if anyone was hurt and did they need an ambulance, get the correct location and their names." As any 911 operator can testify, those just involved in accidents can be hysterical or in shock and not especially helpful. "This was quite a responsibility for some of us who were only in grade school," Dode wrote. Dode also reported how her father expected his girls to serve as examples to the community, "and we were always aware that if we got into trouble we'd be sitting on the other side of the bars for the full extent of our time."

Young Gary and Larry Lee rode patrol with their dad when they were no more than six and eight. It became a family tradition to patrol with Orville during his twenty-three years in office. Even grandson Dusty happily patrolled with grandpa toward the end of his service in Van Buren County, Iowa. The Lee family started sheriffing in 1956. While out on patrol one night, a call came over the radio that there had been a wreck in Farmington. A family from just across the state line in Missouri were always in trouble. One of their boys was involved in the wreck due to having too much to drink. He'd decided to drive backward down a one-way street and plowed into another car.

It being a cold night, the Lee boys sat inside a building with the drunken thug while the sheriff and town marshal investigated the damage. The drunk, not knowing or not caring who the little boys were, started bad-mouthing the sheriff, calling him names and saying he'd not be in trouble if it weren't for "that Podunk sheriff interfering." After listening to all of this for what felt like way too long, Larry "stated the obvious, that the guy wouldn't be under arrest if he'd not been driving backwards down a one-way street, which infuriated the drunk." The drunk leapt up and Larry thought he was going to have his block knocked off. Gary stood up to intervene but at that moment, dad and the marshal came into the room and prevented the boys from getting their "clocks cleaned."

LIFE IN A FISH BOWL

Richard Edinger in McHenry County, Illinois, noted that "the detrimental part was the fact I couldn't do much that dad didn't hear about." He found as compensation the fact that on weekends he could play in the courthouse. "Living downtown was a bonus as the theater was but a block away and there were concerts on the square" across from their home.

Kids will be kids even if they are related to the top lawman. Charlie Ross, son of Jackson County, Missouri, Marshal JB Ross and his wife, Ella, wasn't above playing hooky. Charlie entered the third grade two years younger than his classmates as a result of the excellent home schooling of his mom. Skipping school with his new friends seemed like a lovely idea from time to time. Charlie and his friends used to play around the old flour mill in Independence. One day, the school janitor came looking for the truants. The "little old man named Speck who had chin whiskers"[18] came down to the flour mill. The boys ran down the train tracks in retreat. "Charlie Ross fell down and cut his nose. It just bled like the dickens and it left a scar for the rest of his life."[19] Ella asked her son how he came to have the scab on his nose and Charlie just stood there and lied to her: "when I leaned down to get a drink of water at the spring, a frog bit me."[20] Charlie Ross grew up to win the Pulitzer prize before going to work for his friend Harry Truman.

Maureen Elston, Mrs. Sheriff of Wright County, Iowa, observed that her children were treated in school like any other kids. "They just weren't told where the beer parties were going to be held." Neither were the Jahnel girls. Kathy reported that if a sheriff's patrol broke up a beer party and brought the kids in for underage drinking, "mom would check and make sure we were in bed because she knew dad would question us. One time a young guy was brought in and when he opened his wallet, my picture was the first thing my dad saw!"

Leila Pedersen's daughter, Marge, recalled that she helped to feed World War II prisoners of war. The German captives worked on area farms in Chippewa County, Minnesota. "We fed them out on the jail lawn before they went back to camp at Ortonville."[21] Marge noted that it was difficult to get help at the jail during the war because the men joined the service and women went to work in war plants. "There were fewer prisoners, and the ones who were there were more dangerous."[22] As a result, she helped Leila feed prisoners by taking the breakfasts around, "getting done just in time to run to classes up the street at Central School. The kids called me 'hash slinger.' "[23]

Gloria Bridenhagen of Door County, Wisconsin, recalled that in the 1960s, "the children lived in a fish bowl." Sheriffs couldn't help but make enemies in pursuit of their duties and Gloria's husband was one of those who broke up corruption in his county. His enemies "weren't above picking on your kids."

After the Werth's retired from sheriffing in Ellis County, Kansas, in 1975, Anne's children told them that they were sometimes "ridiculed for being law enforcement and living in so public a house." Anne didn't find out until it was all over that her daughter's life had been threatened by a neighbor who was in trouble with the sheriff on more than a few occasions. "He indicated he knew who our daughter was and could take care of her any time. Many years later, I learned she had discreet police protection for a long time."

A situation that must have proved traumatic for a young boy occurred in Berkley County, South Carolina, in November of 1887. The local paper reported that seventy-year-old Stephen Bailey worked as an engineer at the steam saw mill. Bailey had married a woman much younger than himself and began to suspect her of infidelity. He confessed that he "laid in wait for her and killed her with an axe."[24] When night fell, he loaded her body onto his wheelbarrow and put it in the furnace of the saw mill. For some reason, he took her outer clothing off before cremating her, but "in his distress, he failed to dispose of the bloody garments in front of the furnace."[25] He went home and sometime the next day, his wife was missed. It didn't take Sherlock Holmes to connect the missing woman with the pile of bloody clothes in front of the furnace. The sheriff took Bailey to the furnace where he confessed that those were his wife's clothes and what he'd done. While he investigated, the sheriff handcuffed Bailey's arms in front of him and tied him to a post to keep him from running off. The unnamed sheriff then asked his little boy to watch the prisoner.

Bailey managed to dig his pipe out of his pocket and retrieve his tobacco pouch. He asked the little boy if he had a pocketknife so he could clean his pipe before filling it. The boy had one and handed it over to the prisoner. "Bailey then attempted to commit suicide by slitting his throat [in front of the boy], but the dullness of the boy's knife and the fact that Bailey's hands were manacled prevented immediate success."[26]

The frightened boy ran screaming to his father who called the doctor and Bailey was taken to the jail to be tended by the sheriff's wife. It appeared that Bailey was going to recuperate but he took a turn for the worse and died by the end of the month. "However, before doing so, Stephen Bailey confessed to killing all three of his wives. The first, Catherine, he 'killed with a club and buried her in the garden.' His second wife, Mary, was killed with a brick but Bailey refused to say what he'd done with her body."[27] His third had landed him in the care of the sheriff's young son, the sheriff's wife and the undertaker.

All family members joined in the effort to smoothly run the jail. For most of the mom-and-pop jail era, food preparation took up the largest portion of the day. Meals were prepared from scratch, not poured out of a box or popped into the microwave. In the next chapter, we will explore the role of the jailhouse cook, the role for which most sheriffs' wives were noted.

10

With a Pistol in Her (Apron) Pocket

> Jail feeding must generally be on a low cost level. The amount of money available for spending limits the kind of food that may be purchased. But, there is no limit on the way in which food can be prepared. For example, one cut of beef may be roasted; it may be sliced and braised as a Swiss steak; it may be cut into pieces and served as braised beef with noodles; it may be made into a stew or a meat pie; it may be made into many different types of casserole dishes; it may be ground and served as hamburger, meat loaf, or as a meat sauce on spaghetti. These are only a few of the possibilities.
>
> —1961 *Handbook of Jail Food Service*

> Tarrant County, Texas suffered through the Mustard Greens Riot of 1952. Mrs. Harlan Wright boiled her mustard greens in water with just a little salt. This was how she'd always done it and this was how her family liked them. This was how the inmates were served. As a result, drains were stopped up, floors were littered with food and paper shreds, faucets were turned on and water was channeled into the corridors of the jail with magazines. The sheriff was not amused. The inmates were forced to clean things up, and the next day, were served mustard greens again . . . this time, riot-free.
>
> —From *The Texas Sheriff* by Thad Sitton.

In the first nine chapters, we have stepped across the jailhouse threshold, touched on roles required of the sheriff's or jailor's wife, and identified those who worked with her to keep the jail running 24/7, as we say today. No one knew better than jailhouse families what that bit of jargon means.

Because so much of the work at the jail revolved around food—getting it to the kitchen, preparing it for consumption, cleaning up after a meal, and starting all over again for the next meal—it deserves its own chapter. During most of the era of the mom-and-pop jail, work in a kitchen was arduous even for a small household. Food preparation was time-consuming and dangerous. For a large portion of the era, kitchens were built as outbuildings to protect homes from the frequent fires. County commissioners were reluctant to spend tax dollars to update the jail kitchen once it was included in structures built during the Victorian era, so even as late as the midpoint of the twentieth century, many kitchens still came equipped with woodstoves and food was cooled in ice boxes.

As a holdover from the rigid social rules of the Victorian era, mornings at home for at least half of the twentieth century were reserved for cleaning, baking, cooking, and household chores of all kinds. Mary Drenton recalled being told that during morning hours, her grandmother, Mary Lugten, wore her "work apron" around the Allegan County, Michigan, family quarters during the 1920s. After the noontime meal was eaten and cleared, Mary Lugten changed into her "good apron when callers might come. She also put on her beads in order to look presentable." What no one but family knew was that at mealtimes, as Mary Lugten passed food she'd prepared for the inmates through the opening in her kitchen door, she kept a Defender 89 pistol in her apron pocket, just in case.

At the same time, when Leila Pedersen heard from trustees at the Chippewa County, Minnesota, jail that the Bonrud Gang were planning a break—after it had taken a shoot-out to get them behind bars—she too took to sporting a small pistol in her apron pocket. Her daughter, Marge, remembered that it was the only time her mother did such a thing. Leila continued to carry her gun until the four men were found guilty and safely transferred to the penitentiary.

ALL'S QUIET IN THE CELLS

It became a tenet in sheriffing families that well-fed prisoners were good prisoners. Bad food led to bedding being stuffed into the plumbing which led to flooded jails. It also led to cranky inmates participating in the traditional rasping of cell bars with their metal cups. This time-honored method of protest among inmates was once tried on Maureen Elston in Wright County, Iowa. "On one occasion when we'd returned from church on Sunday—before we could get dinner back to them—the inmates took their 'tin cups' and scraped them across the bars, chanting 'where's the beef?' I had my husband go back and tell them 'if you don't quit that racket, there won't be any beef!' Sometimes the antics of the prisoners were quite amusing."

Helen Haugerud found an opportunity or two to amuse her inmates. As she prepared turkey for the Sunday afternoon meal, the inmates started "acting up" so Neil threatened to withhold the turkey dinner if they didn't settle down. As a joke, Helen sent the inmates "a big bowl of necks, wings and innards as their 'punishment' at noon. At 3 P.M. everyone enjoyed some lovely roasted turkey for their Sunday dinner."

The inmates of the Clarion County, Pennsylvania, jail in the 1960s were not the victims of a harmless prank when they were forced to wait for their chicken dinner one night. In 1962, the sheriff and his family moved out of the family quarters and the job of jailor was taken over by a deputy and his family. The only time the sheriff's wife cooked for inmates after 1962 was when the deputy and family took a vacation or time away for the holidays. One of the sheriffs' wives prepared what looked to be a lovely meal of fried chicken with all the trimmings, "but the oil must have been too hot because the inside of the chicken was still raw. The prisoners waited patiently as she recooked the chicken and apologized for serving it in such a state."[1]

Not all Mrs. Sheriffs could be great cooks, or even good cooks. Allegan County, Michigan's Viola White fell into this category. Her grandchildren remarked that as a cook, Viola "stunk" and had absolutely no sense of what foods went together. "Instead of cooking something that required 2½ hours at 325 degrees, she would cook it for one hour at 400 degrees. She could make a perfectly good chicken and dumplings and then add green beans to it, and ruin it." When anyone asked her why she'd done such a thing, she'd reply that it sounded good when she thought of it. "She served green beans with spaghetti. She took up needlepoint and quilting, which she did beautifully, and time would get away from her so she'd go into the kitchen and throw together anything."

However, Viola always kept cupcakes in the freezer because it was one of Bob's traditions to issue a cupcake along with the new driver's license on a teen's sixteenth birthday. The kids knew they could come to the sheriff's office at midnight and start their natal day with birthday wishes, a much anticipated driver's license, and a candle in their cupcake.

With bread and water defining the lowest range of the inmate food continuum, some prisoners actually enjoyed the efforts of jailhouse cooks like Dorothy Everson of Boulder, Colorado. Not only had inmates appreciated her meals during the 1940s and 1950s, but when they left, they often asked for her recipes. The same was reported by Maureen Elston of Wright County, Iowa: "I washed a lot of sheets, pillow cases and blankets! I really liked cooking for the prisoners and we fed them well. I remember that one kid on work release brought 'home' fresh asparagus he'd picked and asked if I would fix it for supper that night. I did. Another kid who had done his time asked when he left if he could have my baked-bean recipe to give to his mom."

Trading recipes took place between trustees and jail families. Marian Edinger's son, Sid, reported that "one of my favorite stories regarding a bootlegger from around 1932 involved Nick D. He was from a 'good' Italian family in Chicago (I think his brother was shot to death in his driveway). His wife would come to Woodstock [McHenry County, Illinois] to visit him. Nick missed his Italian spaghetti so she would make spaghetti and sauce in our kitchen. It was a terrific sauce and it became our family recipe. In 1952, I was home on leave from the Navy and my wife and I were invited to dinner with several of her fellow teachers. They served spaghetti with sauce just like my mother made. I remarked on that and said my mother got the recipe from the wife of a bootlegger named Nick D. The girl serving the meal said 'Uncle Nick!' She was engaged to Nick's nephew and knew all about his past."

HOLIDAYS AND SPECIAL OCCASIONS

The word on the street is that prior to 1933, a few Mrs. Sheriffs of Allegan County, Michigan, were prone to taking the easy way out of feeding inmates by serving bologna sandwiches, sometimes twice a day. But things picked up when Bertha Miller put on the county apron. She was a good cook and for holidays she prepared turkey or ham dinners with all the trimmings, as did so many of her sister matrons through the decades.

Neva Allen's hubby helped the inmates celebrate holidays by allowing them to drink sodas with their holiday feast. In the 1950s, pop or sodas were not the everyday drink that they are today so when the Sheriff brought pop in with the meal, the inmates knew it was a special occasion.

Betty Vinson in Lyon County, Iowa, fed her husband, Craig, two grown children with spouses and three children apiece, two dogs and a cat plus inmates in residence when holidays rolled around. It was not uncommon for a Mrs. Sheriff to serve as many as twenty in the family quarters and another twenty in the larger jails on any given Thanksgiving or Christmas, all enjoying the same food.

Up in Walworth County, Wisconsin, Ella Banks Wylie and family celebrated Christmas in 1923 in the traditional fashion for a jailhouse:

> Most prisoners were allowed to receive packages of presents such as candy, fruit, and books and were visited by family members. . . . The prisoners were also served a delectable Christmas dinner of roast chicken, dressing, mashed potatoes, gravy, cranberry sauce, dessert, and coffee. And to top off the day, Elkhorn pastor AB Bell brought his church choir to entertain the inmates with a vocal and instrumental Christmas concert. . . . The day after the holiday, harsh reality returned as several convicted prisoners were shipped off to state institutions to begin their sentences. . . . [2]

In the late 1920s and 1930s, Leila Pedersen purchased live fowl for holiday meals. "The prisoners would dress them, and Mrs. Pedersen would cook a festive dinner."[3] The same report noted that Leila fed twenty-three inmates one winter in the Chippewa County, Minnesota, jail.

For the holidays from 1927 until the outbreak of World War II, Marge Pedersen reported that her

> Mom had a special Christmas dinner, usually baked chicken, for the prisoners and our family, and afterwards, Mr. Bergman read scripture. We stood in the area in front of the cells and the prisoners would join the family as we sang Christmas carols. Then we told them to hang their stockings on the bars, and we went to church ourselves, just across the street to the Baptist Church. We hung our own socks by the fireplace when we came home, and then went to the jail where dad would have oranges, apples, nuts, playing cards, Christmas candy, mouth organs and new socks which we'd slip into the [inmates'] Christmas socks. Though most of the prisoners were from right around here, some of them had never had a Christmas before.[4]

A Christmas tradition during the dozen years that Dorothy Everson and family lived above the courthouse in Boulder County, Colorado, involved young Bob. "Every year, Boulder firemen put up elaborate Christmas decorations on the outside of the courthouse. In coordination with the visual displays, loud speakers projected holiday songs from a record player in Bob's bedroom, where he changed the records as needed."[5]

CHOW TIME

By dinnertime, most Mrs. Sheriffs knew exactly how many mouths she had to feed. With families ranging in size from one to ten children, live-in parents, sheriff's staff for every meal, those rare meals when there were no inmates still required a huge amount of time and organization to prepare. Anne Werth reported that because their jail was approved to hold federal prisoners in transit, the federal jail inspector might pop in unannounced at any time to check on the state of the jail and condition of the meals being served. "He gave me a book of menus and recipes that I was very pleased to have and still have." [Anne shared that book with us and it is the source of the quotes that begin each chapter of this book.] "All the food I prepared was the same that our family and guests ate. When prisoners showed up at dinner time, all the food went to them and we went out for burgers."

When Marjorie Price donned the Randolph County, Missouri, apron in 1969, she kept a notebook of her menus. Marjorie reported that "sometimes, if a prisoner had a health problem, I would cook differently for them. Like one prisoner had something wrong with his liver and could not eat things like onions, cabbage and spices, etc. He painted a picture in oils for me. Then he died while in state prison."

Deb Wood reported how in Ida County, Iowa, her mother was "a soft touch. Dell Gebers cooked favorite foods for some of the long-term prisoners. Mom was famous for her strong black coffee and chocolate chip cookies. Everyone in town knew they could stop and be treated with compassion no matter what their problem was."

Some states required that inmates be fed three times a day—breakfast, lunch, and dinner—while others required only brunch and supper. On Sundays and holidays, just as it was traditional for many families to sit down to a hearty breakfast and a Sunday dinner at 3:00 p.m., some jails followed suit. Mrs. Sheriff might augment that schedule with a light snack before lights-out on Sunday.

For Fillmore County, Minnesota, during the years that Helen Haugerud lived in the family quarters, breakfast consisted of toast or rolls, eggs, and coffee. Helen fixed a noon meal that consisted of "a small hot dish of some sort or sandwiches." The main meal was served at supper and the inmates ate the same as the family.

Edith Weiss, twenty years earlier, served cereal with milk and sugar, bread and margarine "and perhaps a little jam" with coffee for breakfast. She served the main meal of the day at noon and it consisted of a meat, potatoes, vegetable, bread and margarine, coffee, fruit, cake or pie. Soup and sandwiches were served for supper, or sometimes the inmates finished off leftovers in the ice box at the Holmes County, Ohio, jail.

Lily Serles noted that it was against the law to use margarine in Wisconsin when she took up her Adams County apron in 1955. Given that Wisconsin is the Dairy State, that makes sense once it is given a little thought. Lily was issued a nutrition sheet to help her prepare meals for the prisoners. Everyone ate the same no matter which side of the kitchen door they had their meals, "except on those special occasions when the family had steaks." She reported that she "did make Swiss steak because it went a long ways. Everyone had fruit every day and juice in the morning."

With appreciation still evident in her voice forty-five years later, Lily reported that in 1957 her in-laws presented her with a gift of a dishwasher to make life easier. Lily Serles still had that dishwasher at the time of her interview.

During World War II in Allegan County, Michigan, Mildred Johnson always fixed her inmates healthy meals, although they did not eat the same food as the family. Mildred was fond of saying, "I'm not here to make money off the prisoners!" For breakfast, inmates ate oatmeal, bread and coffee. On weekends, a fruit such as oranges, apples, peaches or pears was added to the enamelware dishes. For lunch, she served her main meal of the day that consisted of meat loaf, baked beans with meat in it, goulash, tuna casserole or stew. Canned veggies and canned fruit were commonly served. Salads consisted of cabbage or sliced tomatoes in season. Along with that, the inmates drank coffee, iced tea or lemonade. For an evening meal, Mildred served bologna or hot dogs with fried potatoes and more of the drinks served at lunch. Water was always available to the inmates.

During the same time frame, prisoners ate a breakfast of sweet rolls and coffee at the Boulder County, Colorado, jail. Dorothy Everson sent her children, Shirley and Pat, to pick up the rolls at the Boulder City Bakery every morning. Then off the kids would run to school. The main meal of the day was served at noon and Dorothy's kids came home to eat with their mom and sometimes their dad. Trustees took pots and pans of meat loaf or roast beef with veggies, either a salad or coleslaw, and dessert into the bullpen, filled the metal plates and served the prisoners. Shirley reported that the inmates' favorite desserts were her mom's coconut cakes and cherry pies. When the meal was finished, the prisoners washed their own dishes and utensils and set them aside for collection when someone had time to take them to the kitchen.

Like Dorothy's coconut cakes and cherry pies, the inmates remembered Maud Tanner's pies in Antrim County, Michigan. "The meals were very good for everyone including the prisoners— chicken and biscuits on Sunday. We occasionally got Christmas cards from former prisoners. They nearly always mentioned the food. They often had homemade pies served to them."

Harriet Moore, daughter of Sheriff Abel Moore, has come down through history to us because of her pies. In 1845, the Middlesex County Hotel in Massachusetts burned. After the sheriff's family moved into the new county hotel, "one Thanksgiving Day, a visitor to the sheriff's [home] found Abel Moore's daughter, Harriet,

2 Jeremiah Lynch	May 30	June 18	Drunkenness
Elijah Gregory	" 30	" 28	stubborn Child
Ebenezer Bassett	" 31	" 29	Drunkenness
John Gibbs	June 1	July 30	" "

In a Bristol County, Massachusetts, jail log for 1847, those incarcerated were noted along with the first and last day of their stay, as well as why they were arrested. Note the second entry for Elijah Gregory who served a month for being a stubborn child. A similar entry occurred later in the same document but for a different boy. (From author's collection)

making sixty-nine apple, squash, and mince pies, one of each for each of twenty-three prisoners."[6] We should all remember Harriet Moore when we bake our two or three pumpkin pies each November.

The staff at the Old Lincoln County Jail in Maine tell their visitors that prisoners lived on "tea, gingerbread, soup, and biscuits."[7] A short menu can still have its fans. Madge Harris recalled how the inmates loved her cold-weather Saturday night meal of ham and beans, corn bread with applesauce.

Down in Texas, home of 219 counties and their jails, many a bean was served. In Brown County, it is reported that pinto beans were served every day. They were prepared in a large pressure cooker "with plenty of salt pork"[8] during the 1930s. Inmates were given a serving of about $1\frac{1}{2}$ cups of beans. "Corn or potatoes were served with the beans. Every inmate was given seven thick slices of bread at noon that was to last until next noon meal. On Sunday, meat was added to the plate. All the coffee they wanted was served at breakfast and they had access to water at any time. Bacon was served at breakfast on Sunday and if they had a slice of bread left, it made a pretty good meal. On Christmas and Thanksgiving, the inmates were served traditional meals."[9]

As jail inspection reports were compiled and prison reform filtered down to the county and city jails, states created regulations to govern all of their incarceration facilities. It was noted in the 1950s in Hamilton County, Florida, that prisoners were fed three meals a day. In Hamilton County that meant breakfast, a main meal at noon, and two sandwiches and either soup or chili for the evening meal. The new regulations required that inmates be served 2,000 to 3,000 calories each day. Eggs were served on occasion.[10]

In Hamilton County, even before regulations were created, inmates seem always to have been fed well. When Grace McGhin served as matron in 1941 for her husband, Eddie, most days Viola Robinson wore the cook's apron. Viola fed the prisoners beef and potato stew, sweet potatoes, peas, beans, various greens, fatback pork, biscuits, coffee, corn bread, and the occasional peach pie. There were two or three meals a day. Tin or aluminum plates and cups were used. It was noted that ice was expensive at the time so no one got much iced tea with meals. Viola prepared meals on a woodstove. She also cooked for Judge Hal Adams, and she was pleased to fix him his favorite dish of black-eyed peas.[11]

Regional cooking was always a hit with the local inmates but caused a problem for those incarcerated from elsewhere. During a 1958 newspaper interview with Olivia Cormier, jail cook in Lafayette, Louisiana, the following details came to light:

> With efficient swiftness, Mrs. Joe Cormier ladled stew gravy and meat over a mound of rice in the aluminum plate, added a generous serving of lima beans, cole slaw and bread. She did this eleven times. Mrs. Cormier cooks for the prisoners at the city jail. She has been at this job for five years. Mrs. Cormier likes her work, spends the better part of each day, seven days a week, in the green and white tile walled kitchen at city hall. The jailhouse cook takes pride in serving good meals to the prisoners. She is an excellent cook, in the best French-Arcadian tradition, and knows what to do with a bottle of pepper, a bit of garlic and some stew meat or chicken. Sometimes there are more than twenty prisoners to feed each day. At other times there are only five or six, but seldom less than this, Mrs. Cormier says. Breakfast and supper are always the same: three slices of bread, one roll and a big cup of café-au-lait. Dinner, the noon meal, varies. Usually there is stew gravy with rice, meat, beans, bread and a salad varied with steak or stewed chicken. Sundays, there is always chicken and potato salad. It is noted that Mrs. Cormier got Christmas Day off and the prisoners meals were catered by local restaurants. She got a few complaints about the food: "Sometimes, she says, strangers to these parts object to the coffee or the rice she serves because the coffee is strong, and they're not used to rice and gravy."[12]

Olivia Cormier was allowed to concentrate on cooking for her own family on Christmas Day while the prisoners ate restaurant food brought in for them. For over thirty years, inmates were fed restaurant food each night for supper, and not in their cells at the Summit County jail in Colorado. In the 1940s, Anna Mumford cleaned the jail, cooked breakfast and lunch for the inmates, but she put her foot down over evening meals. Her husband, Judge Russell Mumford, who also served as jailor and driver's license examiner, took the "inmates out to dinner at either the Gold Pan Saloon, Colorado House, or Brown Hotel. A County Commissioner, Sheriff, or Assessor usually accompanied them. Such 'dining out' wasn't extravagant."[13] When Anna just said no to dinner, taking the boys out every night was cheaper than hiring a live-in cook. The practice became a tradition that lasted into the 1970s, and no escapes took place during the transfer of prisoners to and from the eateries.

In Nassau County, Florida, when Annis Moore served her county, she donned her county apron only on Sundays and holidays. Six days a week, Mrs. Guest walked across the street from her own home and prepared meals for the inmates. Trays for breakfast held scrambled eggs and grits, homemade biscuits with milk and coffee. The main meal was served at noon and consisted of lima beans, corn bread and water. Dinner was a lighter meal of a sandwich (ham, bologna, peanut butter, or banana) and milk. "Some of the local farms provided fresh produce and the eggs came from a county farm."[14] When Annis prepared the noon meal on

Sunday, it was the traditional fried chicken with all the fixings. For holidays, she prepared turkey with all the trimmings.

Madge Harris in Wilson County, Kansas, like many of her peers, went the extra mile for her inmates. Not only did she serve them good food on a daily basis but when Valentine's Day rolled around, she served them their own heart-shaped cake with pink icing. Delighted inmates enjoyed that cake with ice cream. Because she had access to the inmate records in her husband's office, Madge knew the birth date of all those incarcerated at any given time. Prisoners celebrated their birthdays behind bars with their fellow inmates. Everyone was served cupcakes, and the birthday boy's cupcake was decorated with a candle.

In the next chapter we will explore how food made its way to the jailhouse kitchen. We will also see how sheriffing families were reimbursed for feeding prisoners, lawmen, and any others who made their way to the jail at mealtime.

—11—

Here's the Grocery Bill, Honey

When available, fresh fruits can do wonders for a jail menu. In addition, they are associated with good health by reason of their high nutritional content. You must have heard the saying that 'an apple a day keeps the doctor away!' Keep in close touch with your local wholesalers of produce or a farmer or two if you live in or near a country area. Many times very good buys in fruits can be obtained when either the wholesaler or farmer is left with merchandise on his hands that will spoil quickly. Usually they are willing to sell these 'distress' items at much less than regular cost.

—1961 *Handbook of Jail Food Service*

In Dubuque County, Iowa, "two prisoners got past the jailor as meals were being served. Mom and Dad were in the kitchen and both were knocked down by the escapees. The inmates ran through the door leading to the back porch, which opened onto the alley. The back door, however, was locked and they were captured by deputies before they could fully escape. It was a harrowing experience for my parents."

—About Geraldine Spielman who
served alongside Sheriff Frank
Spielman from 1958 to 1964,
reported by daughter, Shirley.

County commissioners, notoriously tight with the county tax dollars, were not always fully prepared to foot the bills presented by their sheriffs. In 1878, Sheriff JG Weakley presented the new Democrat county commissioners with his bills for expenses from the previous quarter when a Republican county commission sat. He asked for reimbursement in the amount of $128.72 for items such as travel expenses to pick up prisoners, fees for notifying jurors to come to the courthouse when the district court met, serving subpoenas, and boarding prisoners. The new county commissioners wrangled over the expenses and finally agreed to pay Sheriff Weakley $70.82. Russell County, Kansas, did not have a happy sheriff after that.

County commissioners in general were no different in 1954 when Mary Ann Darrow settled into life in the 1873 jail and family quarters of Powell County, Montana. "I visited the County Commissioners and requested that the kitchen sink be raised. I found it quite difficult to wash dishes at a sink that hit me at my knee caps. Ed hired a carpenter to build a cupboard so at least I had a counter top and some storage for dishes and utensils."

> I also asked the Commissioners if the wall in front of the stove could be taken out. [When the oven door was open, Mary Ann could take food out or put food in only if she stood to the side.] They refused this request. After burning myself several times removing things from the oven at the awkward side angle, I lost my temper. I went to see the maintenance man at the courthouse to ask him for a crowbar. He wondered what I was planning to do with it. I told him I was going to tear out the kitchen wall in front of my stove. He said, 'You can't do that!' I just looked him in the eye and said 'watch me.'
>
> Ed heard the noise in the apartment and came upstairs to see what was going on. He saw me tearing out that darn wall and just turned around and left me to my task of demolition. After I had the wall out (it took the better part of a day) I returned to the County Commissioners office and told them what I had done. I said to them, 'now you can send someone over to fix the floor and paint the entire apartment. There has been nothing done over there since 1928 to make it more livable. This is 1954 and I think it is about time.' Arrangements were made to have the entire apartment painted and new linoleum was ordered for the dining room and the kitchen. A storage cupboard was built in an area of wasted space between the bathroom and the bedroom. With new paint on the walls, new linoleum and best of all, another storage cupboard, I was more content to live in the jail."

Mary Ann served as matron for female and juvenile prisoners, filled in on phone duty as needed, served her county in a variety of ways as seen in other chapters and prepared two meals a day for the inmates. They ate a hearty breakfast at 10:00 in the morning and the evening meal was served at 5:30. For all of this, Mary Ann was reimbursed $1.75 a day (not for each meal) for each prisoner to cover the cost of food.

The disparity in what a county would pay for feeding of inmates varied widely. It was reported that Edith Weiss served her Holmes County, Ohio, inmates well on the 17 cents per meal for each prisoner during the Depression, and served them turkey or chicken for holidays, complete with mashed potatoes, dressing, vegetables, pies or cakes or some other dessert. Neva Allen was paid $3 per meal per prisoner by Poweshiek County, Iowa, twenty years later, which turned out to be generous compared to her peers around the nation at that time and well into the future.

Going back as far as 1873, there exists a contract signed by a Mrs. Knowles stating that the Board of Supervisors of San Diego County, California, would pay her the sum of 48 cents per day for feeding each of the county's prisoners twice a day. Twenty years later on the other side of the nation, in Hamilton County,

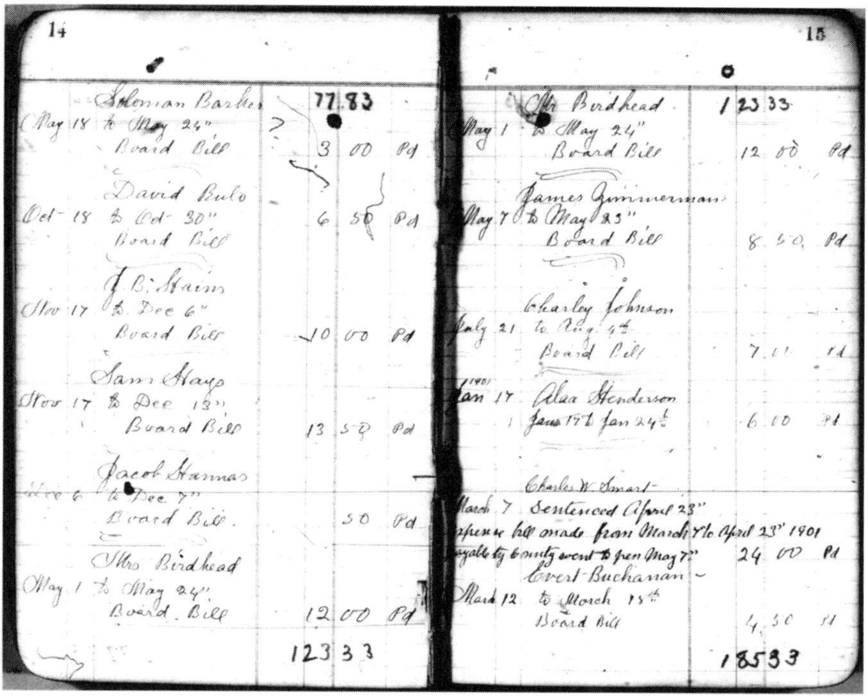
14

Solomon Barker 77.83
May 18 to May 24" Board Bill 3 00 Pd
David Bulo
Oct 18 to Oct 30" Board Bill 6 50 Pd
J. B. Stairs
Nov 17 to Dec 6" Board Bill 10 00 Pd
Sam Hays
Nov 17 to Dec 13" Board Bill 13 50 Pd
Jacob Hannas
Dec 6 to Dec 7" Board Bill 50 Pd
Mrs Birdhead
May 1 to May 24" Board Bill 12 00 Pd
123 33

15

Mr Birdhead 123 33
May 1 to May 24" Board Bill 12 00 Pd
James Zimmerman
May 7 to May 25" Board Bill 8 50 Pd
Charley Johnson
July 21 to Aug 4th Board Bill 7 00 Pd
1901 Jan 17 Alex Henderson Jan 17th Jan 24th 6 00 Pd
Charles W. Smart
March 7 Sentenced April 23"
Expense bill made from March 7 to April 23" 1901
payable by county went to pen May 7" 24 00 Pd
Evert Buchanan
March 12 to March 15th Board Bill 4 50 Pd
185 33

A page from Mary Crandall's boarding records from 1900. Note the female inmate, Mrs. Birdhead, who had been incarcerated for murder. Mr. Birdhead also sat in the Knox County, Nebraska, jail, charged with being an accessory to the murder. (Courtesy of the Nebraska State Historical Society at Lincoln.)

Florida, Laura Polhill was reimbursed 30 cents per meal for the first five prisoners in her care on any given day. If she cooked for more than five inmates one meal, the additional food warranted reimbursement of only 25 cents per meal.

In 1928 and after, while Martha Bulman prepared meals for the prisoners in the Allamakee County, Iowa, jail "she gave them big meals with meat, vegetable, salad, pie or dessert and homemade bread" for 20 cents per meal for each prisoner.

Burton Drury, raised in the jail at St. Genevieve County, Missouri, reported that his mother, Philomena, fed her family and the prisoners twice a day for which she received 35 cents per meal for the inmates' meals. Everyone ate the same food and received good, healthy servings. "Those were lean years for everyone just after the Depression, but mom and dad raised five girls and me, the only son."

Times remained lean after the Depression and World War II when it came to county jails. In 1955, Betty Swanson in Lucas County, Iowa, was paid the same 35 cents a meal for each prisoner. Betty says, "we bought the groceries with our own money. We fed the prisoners the same food we had and plenty of it. We never, ever, had any complaints about meals from the prisoners. I wore out pots, pans, appliances, etc."

In Kansas in the 1960s, the sheriff was reimbursed at the rate of 50 cents per meal per inmate. Elma Sinclair in Hodgeman County reported that she had to be resourceful in her buying. "I cooked from scratch while holding down a full time job outside the home for the first four years." Elma went on to be elected sheriff when her husband ran into term limitations so gave up her full-time job. She continued to feed the prisoners from scratch as sheriff and then later when she served as her husband's undersheriff.

During the 1960s, Anne Werth was reimbursed the same 50 cents per meal per prisoner as was every other Mrs. Sheriff in Kansas, with no salary for all of the work they performed. The Werth's lost the next election in Ellis County, and when they won the office once again, she "was paid $1.50 per meal per inmate and a small salary for her effort. Things got a lot easier. I'm not sure what happened while we were away but it sure helped."

What happened was the lawsuit that the Schumaker's filed against the state of Kansas after they lost almost every cent they had put aside while serving Ellis County as sheriff. Agnes Schumaker cooked for as many as 20 extra people at any given time. With her physical health failing and their financial health in ruins, Agnes and Hilly took on the state of Kansas to change the law governing how much sheriffs were reimbursed for feeding each prisoner. It required a court battle. When the family went into sheriffing, they were financially sound. By the time Hilly resigned, the couple was deeply in debt from feeding all of the people who depended on them. Agnes burned out and her daughter, Peggy, reported that Agnes hated to cook for the rest of her life. Agnes suffered from exhaustion and then developed a heart condition. Her husband resigned, but not before they won the court battle to increase the food allowance for prisoners, making life better for all of the Kansas sheriffs in office then and after.

When Anne and Clarence Werth entered the total amount of the money they spent on the prisoners as a line item in the expense portion of their tax form, they offset it by the total income they received. When this came across the desk of someone at the Internal Revenue Service, alarms went off, lights flashed, a hubbub ensured, suspicions were raised and an audit was required. "The auditor said he couldn't allow such a thing without receipts, it was unheard of." So Anne pulled out every receipt for food money she'd spent on the prisoners, from the grocery store to the burger joint. "The auditor allowed it as a legitimate expense."

FILLING THE PANTRY

At the beginning of legal life for many counties, the location of the county seat was often a hard fought battle that lasted for years if two or more towns in a new county wanted the honor. Once the dust settled, the fortunate town so designated prospered. Businesses built up and citizens bought lots to build their homes. Those counties that came early in our nation's history were built on the European tradition of farmers living in town and commuting to their land to work. As the frontier moved west, pioneers had to wear many hats. Many who settled on the prairie built homes in town, became businessmen or tradesmen, and broke the prairie in their section of land as they could.

As the majority of sheriffing families moved to the county seat, the food they acquired for themselves and their inmates often came from local grocers. If there were more than one grocery store in town, some Mrs. Sheriffs utilized them all. Other sheriffs set up accounts at one store. The store-bought groceries were augmented in various ways to economize, given the scanty rates per meal that most county commissioners were willing to pay.

The following sources of food is presented in chronological order to show how things changed or didn't change in the twentieth century. In 1902 Bath County, Virginia, Lollie Jane Gum kept chickens in the backyard of the jailhouse. Her daughters, Montague and Lucille, gathered eggs each morning as one of their regular chores.

In 1935 Holmes County, Ohio, Sheriff Weiss and the boys hunted grouse, pheasants, and rabbits to put on the table. As he was able to afford, the sheriff also purchased a farm on which there was an orchard. The family put in two and then a third large garden to help feed everyone. Edith Weiss raised seven children. Everyone worked hard to feed themselves and the inmates. The gardens produced potatoes, string beans, corn, "just about any vegetable," Edith's daughter, Evelyn, reported. They also put up one hundred quarts of applesauce every year.

Evelyn worked at the local department store but when her Wednesday afternoon off rolled around, she rolled right out to the farm to help garden. She remembers going out to the farm to can all of the produce as it came into season. "That meant canning hundreds of quarts of vegetables as well as all kinds of fruit. Some of the prisoners gained weight."

Howard A. Tanner recalled how he and his father hunted and fished a lot. His mother and grandmother, Maud and Donnie, canned produce from their big vegetable garden after they moved into the family quarters in 1937 in Antrim County, Michigan. When meat rationing went into effect during World War II, the family raised rabbits. As in many counties, when officers confiscated game while making an arrest for hunting out of season, the game was given to the sheriff in order to help feed the prisoners.

In Tolland County, Connecticut, during the same war, Mabel Cook canned hundreds of jars of vegetables for winter. The county farm was still in existence at that time, which proved to be quite helpful as rationing took effect. Barbara Cook remembers that a team of workhorses was still in use on the farm during the 1940s. The horses came in handy when gasoline was difficult to come by even for farmers. "The large barn housed five milking cows plus young stock. There were pigs, chickens, and at various times, turkeys, ducks and sheep. There was a huge garden area where vegetables were grown, and a large raspberry patch. Animals were butchered, lard was tried, sauerkraut and pickles were put up. Those chickens had to be cleaned (and sometimes killed and plucked) by Mother. Butter had to be churned. A hundred-acre farm about a mile away raised hay, pumpkins, squash, root crops, and provided pasture for the herd during the summer. The cows were driven down the road in spring and returned in the fall. Thanksgiving and Christmas were celebrated with special meals and numerous pumpkin pies."

During World War II when any number of household items and various foods were rationed, many Mrs. Sheriffs stood in long lines to be able to feed their families and inmates. Shirley Everson shared her mother's tale of how precious sugar was in the jail kitchen during those years. One night, Art brought in a drunk who was determined not to go to a cell. A fight broke out in Shirley's kitchen. During the scuffle, the drunk kicked the table. The sugar bowl flew off the table and fell to the floor, spilling sugar everywhere. "The loss of what today is a common kitchen item much taken for granted was sorely grieved that night because everyone knew how long Dorothy had stood in line to get the sugar."

Viola White's husband, Bob, left his duties in Leelanau County, Michigan, only once a year after he took office in 1948: to go hunting with his sons. The deer the men brought home was turned into venison stew and was eaten by both the family and inmates. Confiscated game in Coleman County, Texas, after World War II was used by Loretta Fenton to augment the red beans she purchased in hundred-pound bags. She recalled that she made a lot of gravy to extend meals. "Eggs were 10 cents a dozen. Bread was even cheaper."[1] The Fentons put in a garden and others in town brought their excess garden produce to the jail to help. Loretta remembers being invited to pick through other people's gardens to take home anything she could salvage.

At the same time, in Burnet County, Texas, Essie Riddell kept a cow and four hogs in the back lot behind the jail plus numerous "chickens [that] had no hen house, so they roosted in trees around the courthouse square. Late fall hog butcheries took place at the Riddells' jail home [behind] the courthouse square just as they had previously at the family's farm and the pork went into the smokehouse."[2] Essie recalled how her family visited Wallace's parent's several times a year to harvest their large garden and help can produce. Their share was used at the jail. Wallace hunted every fall with his pa and brothers "to kill several whitetail deer to cook and can for the jail."[3]

In 1954 Powell County, Montana, Mary Ann Darrow purchased "sweet rolls and Pullman cakes at a discount after they were pulled from the shelf and I'd freeze them. Pullman cakes were three layer cakes three inches high, three inches wide and about nine inches long. They were common before the advent of in-store bakeries. The prisoners appreciated a piece of cake or a sweet roll as a part of their diet."

Ten years later, Mary Jahnel was raising tomatoes in the flower beds in front of the sheriff's office in Mitchell County, Iowa. Marjorie Price of Randolph County, Missouri, did her grocery shopping at the end of the 1960s in two towns. "I shopped once a week in Moberly, seven miles away, for groceries and supplies. During the week I shopped with the two local grocery stores in Huntsville, which is the county seat. I made out menus and cooked for the prisoners first. And then I prepared my family's meal."

During the one year that Nancy and Tom Fitzpatrick lived in the family quarters attached to the jail in Kossuth County, Iowa, "Tom hunted as most of the guys in that area did, and came home with geese and pheasant for the table. The prisoners ate what the family ate, so if I had one in the cell in time for supper, he partook also."

Nancy also put in "a big garden full of tomatoes, corn, peas and beans." She inherited a huge asparagus patch and rhubarb from former Mrs. Sheriffs. When it came time to harvest that year, Nancy was pregnant with daughter, Laura. While she didn't suffer from morning sickness, "certain foods set me off." She'd organized all that was needed to can quarts and quarts of tomatoes only to discover that the smell of cooked tomatoes made her violently nauseous. "There was nothing to be done but to keep ladling the cooked tomatoes into the jars as fast as I could before I had to be sick." Nancy reported that it was easier to run out the back door and be sick off the steps than to run upstairs to the bathroom.

SOUP'S ON!

We have followed the food trail from garden or grocery to kitchen. How did food make it from the kitchen to the inmates? Sam Cooper spent his teens in the Greenwood County, South Carolina, jail when his mother, Vernice, served as Mrs. Sheriff during the 1960s. The majority of the household work was taken care of by three trustees: Dot, Fox, and Junior. Sam noted that "the kitchen was the place where the world of the jail and the world of the home met." In the majority of jails with family quarters this was so. But how the two worlds intersected differed from jail to jail.

Mary Jahnel's daughter, Dode, recalled that "prisoner trays were lined up around the kitchen on the limited countertop space and table. Trays were always filled first and several of us would march single file carrying them through the living room to the short hall that separated our lives from the prisoners. Mom was paid around $1.25 per day per prisoner to cook the meals and the food expense came out of that money. A woman prisoner's family would come often from a neighboring state on visiting day and mother would have tea and a sweet treat ready for them to enjoy."

Kathy Jahnel Stammer wrote that she recalled the many times her mother "had the counter full with prisoners' trays. Mother had to share what little counter space she had in the kitchen with a 24-hour blasting sheriff radio and phone. These were also left to her to answer if nobody was in the one-room sheriff's office in the front of the house." Kathy noted that "prisoners washed their own dishes after they ate. If they refused, dad told them 'no food if no dishes!' Usually, missing one meal turned the rebel around."

Annis Moore-Littles of Nassau County, Florida, reported that they had a large jail kitchen, a fact that was much appreciated. The family had their own small kitchen that had been tacked on later by enclosing a small porch at the back of the jail. When the jail cook was finished cooking for the inmates, the trustees came by the steel kitchen door to pick up trays and deliver them to the inmates.

During the Depression, Edith Weiss in Holmes County, Ohio, prepared all of her meals in a very small kitchen. In the wall between the kitchen and cell area had been built a slot "just large enough for a table top and plates to move through. There was a locking mechanism that had to be unlatched when the table top was brought down from the upright (storage) position. Then Edith and Evelyn set out the food for the inmates and slipped the table through the wall to the common space in the jail on the first floor. The inmates pulled chairs up to the table top and ate. They washed their own dishes and when they were finished, they passed the table top back through the wall and it was secured against the wall."

More difficult prisoners were housed on the second floor of Edith's jail and ate in their cells. The sheriff and his kids took trays of food to those who had to remain under lock and key. They slid the trays through the slot in the cell door.

Evelyn Weiss reported that when the first-floor inmates needed supplies like clean towels, soap or other toiletries, they sent a note across to Edith along with the clean meal dishes. Edith and the children then "filled the request" and sent the items back to the inmates through the slot in the wall before securing the tabletop to the kitchen wall. When the tabletop was in the down position, it took up most of the small kitchen.

When jails were built during the end of the Victorian era, many of them came equipped with dumb waiters. Mary Ann Darrow and Helen Haugerud lived in two such facilities. Both women reported that their young children were fascinated by the contraption. Mary Ann wrote that "under close supervision, Barry at age 5, loved to demonstrate how it worked for all his friends. The food was sent down in pots and pans in which it was prepared. The prisoners returned the pots and pans after they were washed and dried."

In Ellis County, Kansas, during the 1960s, Anne Werth often served female prisoners at the family table. The men's meals were served "family style" with pots of food put on a cart and wheeled into the cell area and served by a trustee. Female prisoners held in Allegan County, Michigan, during World War II were fed in their cells. The men lined up for food through the 2½ x 2½ foot pass-through in the steel kitchen door.

Leona Banister wrote of the system they used in the Coleman County, Texas, jail after 1914. Emma Banister was fortunate to have the help of a cook to prepare the food. "Great pots of meat and vegetables were cooked on the big coal stove, and such other foods as were added to our own table were in smaller pots. [Mother] believed that hot breads make a feast of a common meal, and she saw to it that they were on the generous trays of prisoners' foods twice a day."[4] She added that the family's

> meals were cooked and served, and our dishes put away in one of the butler's pantry cabinets. The trays of food, just about the same as were on our table, were then prepared for the prisoners; Papa or a deputy carried the big tassel of keys to the cell doors, and the

trays were taken upstairs by the cook and one or more of us children. Papa always ordered the prisoners to stand well back as the foods were placed on an empty iron cot. Later, the trays were brought back to the kitchen, washed, scalded and put into their own cabinet.[5]

In 1906 Jackson County, Missouri, Mama Hulse was the county marshal's wife and she had her own kitchen for family meal preparation. Her granddaughter, Alice, who came to live in the marshal's quarters while she attended high school, recalled that "in the mornings we ate breakfast in the big old kitchen because Mama Hulse always had a hot fire in the old cook stove."[6] From the kitchen, a stairway led to Mama's laundry. Down more steps, one came to the jail kitchen located in the basement. In the late 1950s, when Alice toured the Jail Museum that she used to call home, "memories of the delicious food which the trustee cooks concocted came back. Prisoners really ate good in those days. When I came home from school, hungry as a bear, I used to slip down to the old kitchen and get some beans and cornbread before my grandmother got our supper ready up in her kitchen."[7]

Eileen Chesbro reported that the trustees cooked for the prisoners in the basement of the Oswego County, New York, jail as well. Male inmates ate there at long trestle tables. It was a large basement and part of it was used to butcher meat from the county farm and prepare it for the freezer. She recalled how every year they were inspected by the grand jury. During the inspection, the jurors were always treated to a sit-down dinner at those trestle tables in the basement and "for some reason they always found it fascinating, entertaining, as well as delicious. There is something about getting that glimpse at the other side of life that intrigues the more law abiding of us."

For those Mrs. Sheriffs who did not live in but near the jail, they turned their kitchens into an assembly line also. Rose Singler, first a Mrs. Sheriff and then the poorly paid cook for the Jackson County, Oregon, jail for several years after 1913, sent food to the prisoners by way of big baskets. The jailor walked across from the jail, loaded up the pots, pans, crocks and bundles of bread, and walked it all over to the cells. Later, he'd bring back[8] the empties so she, like her sister Mrs. Sheriffs down through the ages, could start all over again for the next meal.

Food arrived at the jailhouse from stores, gardens, hunts, and county farms. Everyone partook of it. In the following chapter, we will see who, besides the family, came to the table through the years.

12

Loaves and Fishes

> Economical coffee can be brewed by using 1/3 lb. dry coffee to one gallon of water. If further economy is desired, a blend of chicory and coffee is quite acceptable. Using 70% coffee and 30% chicory will reduce the pound cost by one-third. Buy coffee in small lots that are quickly used up. Coffee beans or ground coffee lose a great deal of flavor on standing and even if you issue a contract for large amounts, you should ask that frequent small shipments be sent rather than having the entire load delivered at one time.
>
> —1961 *Handbook of Jail Food Service*

> One morning in 1910 Martin County, Minnesota, the milkman knocked on the back door to the home of Mrs. Sheriff Mose Denman. As he dropped off the dairy goods, he nonchalantly inquired if they were hanging laundry out to dry at the jail? Mrs. Denman looked across the way and sure enough, sheets were flapping in the breeze. Two prisoners had cut their way through the bars and made their exit.
>
> —From the Martin County Jail Stories Web site.

Who besides family members and inmates ate the food that the sheriff included in his expense report to the county commissioners on a quarterly basis? In this chapter, the answer to that question will be explored and there may be some surprises. People from the top of the social ladder to the bottom, to put it bluntly, thought nothing of catching a meal in the jailhouse dining room, and that resulted in stretching the pantry contents as far as possible.

The appropriately named Mabel Cook of Tolland County, Connecticut, "prepared a fine dinner at noon each month for the Commissioners' meeting." Mabel's daughter, Barbara, recalled that her mother also "fed on a regular basis any State Troopers, missionary, doctors, ministers, barbers, blacksmiths, the sheriff himself and others who might find themselves (accidentally or perhaps not) present at mealtimes. The family had a dining room connected to the jail kitchen where prisoners employed on the [county] farm and in the kitchen took their meals. The family gave up this dining room once a month when the County Commissioners came" for their meeting and meal.

The Cook family "had our own small refrigerator in the dining room, to stash milk for the baby and ice cream and other private treats but in general, everyone ate the same thing, as my mother prepared it all in the jail kitchen on two large wood stoves. Occasionally a prisoner would take over some cooking but mostly she was happy to have somebody to prepare vegetables, wash dishes, fill the wood box, and maybe kill and pluck a couple of chickens for dinner. When there was no trustee to help, she did those things herself."

In 1885 Lawrence County, Kentucky, Virginia Vinson served plenty of guests around her table while court was in session. "The judge, as well as the commonwealth attorney and other lawyers, boarded at the Vinson home [sheriff's quarters next to the jail], and they allowed [Virginia's son, Fred] to listen in to their conversations, which naturally were liberally sprinkled with discussions of the law and politics."[1] This influenced Fred and he grew up to become chief justice of the U.S. Supreme Court. He also resigned that position to become secretary of the treasury under Harry Truman, who knew the value of keeping former jailhouse kids around him. Truman's press secretary was another such kid and lifelong friend, Charles Ross, who grew up in the Jackson County, Missouri, jail.

In Republic County, Kansas, Gloria Peterka Nondorf recalled that the family quarters were situated on the same floor in the courthouse as the sheriff's office, so lawmen of all kinds thought nothing of stopping in Christina Peterka's kitchen "for coffee and a snack, or lunch. Only the special ones were invited to dinner."

While Helen Haugerud in Fillmore County, Minnesota, recalled that she rarely had visiting lawmen in for coffee and never for meals, Fulton County, Indiana's Marguerite Norris found herself tripping over lawmen needing coffee and meals after her husband, Lawrence, arrested sixteen members of a robbery gang. Included in the arrest were two women who were either the wife or girlfriend of others in the gang, so Marguerite's attention was required for them in the capacity of their matron. Each of the Norris inmates had to be housed in a separate cell to keep them from harming each other, some having been threatened with violence if they talked. The gang had robbed at least 200 places in eight Indiana counties as well as Illinois and Michigan. "The sheriff's office [and Marguerite's kitchen] was jumping for days with law enforcement coming in from all over to clear pending case files."[2]

Marian Edinger "had to be ready for anything," reported her son, Sid. "Being right on the town square, it was not unusual for people to come to the door wanting to see the sheriff. I recall one evening just as we sat down for dinner there was a knock on the back door. It was Elmer S., a forger who was wanted in Illinois and California. He decided to turn himself in because mom was such a good cook and he figured that if he was picked up elsewhere, he would not be as well fed. He was a regular customer, almost a member of the family."

Larry Robinson of Windham County, Vermont, noted something similar. Hobos, known locally as the "Knights of the Road," knew where the best places for food could be found and would get incarcerated routinely at their favorite jails.

ALWAYS ROOM FOR ONE MORE

As in many places, trustees ate with Martha Terrell's family at the Garfield County, Colorado, jail kitchen or dining room table during the latter years of the Depression. And many, like Agnes Schumaker in Ellis County, Kansas, fed families of prisoners too. It was noted that she often had the families of incarcerated drunks at her table on a Sunday afternoon.

When Irene and Jack Gray lived in the Saguache County, Colorado, jail during the 1950s, she fed "a few drunks in town who would not want to go home." Irene also remembers a "family who was out of work and they wanted to spend the night. I fed them supper. In the morning, they wanted pop instead of milk for the kids for breakfast. They got milk."

Stories were shared by many sheriffing families of housing various people who were there, like the family above, not because they deserved incarceration, but because of other circumstance. Before the days of social service agencies, people in trouble turned to ministers and priests, or to the sheriff. Anne Werth in Ellis County, Kansas, supplied several typical stories. An older gentleman traveling across country on a bus was taken off in Hays and Clarence was asked to take him in. The man had become disoriented during the trip; he was later diagnosed with Alzheimer's. Clarence made the elderly gentleman comfortable in a cell in the men's area, but Anne fed him at their table with the family.

On another occasion, a woman riding across country on her motorcycle stopped and asked for shelter, so Anne made her a bed on their couch. The woman enjoyed supper and breakfast before she started on her trip again, grateful for having had a safe place to stay the night.

Another young woman came to Anne under much more trying circumstances. She'd been keeping company with a man in Oklahoma and one day, while they were out, the man drove her across the Kansas border and just kept going. Frightened, the young woman managed to escape from the fellow while they were in Hays and came to Anne and Clarence for protection. The Werth's took her in, gave her the couch to sleep on and provided her with meals until they could arrange for her to get home again on the bus.

Something similar but more sinister took place at another time. A young lady was kidnapped by her boyfriend and his friend. On their way through the area, they stopped at a motel on the edge of Hays. The two young men robbed and killed the desk clerk and drove away with the girl. She eventually assisted the authorities in Indiana in their apprehension of the two men and came back to Ellis County as a material witness. As it turned out, she lived with the Werths in the family quarters for several years while the trials took place, and became like one of their own.

A family came through Ellis County on their way West. They'd run out of money by that time, so stopped at the sheriff's office. The head of the migrating family offered to sell Clarence a "very nice gun" for an amount of money that would see them through to their destination and a new job. Clarence looked the gun over, observed that it truly was "very nice," and agreed. The family was fed, gasoline was put in their automobile, and off they went. It wasn't too long, just a matter of months, before Clarence received the full amount of the loan and he was pleased to be able to return the gun to its owner.

THE AMBIANCE LEFT SOMETHING TO BE DESIRED

During the time that Anne Werth was taking care of grateful people from all over the nation, Elma Sinclair's family lived in the Hodgeman County, Kansas, jail. The cells and sheriff's office were located just outside of the family apartment. "I served three meals a day to the prisoners. One unruly bunch of inmates would not settle down but continued their loud behavior. Finally I told them I was going to withhold their meals until they complied. They missed two meals before they apologized and decided to change their actions."

Another ingrate was reported by Nancy Fitzpatrick of Kossuth County, Iowa, during the following decade. Still chuckling at the time of her interview, Nancy recalled that the local movie theater manager was incarcerated for drunk driving one evening. "I fixed him the standard ham and eggs breakfast that everyone else ate. When my husband brought the tray back later, the food was untouched except for being used as an ashtray for a half dozen cigarette stubs. The man told my husband that he couldn't eat eggs because he had a bad heart. I laughed and laughed that a drinking smoker was concerned about eating eggs!"

When a jail building fell on hard times and the county could not pay for repairs or to build a new one due to their own hard times, sometimes there was nothing left to do but to take your prisoners to a neighboring jail. Nancy Fitzpatrick lived in such a jail, so decrepit that it had been condemned and was capable of holding only one male prisoner for one night. Maud Tanner's jail deteriorated and then caught fire, so Howard had to transport prisoners back and forth to the next county, sometimes three times a day for five years. Not having to tend to the needs of numerous inmates on a daily basis made life easier for both Nancy and Maud, but what of the Mrs. Sheriffs on the other end of the car ride? One of those, Dolores Lee of Van Buren County, Iowa, fed prisoners from several other counties toward the end of her tenure as Mrs. Sheriff. Her son noted that it was a tremendous amount of work to put on Dolores but the county commissioners looked upon this as a fine moneymaker for the county coffers.

TWELVE GOOD MEN AND HUNGRY

For most of the history of our nation, jury members were exclusively male. As alluded to previously, the sheriff and his wife housed and fed sitting juries in many locations. Not many counties could afford to cater food for a sitting jury. The burden of feeding them and their bailiff, if the county bailiff was other than the sheriff himself, fell on the sheriff's or jailor's wife. The jails of this period often were built with jury deliberation rooms. As noted, many of the jails built during the late Victorian era came equipped with a dumbwaiter. The inclusion of a dumbwaiter in the family quarters was much appreciated by both the bailiff and sheriff's wife. Without that newfangled contraption, they would have lugged food to the jury and the dirty dishes back down again via the stairs.

With all of those extra mouths to feed when unexpected company dropped in, many a jailhouse wife grew a bit frazzled. Sometimes trustees went the extra mile to help with the jailhouse children. Next, we will investigate the mix of jail life and children.

—13—

Bootlegging Babysitters, Straight Pins, and Whirligigs

> A three compartment sink is the ideal thing for hand washing. One compartment is used for washing, another for rinsing, and the third for chemical sanitizing. Your local health department will be glad to give you information as to what detergents and chemicals are best to use.
>
> —1961 *Handbook of Jail Food Service*

> In Holmes County, Ohio, during the 1930s, if a call came in during the night about something happening in town, "all of the kids and mom would stand at the window and wait for him to come back. I remember nights when we would be waiting and heard shots ring out, not knowing if dad had been shot or if anyone had been shot. All of these years later, I can still feel the fear in my stomach when I remember such nights."
>
> —About Edith Weiss who served alongside Sheriff Harry Weiss from 1935 to 1966 (with gaps), reported by daughter, Evelyn.

There seems always to have been children around the county jail during the entire history of the mom-and-pop jail. There were many reports about the jailhouse kids learning to be discreet. Some families didn't allow sleepovers in the family quarters. Some parents kept things from the kids, if possible, so the youngsters didn't have to lie. But in the main, children living in a jailhouse knew plenty and kept their mouths shut.

Not all of the children around the jail were related to the woman in charge. Every year the teachers of Oswego County, New York, brought their grade school children to visit the jail. The children were divided into two groups according to sex. Deputies escorted the boys through the men's facility and the boys always thought it was a grand adventure. Eileen Chesbro and the teacher escorted the girls through the women's jail. Eileen observed how "girls of that age inevitably giggled and thought everything was funny." Entering a cell, Eileen invited the girls to come in to get a closer look. In they'd come, giggling. Eileen then stepped out and with the girls inside, locked the door. Immediately, giggles stopped and the girls got a tiny taste of what it might be like to be incarcerated.

Eileen also reported about the time she'd asked a friend for lunch and the friend brought her young daughter. Of course, this was one of those days when an inmate chose to be troublesome. The door between kitchen and cell area, being steel, reverberated loudly each time the inmate scored a direct hit with stones he'd obtained somehow. Every time a stone clanked against the door, the little girl became more frightened. It was not a happy lunch.

Other children made regular visits to the jail because of the hospitality of the Mrs. Sheriff. Harold Pletcher, Jr., remembers stopping at the Clarion County, Pennsylvania, jail as a child in the 1940s and being given fresh-baked cookies. He and his friends were sometimes served sandwiches as well. The kitchen was not the only hangout for the boys. Harold recalls that he "was allowed to target shoot in the basement along with the officers."

Unhappy circumstances brought children to Mildred Johnson's jail in Allegan County, Michigan. Her daughter, Florine, remembered how her mom welcomed a young boy into their home overnight after he'd accidentally been left behind during a field trip to the area. The boy, when discovered, was turned over to the sheriff. The child had lots to talk about when he finally got home. Not only did he get to spend the night in the jail, which must have made him the envy of all his friends, but he also took a bus home, all by himself, just like a big kid.

When Ida County, Iowa's sheriff, Don Gebers, arrested a couple, his wife, Dell, brought the couple's children home with her. She bathed them, washed their clothing, fed them for two days and tucked them into bed for two nights until other members of the suspects' family could make arrangements for their care.

Pauline Folkers of Chickasaw County, Iowa, also took in four young children. Paulette, her daughter, recalled that when she "was about eight years old, dad was called out to an accident. A young couple died in the crash. They were pulling a camper trailer with four small children asleep in the back of it. The children weren't hurt. In the midst of all the confusion and investigation, dad brought those four little ones for mom to take care of. I watched her as she gave them hugs, rocked them, read them stories and tried to dry their tears. She never left them for a minute and they never left her side. Relatives came later the next day and got them."

In Republic County, Kansas, Christina Peterka opened her home for four days to a girl in her early teens after the girl's father attempted to shoot his daughter. Fortunately the girl's mother grabbed the gun to prevent him from killing the girl, but the gun fired and the bullet entered the mother's leg. At this, the man "freaked out and ran away." Charlie went out to see what could be done, got the mother to the hospital, and brought the girl to Christina for protection in case the father came looking for her. The sheriff "couldn't see putting her in the women's cell" so she stayed in the family quarters. "On the fourth day, the father was found dead on his mother's grave, a suicide." The girl returned home and helped her mother recuperate from her gunshot.

Priscilla Campbell of the Converse County, Wyoming, jail took into her home and her heart an orphaned boy whom Malcolm brought home from a trip to Laramie in the 1890s. She altered a pair of Malcolm's trousers so they would fit the boy to replace the rags he'd been wearing. The boy "was very proud of them [his trousers], but over at the hotel one day some of the cowboys began scrapping with him, handling him so roughly that the trousers were torn."[1] The roughhousing stopped when the young men realized what they'd done. They felt so bad about it, they took up a collection and one of them hopped the next stage to Laramie. He brought the boy a "brand new suit of clothes"[2] to make up for the ones they'd damaged.

During the Depression, a local boy decided to stay in town to finish high school when his family moved away, so his parents arranged for the kid to move into the family quarters at the Garfield County, Colorado, jail. Martha Terrell's son, Hal, disliked this kid "because he was a bully." Bigger than Hal by quite a bit, Hal still challenged him one day for bullying a handicapped child in their class. Hal related the event during his interview: "We went over behind the grocery store and had a fist fight, and I got the worst of it, but wouldn't quit. Finally, when both of my eyes were nearly shut from the swelling, the other boy 'gave up' just to put an end to the ordeal. This satisfied me. The boy picked up two handfuls of snow to put on my swollen face and we walked home to supper." Martha took one look at Hal and demanded to know who had done this to him. "When I nodded to the boy standing beside me, all mom said was 'well, okay then, go wash up for supper.'" Hal reported that after that, the two boys became friends and the other boy's need to bully diminished greatly.

Martha got a few licks in of her own. Hal described his mother as "loving but formidable" as a preface to the following story: "Two of my father's grown sisters fought over something and refused to speak to each other for several years. The pair made family get-togethers unpleasant for everyone by continuing the spat. At one such gathering, mom grabbed first Aunt Peg and then Aunt Esma and spanked both of them" as if they were misbehaving children. "She then informed them that the family had had enough of their antics, and so ended the feud."

Lucille Ingalsbee, a niece of Sheriff Fred and Bertha Miller who lived in the Allegan County, Michigan, jail during the Depression, came to stay with them for a year to finish high school. Lucille helped Bertha with the cooking and inmate care. Lucille reported that "a scarlet fever epidemic went through our town and my cousin [Bertha's son] got it so my aunt isolated herself and her son in a bedroom upstairs. None of the rest of us got it. The doctor would not put a quarantine sign on the building as it was a public building."

The daughter of Sheriff Lewis Clay Sheets, Marty Jill, twenty years earlier in Fulton County, Indiana, was around to describe how their jail succeeded in becoming the site of a quarantine. A few months into their 1917 term, Marty's brother, Donald, came down with diphtheria, an often fatal disease. Mrs. Sheets took him to an upstairs bedroom. Her other two children brought food and supplies as needed, but no one was allowed into the room. The sheriff, not home when the diagnosis came in and the quarantine started, moved in with his mother for the eight to ten weeks it was in force.

On the day the quarantine commenced, the Fulton County jail was full of drunks and prisoners awaiting sentencing. Except for the drunks who were kept overnight, given breakfast and let go, the sheriff took his prisoners to a restaurant for their meals and brought them back to the jail until room could be found for them at the penal farm or prison. Once the jail was emptied, it stayed empty until quarantine was lifted.

Marty described the quarantine: "Our schoolmates came up on the front porch and looked in at us through the window. The teachers weren't allowed to send us our books, so my other brother and I had a field day."[3] Donald's siblings received vaccinations against diphtheria that had just come out so did not contract the disease. Marty reported that Donald survived due to the excellent nursing of their mother. "When the quarantine was lifted, we gathered our clean clothes together and went into the jail and stayed there until our living quarters were ready after many formaldehyde candles were burnt, as a disinfectant."[4] It was the only time the Fulton County jail was closed for business until it closed for good when the new jail was built.

ALL WORK AND NO PLAY . . .

In her oral history conducted sixty-eight years after living behind the Jackson County, Oregon, after Sheriff Singler took up the star, Zita Singler Maddox recalled how the children played: "We didn't have dolls or anything like that. We used to sit on the ground and make little houses, you know, like with dirt and there'd be rooms. And we'd take acorns, dress 'em, and make dolls out of them. We'd take toothpicks and make the arms and legs. Make them little tiny dresses. Of course, they had these big caps."[5] The girls would play with their acorn dolls in the rooms of the dirt houses.

The Singler children, like so many other county seat children, loved to climb the window bars of the jail to sit on the sills and talk to the inmates. The bored inmates loved the diversion. In the case of the Singlers, Jailor Basye, chased the kids away when he discovered them. Then the children would do something else like skate around the courthouse on the only sidewalks in town.

Mrs. Mervin McKinley's daughter in Clarion County, Pennsylvania, used to climb the bars to talk and sing for the prisoners. When the little girl died while her father still served as sheriff, "the prisoners took up a collection for flowers to be put near her coffin."[6]

In 1905, Alice Ketchum gave birth to a son, Dorsey, while living in the Wayne County, West Virginia, jail. Her granddaughter later recalled how Dorsey was known for "running the lawn, the sidewalk, and jail while still in diapers." It

Children playing with a sulky behind the jail during the term of Sheriff Benjamin and Mary Lugten in Allegan County, Michigan, during the late 1920s. Note the two floors of barred windows on the cells. The lower level was used for inmates incarcerated for lesser crimes while the upstairs cells were reserved for violent criminals or those deemed escape risks. The children are (l–r) Henrietta Veneklasen, Florence Lugten, and Hilda Rankens. (Courtesy of Mary Drenten.)

seems that Dorsey would stop just about anyone handy to request help pulling up his diapers when they drooped. He'd always come home "with a few pennies in his pudgy little hand" and Alice finally "read him the riot act" because she thought he was begging for money. Dorsey wasn't begging, he was just so darned cute with those droopy diapers and his need to explore that people couldn't help but pay for the privilege of pulling up those diapers so he could explore some more.

As many jailhouse kids grew up in the heart of their county seat, they experienced life under the watchful eyes of just about everyone in town. This was true for the Edinger children of Prohibition-era McHenry County, Illinois. Sid Edinger shared a tale about his older brother, Richard, that took place when he was just a tyke. Marian "always had to be aware of appearances. When my older brother, Dick, was about three or four, he received a pair of cowboy chaps. He did not know that cowboys wore jeans underneath their chaps. He put them on with nothing underneath and paraded around the square." This became one of Marian's favorite stories and it was told many times by her in later years.

Life around the town square and the courthouse influenced more than one jailhouse kid. In 1885 Lawrence County, Kentucky, Jim Vinson took on the job of jailor. He moved his family from the farm to Louisa. They were fortunate to live in the "newly built eight-room, two-story, red brick home on the courthouse square, not the jail, which was a small separate building in the back."[7] Five years later, Virginia gave birth to Fred, her youngest. Fred recalled how he grew up with the town square as his playground. Living near the courthouse, Fred also managed to get near the legal action. "The circuit judge at the time, Stephen Gerard Kinner at Catlettsburg, a friend of Jim Vinson's, occasionally let Fred sit beside him on the bench while court was in session."[8]

As mentioned before, Harry Truman brought two jailhouse kids into his administration: Fred Vinson and Charlie Ross. In a letter written while Charlie worked as press secretary at the White House, he told the tale of how his dad had been instrumental in heading off a jail break. A regional manhunt after a family had been killed netted the Taylor brothers who were tried, convicted, and scheduled to hang. Lawmen in the region and local firemen were invited to witness the hanging of Bill Taylor so County Marshal Ross accepted.

> A day or so prior to the hanging, Taylor was paraded in front of these visiting firemen. My father noticed that Taylor's mouth on one side appeared swollen, as if he had a large chew of tobacco in it. He went to Taylor and made him open his mouth, and Taylor disgorged a bunch of thin jail-breaking saws, a little packet containing poison, and a slip of paper on which was written the key to a very simple cipher [code]. My father gave me this cipher key, and it made me a great hero among my schoolmates.[9]

When one actually lived inside the courthouse, it became one big playhouse after the staff went home. When Bob and Shirley Everson lived on the fifth and sixth floors of the Boulder County, Colorado, jail and courthouse, their playroom under the clock tower did not always prove adequate for their needs. After the courthouse closed for business, the siblings played ball in the long hallways, "sometimes with the really neat night janitor."

Shirley Everson didn't mind living downtown. While she had no girlfriends living near her, she enjoyed roller-skating on the sidewalks. "The bus went right by the courthouse and I could take it, but mostly I walked. There were three movie theaters around the courthouse and dad loved Westerns. On weekends, he'd say 'I'll pay your way if you let me go to the movies with you!' and he'd always be taken up on it."

The Republic County, Kansas, courthouse was also available to Christina Peterka's grandkids when they came to visit. Gloria, Christina's daughter and mother of the kids, did not allow them to help Christina pass out meals to the inmates, but they did find the courthouse hallways very entertaining.

During an earlier era, in Ellis County, Kansas, Agnes Schumaker's children were allowed to play in the entire courthouse after hours. Daughter Peggy reported that they played in the judges' chambers and ran around everywhere. The Everson kids and Peterka grandchildren came along during the era when offices were locked at night, so didn't enjoy the mock trials that the Schumaker children acted out after vying for the honor of playing "Your Honor" and the lawyers.

Shirley Everson reported that brother Bob was not very happy about moving to the top of the Boulder County courthouse but "he was fortunate in that just a block away were several friends for him to play football with on the courthouse lawn." Edith Weiss's kids also played football on the lawn of the courthouse in Holmes County, Ohio. David Weiss, Edith's grandson, included a story on the Sheriff's Department Web site about how the grass turned to mud because so many games of football were played not only by the Weiss kids but also the town's children.[10]

PLAYING IN THE JAIL

Sports of all types had a place in the lives of jailhouse families. Martha Terrell's son, Hal, was taught to box by one of the inmates who happened to have learned as part of the Golden Gloves program. Sean Fenton in Coleman County, Texas, learned to pitch through the efforts of an inmate. Anne Werth of Ellis County, Kansas, recalled that during the 1960s, her children enjoyed the games between the town baseball team and inmates from Lansing prison. The latter team members required locked accommodations after the game so were housed in their jail. She noted that "they were very appreciative of their treatment and thanked us with a signed baseball. We also had Lansing prisoners who were touring the state and talking to high school students about 'staying straight.'"

Lulu Knapp alluded to driving their inmates crazy when she shared the following anecdote. She was four years old when her parents moved into the Griggs County, North Dakota, jail in 1907. Between the cells in the basement jail, a long hallway led to the furnace room. "This made a wonderful place to roller skate. Papa bought me a pair after he found out I could skate so well on borrowed ones. Oh, what fun we had! Other children came there and skated too. Now I wonder how well the prisoners like it—all that noise."[11]

One could also wonder how well the prisoners liked it in Powell County, Montana, when five-year-old Barry Darrow was discovered in the kitchen, shooting prisoners through the connecting jail door. The door between the kitchen and the cell block was covered with a steel grid. In the grid was an open space just large enough to pass the pots and pans of food that was served family style by the trustees. This pass-through was covered by a wooden door on a hinge. Little Barry was found shooting prisoners from the kitchen side of the pass-through with his water pistol.

Vernice Cooper's son, Sam, confessed to a guilty pleasure that he took when the family lived in the jail during the second half of the 1960s. Because he was an adolescent, Sam would take any opportunity to "stroll down the hallway in front of the female inmates cells trying to catch a peek at the women." He also recalled the time when a cross-dressing man was brought in and held in one of the downstairs cells away from the male inmates. For the day or two that the inmate stayed with them, Sam meandered down to that area several times "to try to figure out what he was all about."

Edith Weiss' family in the Holmes County, Ohio, jail was a musical group. Everyone played some kind of instrument. The family played together in the parlor and for the public at community events. Sheriff Weiss arrested a couple for forgery once and while they were incarcerated, it came to light that they, too, played instruments. So the forgers were added to the band and came along to the gigs and played their guitars. The band also included one of the regular inmates when he was being held for drinking too much. He played the banjo. No one in the community ever complained about the prisoners being added to the band from time to time.

During the Depression, two of Pearl Hobbs' grandsons stayed with their grandparents at the Moore County, Tennessee, jail when Alex Stagg was incarcerated while awaiting trial for murder. "It was very simple for small children to crawl through the door opening where the food could be passed through to the prisoner. He was always glad to have the grandchildren of the Sheriff to visit with him on almost a daily basis. There was never any fear or concern from the adults."

Many jailhouse kitchens were equipped with a dumbwaiter, as noted earlier. Food and supplies were "shipped" to prisoners on another floor, or to jurors deliberating the fate of someone on trial. Helen Haugerud's children put their terrier on the dumbwaiter one day and shipped him to the prisoners in the Fillmore County, Minnesota, jail, who enjoyed his company very much.

A game Helen's little girls played for quite some time without the knowledge of their parents is described in detail in Neil's book. The game and the girls may have saved their father's life. Renee, Susan, and at least one of their friends stuck their fingers under the steel door to the bull pen and tried to guess who had been incarcerated by how the inmates grabbed them. Over time, the girls were able to guess the identities of many of those who were locked up regularly.

There came a time when Neil arrested some pretty rough characters from the city who'd been in the county on a burglary spree. While he transferred one of the thugs to the penitentiary, that prisoner informed Neil how lax he was as a sheriff and how unsafe it was for him to be so lax when he incarcerated *real* criminals. Then the prisoner confessed that "any other place, I'd have snuffed you"[12] if it hadn't been for seeing those little girls play "guess the fingers" with the prisoners. He warned Neil that not every prisoner was going to be as kindhearted.

In Adams County, Wisconsin, in the 1950s, Lily Serles' son played cards with prisoners through the kitchen door. The table was set up in the bull pen and butted up against the bars across the door opening. Lily's son sat in the kitchen and played through the bars. Lily thought this was an adequate arrangement and would not allow her son to go beyond the kitchen door.

At about the same time in Bastrop County, Texas, Sheriff Hoskins gave the keys to the cells to the kids in town when there were no prisoners so that they could play in the jail. A decade later, in Hodgeman County, Kansas, Elma Sinclair's daughter, Dot, moved out of the women's cell she'd been using as a bedroom and into her own home. When the grandkids began coming along, they used the women's cell as their playroom. "The few times that the men's cells were empty, the grandchildren begged to play or sleep in there," Elma recalled.

None of this was new or novel in the world of jail kids. Back at the turn of the twentieth century when Esse Bailey's children lived at the Fulton County, Indiana jail, they took full advantage of the usually empty women's cell. They charged other children in town five straight pins for the privilege of being locked up. In the world of children at that time, straight pins were the going legal tender "because money was scarce. Five pins equaled one cent."[13]

NOW, STAY OUT OF TROUBLE

Martha Terrell, a woman of action, did what many mothers have wanted to do from time to time since the dawn of man. When her son, Hal, and a couple of his friends played around the jailhouse and refused to behave themselves, she lost patience with their noise and their wrestling, and tossed them in the padded cell at the Garfield County, Colorado, jail and locked the door. She made them stay in there for several hours to get her point across.

Ethel Hunter of Hamilton County, Florida, was fortunate to have two daughters, age 21 and 17, living at home in 1930. Loy Lee and Inez helped their mother tend to the inmates and care for the family quarters. While participating in an interview at the jail museum many years later, some of the local women told of visiting with Loy and Inez as girls, and "misbehaving slightly. Mrs. Hunter locked us in a cell which was most unpleasant."[14] They also told of going on a picnic and the food was the same as that provided for the prisoners. They all reported to have enjoyed it much more than being incarcerated.

Pauline Folkers made good use of the women's cell in the Chickasaw County, Iowa, jail when her children were young. The cell was located directly above the kitchen. Paulette remembers that "when it was time for mom to go get groceries or run any other errands, she'd march us four, single file, up the iron steps to the women's cell and lock the door. Off she'd go! The four of us would head to the window facing the street. We'd all wave and yell good-bye, and tell her to hurry back. We'd usually holler until she was out of sight. Everyone [around the neighborhood] would laugh and knew mom was headed up town and knew where the four of us were. I think there were a few mothers who were a bit jealous since mom had such a convenient way to make sure the four of us stayed out of trouble."

INMATES AND JAILHOUSE KIDS

With children in and around the jail, it was not unusual for them to form special attachments to some of the long-term or frequent inmates. When children's natural affection was brought to bear during the performance of their chores around the jail, it resulted in prisoners making items to give them as presents. After Charlie Ross purchased tobacco for inmates who had begged coins from farmers hitching their horses beside the Jackson County, Missouri, jail, a small bone knife was carved for him by an inmate. It was later donated to the Old Jail Museum and is now part of their display.

Special relationships could pop up in an instant. Leona Bannister reported coming home from school to discover her eight-year-old brother sitting on the front porch "in the embrace of a huge Negro man whom I had never seen before. They got up as I passed inside, and I could see that they were already good friends."[15] The man turned out to be a local preacher who had just killed a gambler. The gambler had been winning most of the money that the men earned picking cotton, leaving little to feed their children and provide for their wives. The women brought their troubles to their minister who talked to the gambler, asking him to move on and leave the families alone. When the gambler refused to leave such a lucrative situation, the preacher fought with him and ended up killing him. He stayed in the Coleman County jail until his trial was over and he was acquitted on the grounds of self-defense.

Up in Powell County, Montana, Mary Ann Darrow recorded in her family memoirs that they bought a puppy for their kids as a Christmas present. In order for the puppy to make its grand entrance on Christmas Eve, the prisoners took care of it in the cell block for a week.

At about the same time, Lori Swanson in Lucas County, Iowa, received her kitten from an inmate. It all started when a neighborhood cat took to visiting the jailhouse every day. "He would make his way to our living room, jump into a soft chair, stay a couple of hours, go the door and away he would go. Our little girl, Lori, wanted him to stay so badly." One of the inmates, a young man named Calvin, learned of Lori's love for the visiting cat so when he finished serving his time, "he came up to our door with the most beautiful kitten for Lori. It was from a litter his family had at home. We all enjoyed the cat, Snoopy, until he died" many years later. "We thought Calvin, the prisoner, was extra special for thinking of Lori and also for giving Snoopy a good home."

Family pets and inmates were mentioned together in several of the interviews. Dolores Lee's son reported how, in Van Buren County, Iowa, during the late 1950s, he and his brother were taught how to make squirrel traps by the inmates. There were a lot of squirrels that were captured by the traps and released "just for fun. However, one prisoner took a squirrel that the boys caught and tried to tame it as a pet in his cell."

BOOTLEGGING BABYSITTERS

Marian Edinger's son, Sid, described growing up during Prohibition in the McHenry County, Illinois, jail this way: "I was privileged to have 'bootleggers' for babysitters. If a bootlegger was sentenced to a year or more, he would go to the state or federal prison. If sentenced to less than a year, he would go to a county jail. So much of our clientele was from Chicago. I am told that when bootleggers were taking care of me, they would feed me coffee or salami."

During World War II, in Tolland County, Connecticut, Mabel Cook always found her children underfoot while she prepared meals for her large brood and inmates, so inmates became her babysitters. "Especially the baby, who was a great favorite with everybody and the recipient of numerous rides in the wheelbarrow and his little red wagon."

During the Depression, Leila Pedersen of Chippewa County, Minnesota, utilized inmates and deputies to babysit for her children. Marge recalled that "a deputy fixed my doll buggy and trimmed it with crepe paper. It won first prize at Sibley School."[16] Leila also enlisted the babysitting skills of "two young boys [who] were jailed one summer for minor offenses. They helped care for the children and kitchen every day while the other prisoners were building a garage next to the courthouse."[17] Marge recalled that her first crush was on a man in jail for murdering his wife. "I was about four years old at the time. I put my feet between the bars and had him tie my shoes every morning."[18] She went on to say that later in life "one of the trustees taught me to make fudge."[19]

Helen Haugerud in Fillmore County, Minnesota, reported that they often housed the nephew of family friends, incarcerated for drinking too much. The friends lived just a couple of blocks away. When the nephew had sobered up and was serving his time, he'd often take Helen's children to visit his aunt and uncle.

Peggy Schumaker Draper recalled that she spent hours watching "Jake the Snake" upholster furniture in his cell at the Ellis County, Kansas, jail. In grade school at the time, Peggy watched the often incarcerated local con artist for hours with no supervision, and she found Jake's knack for his work to be quite fascinating.

In Adams County, Wisconsin, during the Depression, Lily Serles' five-year-old was quite taken with the excellent tap dancing abilities of an inmate. He'd whistle a tune and tap for the little girl to her great delight. Lily reported that her daughter later took up tap dancing. At about this same time, one of the inmates, a man incarcerated for shooting deer out of season, taught Lily's daughter how to tie her shoes.

Randy Harris remembered tossing a baseball around with some of the prisoners when he was growing up in Wilson County, Kansas, in the 1950s. One frequent inmate named Larry babysat young Randy when both of Randy's parents needed to attend a double funeral. It was extremely difficult for both adults to leave the jail at the same time on most occasions. Randy reported that he and Larry "watched a basketball game together. Another time, Larry came to the door of the jail and said hello to mom while she was trying to shake the rugs, and she offered to let him out to watch a basketball game if he'd shake the rugs for her so he said 'let me out!' I was home sick from school that day but felt good enough by that time to come down to watch the game with Larry."

It wasn't really childcare, but at Harvey County, Kansas, a decade later, Karen Werner recalled how her father "always tried to have a trustee if there was someone trustworthy enough. They would help clean, wash cars, and do a little yard work. Sometimes they even had to play baseball with us." Who could refuse the order to entertain the sheriff's kids with a little baseball? It was a tough job, but somebody had to do it.

In Tishomingo County, Mississippi, during the Depression, Sheriff Clarence Pace's family kept a gigantic garden worked by the trustees. One trustee had as his assigned responsibility the care of one long row of corn and then take young Billy Pace fishing. It worked out well for everyone. Billy's father and grandfather both served as sheriffs.

Some of what inmates taught jailhouse children fell into the "questionable" category, such as when an inmate taught Mary Jahnel's seven daughters how to extricate coins from a laundromat washing machine, a skill the girls claim they never, ever used. Most of the stories reported for this book fell into the "beneficial" category. In nippy Leelanau County, Michigan, each winter, "an old man named Earl got himself arrested when the weather turned cold so he would have a warm place to stay. He served as trustee and helped with chores." He also played with Viola White's children. One memorable winter, "he taught all of us how to construct whirligigs. In the following Spring, the jail lawn sprouted wondrous whirligigs for everyone to enjoy."

Babysitting, prisoners, and kids didn't always occur in the expected arrangement. Theda Jo Wendel was eleven when her parents brought her to the Barton County Jail. "With an air base in Great Bend, the jail was a busy place. I remember one incident when a man walked up on the front porch covered with blood and gave himself up to my mom. He had just killed a man. Mom had him and me sit on the step with a glass of tea while she tried to find someone to lock him up."

Theda Jo Wendel also recalled how her mother, Florence Whelan, "did everything—cook, matron and answering service. She served two meals a day. It was during the war and with rationing she had to be very creative. I remember how she mixed soy meal with hamburger as an extender. I thought it was awful.

There was a lot of gingerbread and oatmeal as I remember. I was pretty young at the time but I remember how hard mom worked. My folks tried to shield me from a lot of things, but I had big ears and sharp eyes."

Who were the people incarcerated in the jail and sharing a life with the jailhouse children with big ears and sharp eyes? In the following chapters we will look at inmates more closely, explore the ways some of them found to get out of their cells, and the ramifications this had on the jailhouse families.

14

Guests of the County

Jail life is a rather monotonous one from the prisoner point of view. He must follow the daily routine as to sleep, work, recreation and meals. Necessarily, he has little choice in the most important things that he does. The hours he must sleep and be awake are selected for him. The work he must do is chosen by someone else. The clothes he must wear are not of his selection. The time of his eating and the food he must eat are also dictated to him. But, it is with this last phase of institutional operations that he may be given the greatest degree of relief. The introduction of good food with elements of variety and surprise is easily possible in a jail mess. It involves no extra cost, but it will do a great deal for morale.

—1961 *Handbook of Jail Food Service*

You see people in the worst circumstances and we all learned a humanity that we would not have learned any other way.

—By Peggy Schumaker Draper, raised in the Ellis County, Kansas, jail.

Throughout this book, there have been countless references to tending to the inmates. For the most part, the vast majority of inmates were male. County citizens broke the law, waited for trial in the county jail, and if found guilty of a lesser charge, served their time in the same facility.

Men found themselves incarcerated for a variety of reasons. In August of 1925, Mary Lugten fed two guests of the Allegan County, Michigan, jail who were being held for stealing a beehive and fifty pounds of honey. Passing bad checks, petty theft and drinking too much were the usual reasons men got hauled in.

One day while the sheriff was away on business, a fellow named Jerry was brought to the Chickasaw County, Iowa, jail by the local police. Jerry had been arrested for being drunk and disorderly. Jerry was also not very happy about the situation. Pauline Folkers and the policemen tried to reason with Jerry; tried to get him to come along peacefully to the cell area. Young Paulette watched as "he grabbed mom's brand new kitchen broom and broke it in half. I don't think I ever saw mom get so mad." That sobered Jerry up pretty quick and he went to his cell and served out his time. "When he was released, he gathered his belongings and put them by the back door. Jerry told the deputy he'd be right back. A short time later, he was back and handed mom a brand new broom along with an apology."

Edith Weiss in Holmes County, Ohio, observed that despite it being the era of The Great Depression, "the inmates always had money." It seemed to come to them from family members who visited. Outside of regular visiting hours, "people used to hang on the bars to the windows of the main floor jail to talk to people inside," just as did the local kids mentioned in an earlier chapter. Edith always assumed that they were family or friends of the inmates.

JAILS DURING DISASTERS

During a time of calamity, many a Mrs. Sheriff had to face the terrible dilemma of whom to save first: her family or her prisoners. Up in the Ontonagon [Michigan], Mrs. Silas Corbett watched over the jail that infamous day in August of 1896 when the Diamond Match Company caught fire and burned the county seat to the ground. In the family quarters of the jailhouse resided Mrs. Corbett's elderly and infirm mother as well as her young children. Locked in their cells sat two inmates, James Redpath and Duncan Beveridge. The sheriff, out of town on business had taken the keys to the cells with him.

The fire burned toward the jail as Mrs. Corbett frantically looked for another set of keys while wondering if she ought to save her mother and children. She kept looking for keys as the men became more and more panic stricken. "The walls of the jail were becoming hot to the touch, sparks were raining down on the wooden roof of the jailhouse"[1] and still she could find no key. Redpath's wife burst in, begged Mrs. Corbett to save her husband, and joined in the search. As the jailhouse filled with smoke, a key was finally located. Immediately the Redpaths and prisoner Beveridge raced for safety. Mrs. Corbett, left alone to save her family, began the arduous task of leading her mother and children slowly down the burning street.

Mrs. Corbett "soon found herself surrounded by burning brush in the cedar swamp. Suddenly, out of the smoke two figures appeared . . . Redpath and Beveridge! One took the children up in his arms and ordered Mrs. Corbett to follow. The other half carried, half dragged the old woman to the east up to the Pigeon Hill area where the fire did not reach."[2] It is also where the two men remained until they could turn themselves in to authorities again.

At 6:45 in the morning on June 29, while the inmates slept or prepared for breakfast, a 6.3 magnitude earthquake struck Santa Barbara. It lasted nineteen seconds. Hardly a chimney withstood the shaking. As seen in the picture below, the county jail suffered severe damage. The Sheffield Dam cracked, allowing a wall of water to wash to the Pacific. Thirteen people died, the business district

Damage to the Santa Barbara County, California, jail after the earthquake of June 29, 1925. Note the collapse of the second floor onto the one below. Note also the ladder propped against what remains of the back wall. (From author's collection.)

was leveled, and had the quake occurred later in the day, the death toll would have been substantially higher.

CELL INHABITANTS

While researching the given names of several of the Mrs. Sheriffs whose stories came from local history archives, the author discovered that there is a wealth of information in the census records for some county jails. The census included not only who was incarcerated on the day the census-taker arrived but some also include details about the prisoners. In 1900 Franklin County, Massachusetts, Myrtle Doan and her husband, Fred, housed twenty-three male inmates between the ages of 66 and 15. They were an international bunch including natives of Italy, Poland, Ireland, French Canada, and a Scot. Only fourteen of the inmates had been born in Massachusetts.

More detail was discovered in the 1870 census for Des Moines County, Iowa. Mollie E. Latty fed nine prisoners the day the census-taker knocked on her door. One was a saloon keeper charged with murder, two blacksmiths awaited trial for rape, Seth Knowles was listed as an insane laborer, and the rest were allegedly thieves. In a note beside the names of the rape suspects, someone entered the information that later they were found guilty and hanged.

While many jails experienced uneventful periods, it was the eventful times that added to the work of the family in charge, to say nothing of the stress. Mollie

Latty, mentioned above, made an interesting Mrs. Sheriff who was up to the task of handling eventful times.

When Mollie's husband, James, was sworn in at the beginning of 1870, his duties kept him away from the jail like almost every other sheriff in the country. His remedy for this was to put Mollie in charge, like so many other sheriffs' wives. With her husband's reputation and reelection at stake, messing with Mollie was something you just didn't want to do. A prisoner, intent on escape, fashioned a straw dummy and tucked it into his bunk. He then hid "elsewhere to wait for an opportunity to get through the jail door. Mrs. Latty, on duty alone that night thought something looked peculiar and went into the cell to investigate. When she discovered the dummy, instead of calling for help, she began searching all of the cells, looking for the prisoner. She discovered him under a bunk, waiting for his chance to escape. She reached in and pulled him out, and ordered him to quit 'fooling around' and return to his cell before she became angry."[3] He did just as he was told.

The other reported incident involved two inmates and the perennial problem of prisoner noise through the walls of the family quarters. Mollie was awakened in the night by two drunks quarreling loudly in their cell. As the argument escalated, profane language was heard and Mollie decided enough was enough. She had two children in the house. She marched into the cell area and told the drunks to "pipe down." Their response was to turn their anger and abusive language toward Mollie. "She left the cell area, secured her whip, and ordered the men to stop, which elicited laughter from the prisoners. She entered their cell and proceeded to whip the men in such a manner as to elicit, not laughter, but requests for mercy."[4] Mollie was able to sleep soundly for the rest of the night.

Some of the prisoners' antics provided a lot of amusement, after the fact. "There was a time I kept smelling beer as I put the meals back into the main cell," reported Betty Swanson of Lucas County, Iowa. This was during the 1950s. "Wayne, my sheriff husband, decided to hide in the garage and see what was going on. Well, someone was standing on the ground with a can of beer, and the prisoner, up above, was sipping beer through a small plastic hose."

Betty went on to add the story of her own two frisky prisoners, who, unlike Mollie Latty's quarrelsome duo above, required first aid. "I had to bring two of the prisoners into the kitchen and do first aid until the sheriff could get there. One had hit the other on the head, resulting in a large gash. Needless to say, it was quite messy. Luckily I had towels handy."

Amusing antics like the contraband beer helped to balance the times when prisoners found their stay in the jail too stressful. Debby, Neva Allen's daughter in Poweshiek County, Iowa, reported that during their stay in the sheriff's quarters, one of the male inmates suffering from the DTs (delirium tremens) during withdrawal from alcohol thought he was being pursued by little green men. He broke the water pipes off the jail walls and used them to break out all of the fourteen windows in the area. Debby recalled that the kids kept hearing the awful racket that seemed to go on and on, until the children decided among themselves that something was terribly wrong. They crept downstairs in a tight little knot. Suddenly, Debby felt a hand grab her arm. She panicked, shook off the hand, turned around and raced back to her bedroom. It was only later that Debby discovered that the hand had belonged to her mom, trying to restrain Debby from going any further. Sheriff Allen decided it was "better to let the crazy man with the pipe have at the windows rather than at him or his deputies."

SUICIDES

Suicides happened in the best of jails. Unless the sheriff knew a prisoner was suicidal and initiated a 24-hour watch, prisoners were not watched every moment. Lorna Werner's daughter recalled that they had a male prisoner who hung himself in the Harvey County, Kansas, jail during the 1960s. The inmate tore his mattress pad in such a manner that he could fashion a noose and with that he hung himself.

Eileen Chesbro in Oswego County, New York, remembered a time, in the middle of the night, when her husband, Ray, was called downstairs to the men's cells. One of the inmates had committed suicide with his belt. It was particularly emotional because the inmate was one of the county's citizens and not a stranger. Eileen commented that she was glad she didn't have to be a part of that investigation.

The Brown County, Texas, jail was the site of an attempted suicide while Mrs. Sheriff Ray Masters served as matron. According to the *Jail Stories* Web site, after a visit from his wife and five children, one prisoner pulled the hose from the gas heater in his cell while his cellmate slept. He wrapped his mouth around the gas hose. When the jailor came in with breakfast, he discovered the suicidal inmate and reported that when he pulled the man's mouth from the hose, gas was spewing at full capacity. The man somehow survived but was transferred to the Huntsville Penitentiary the following day.

Young Howard Tanner came home from college each summer and helped his father with the business of sheriffing just before World War II, babysitting the office and jail while his parents went out occasionally. One Saturday night, "prisoners had been asking for things all evening and banging on the bars to get my attention so they could get water, cards, cigarette papers, and so on. Later on, the banging began again and when I went to see what they wanted this time, one prisoner reported that a cellmate had just committed suicide." Howard discovered when he entered the cell area that the other man had ingested Drano. "He was not dead and had decided he didn't want to die after all, but he was in terrible shape." Howard called the doctor who told him to make the prisoner drink a concoction of soapy water and raw eggs. Then the doctor arrived and pumped the inmate's stomach full of warm water several times and they took him to the hospital. The man survived. "When he was brought back to the jail, he was fed only cold soup for quite some time."

CARING FOR THE INSANE

During her interview, Florine Gooding, daughter of Mildred Johnson of Allegan County, Michigan, commented that by the time insane people were confined to the jail, they were totally out of control. Their families could no longer care for them at home. It was difficult to have most of them in the jail. Thirty years earlier, Leona Bannister found the same to be true in her father's jail. "The ill or demented person was usually cared for in the home as long as possible; but when the family appealed for help, Papa made arrangements for the interview with two doctors adjudging the mental condition, and for transferal to the jail or to a state lunatic asylum, as they were designated until 1950."[5]

When a wagon train came through Coleman County in 1914, they dropped off one of their members who had gone insane on the way West. "The doctors had prescribed a mild sedative for the worst outbursts, and Mama had found that distracting Madden's attention by giving him some delicacy to eat sometimes helped as well. She would have the cook wrap into a piece of newspaper a fried pie, a piece of cake or a banana, and [one of the children] would take it to the ranting man. 'Just don't let him get hold of your hand,' she would tell us.'"[6] Leona's mother, Emma, was not able to persuade the cook to go anywhere near Madden or any of the other insane inmates who were incarcerated during her tenure as Mrs. Sheriff.

Sometime later, Emma Banister used food to good effect once again. Leona included in her book the story of how an old man was brought into the jail as his family could no longer care for him. The man's wife called Emma while he was being brought in and told her that the family had not been able to get him to eat anything for several days. By the time John and Leona, who drove for her father, rolled in with the old gentleman "Mama had prepared a milkshake laced with some of the bootleg whiskey for him."[7] The man ate five meals a day and "Mama would send up ice cream or milkshakes at other times."[8] After regaining some of his strength, the man learned that he could yell for food and it would come. "He could be heard even on the main street in town."[9]

The Kingsbury family of Hillsborough County, New Hampshire, worried about their relative, George, who had emigrated to Kansas and suffered a breakdown in 1877. The story of the event was revealed in a series of three letters from Miami County, Kansas, after George was confined to the care of Mrs. Sheriff Howard. The man's aunt, Sarah, wrote to George's father on June 6th: "I think, myself, it would be a difficult task for you to take George to Michigan. It makes him worse every time he hears from Elva and he was perfectly wild when he found I had a letter from you . . . said he should never see Elva or the children again, he had no idea of going home . . . he is in the Miami County Jail. That was the only course that could be pursued to keep him off the railroad track. I could not bear the thought of his being crushed and mangled by the first train of cars that came along . . . it was utterly impossible for them to take him in at the Asylum as there were four waiting for admission."[10]

On July 6, Sarah reported that "George is very unwell, I will relieve your anxiety in part by saying George B has received the kindest of care in Paola. Mrs. Sheriff Howard has been like a mother to him and tried to persuade him to walk out with her, but he would turn his back to the door, she would tell him to see how beautiful everything looked."[11] Sarah alluded to the other insane man under Mrs. Howard's care and how he'd finally gotten a bed in the asylum, and then described "the next week, after G. went there, it took four men to hold him some of the time."[12] Sarah accounted for how much payment was needed to reimburse the sheriff for keeping George and finished this letter by describing George's suicide attempts. "There is no one in the jail but an old man, put there for shooting a horse, he has to stay until October. He had to hold George one hour one day or he would have beaten his brains out [against the cell wall]. He is very anxious to die, told me a good many times he was dying too slow when he was here. He took some mandrake root twice when he was here and once I thought he was dying."[13]

Two days later, Aunt Sarah wrote to Alice, one of George's daughters. In that letter, she states that "Mrs. Howard, the Sheriff's wife, was very kind to George. She thought one morning that he was dead and she trembled so, she could hardly stand . . . he tried to beat his brains out and the other man in there for shooting a horse held him until they were both wet with sweat."[14] It appears that a Mr. Winchester came to fetch George from the asylum and took him to his family in Michigan. He lived for another twenty years.

THE WOMEN'S JAIL

Not all of the insane inmates were male, and it was just as difficult to care for an insane female inmate. In 1896, Linda Scott cared for Tomacita Jaramilla for several weeks before being able to transfer her to the asylum. When a bed became available in August, Sheriff Scott deputized his wife for the task of making the transfer. Jim figured that Linda was able to manage Mrs. Jaramilla just fine and Linda concurred. The couple were surprised that this decision would thrust Linda into a regional limelight.

A bed became available for Mrs. Jaramilla at the asylum in Phoenix. During the 1890s, the only way to get to Phoenix from St. Johns was to travel by stagecoach to the railhead and finish the trip on the train. Because the seventy-five-mile trip occurred during "monsoon season," the stagecoach suffered many delays due to water racing through the arroyos. Linda watched over her charge, foregoing sleep for two nights, while they slowly made their way to the train and then into Phoenix.

It was noted how surprised the director in charge of the asylum was to answer the knock on his door to find not a patient "accompanied by a big man with guns"[15] but a patient and a "plucky little woman."[16] They went on to say that "the little wife of the efficient sheriff of our neighboring county is as brave as she is efficient."[17]

In 1941 Allegan County, Michigan, the cell upstairs at the jail reserved for females was known as Nellie's cell. Who exactly Nellie had been has been lost to history. Upstairs but some distance from Nellie's cell stood the holding cell for insane people. If the inmate of that cell happened to be female, Mildred Johnson had to take care of her "no matter how violent she was. By the time people got to the sheriff's cell for holding, their family had pretty much given up trying to care for them and taken them to court to be committed. But state insane asylums had waiting lists so sometimes the insane folks stayed quite some time with the sheriff."

During the 1930s, Edith Weiss cared for one woman who was awaiting her room at the mental institution. While in the Holmes County, Ohio, jail, the woman removed her clothing and refused to put them back on again. "Fortunately, she was the only inmate in the women's jail at the time."

Leona Banister reported that in 1917 they housed a woman waiting to go to the asylum who set up a cheery area complete with rocking chair and privacy curtains in the misdemeanor room. She cleaned her cell obsessively while happily waiting to return to the asylum. When the sheriff and Leona prepared to escort her to Austin, "no bride going on her honeymoon could have been happier than Mrs. Moss [as] she packed her traveling case"[18] with her new clothes.

GETTING TO KNOW YOU

When an inmate served a longer sentence or, like the couple below, spent a lot of time in a family's jail awaiting trial and appeals, the family got to know them rather well. During the autumn of 1921 in San Juan County, New Mexico, a married couple named Kutonka hitched a ride to Framington with Billy Kelly and Sam Groy. The couple lived in Pennsylvania. Along the route, Stephen Kutonka killed both Billy and Sam, and drove his wife back home to Scranton in the stolen car.

The following December, Stephen Kutonka irritated his wife no end when he got drunk and burned down their house, killing her little dog in the process. She threatened to get even with him by reporting what he'd done to Billy and Sam. "Rather than face his wife's betrayal,"[19] Stephen notified the authorities himself. He sent a letter, telling all, to Sheriff JC Wynn in New Mexico.

JC sat in his office, scratching his head in disbelief when that letter arrived. Telegrams flew back and forth between the local authorities, and both the Kutonkas were ultimately placed in custody and extradited to Aztec, New Mexico. The couple partook of Mrs. Wynn's meals at the jail before being taken to the state penitentiary prior to trial. Mrs. Wynn welcomed them back to her jail for the duration of the trial. When the Kutonkas were found guilty, they appealed their convictions. The couple were shipped back to the state pen until their appeal was heard.

A year and two months after he murdered Billy and Sam, Stephen Kutonka was hung. Before he went to the gallows, the Wynns had to keep a 24-hour watch on him because of a suicide attempt while he'd been held at the penitentiary. Mrs. Wynn took good care of Mrs. Kutonka while she was in the San Juan County jail, and the murderer's wife served five years of a seven- to ten-year sentence for being an accomplice to the fact.

Madeline Coleman shared a heartwarming story from her tenure as a jailhouse wife between 1975 and 1978. It is a tale of getting to know four teenage girls while they were incarcerated in the Brown County, Nebraska, while awaiting transfer to another state where they were sentenced to "hard labor. Our family went out and picked two five gallon pails of wild grapes and two of plums. I took the girls to the kitchen and sat them in a circle to sort and wash the fruit. Needless to say, they were not happy about their stained hands. I gave them a choice of doing this or housecleaning—they decided the sorting the fruit was better. I sat with them and we all chatted. Of course they hollered to the male prisoners confined in another area how cruel I was to them."

"The next day we made jam and syrup. When I made pancakes and served everyone breakfast the following day, I heard the girls bragging about how good the syrup was and hollering to the men that it was syrup THEY had made. I also took them outside and we planted flowers. When the state where they were wanted came to get them, one of the girls threw herself in my arms and didn't want to leave."

WOMAN'S WORK IS NEVER DONE

In New York State, Eileen Chesbro moved into the Victorian-era house attached to the Oswego County jail and found the place to be rather dilapidated. The Chesbros shared their quarters with two jail matrons, one for the day shift and one for the night. Eileen and the night matron decided to spruce up the place so spent several days wallpapering the rooms with twelve-foot ceilings. In Eileen's jail, the men were held on the main floor, the women on the second floor, and the third floor was used for storage. After Eileen and the night matron got the quarters looking more homey, they tackled the mess on the third floor. Eileen and the night matron found a Stickley rocker tucked among the boxes and dust bunnies on the third floor. Eileen cleaned it up, recovered it and installed it in the common area in the women's jail. When a female prisoner proved to be a good inmate, she was allowed to use the common area to watch television or sit in the comfy rocker and look out over the garden.

During the clearing and cleaning of the third floor, Eileen also discovered the log books for the jail from the early 1800s. She reported that the few women who were incarcerated back then were arrested for prostitution and passing bad checks.

Likewise, when Susan Church, the director of the Old Jail Museum in Jackson County, Missouri shared all of the Mrs. Marshal stories that she knew, she noted that women had been incarcerated for such offenses as petty theft, drunkenness, prostitution, and for performing abortions. One 1880s' Mrs. Marshal at the Old Jail, Lydia Potts, took care of the newborn infant of one inmate serving her sentence for stealing. Born in the jailhouse, the little girl stayed with her mother during the day but Lydia took the baby to the family quarters at night when the woman had to be locked up. The Potts family talked it over and agreed among themselves that no innocent citizen should be locked up in their jail, even if that citizen was only a few hours old.

The Clarion County, Pennsylvania, book, *Jail Tales,* mentions that their Mrs. Sheriff in 1896 provided matron service for one female prisoner before she was sent to the Western Penitentiary. The woman had been arrested for bigamy.

At the time of her arrest, she "had seven husbands and was about to marry the eighth."[20]

From the woman who loved marrying men, the same book mentions another Mrs. Sheriff who matroned for a woman brought in for setting fire to her boyfriend's house after finding him with another woman. The arsonist had to be housed in the high security cell next to the women's cell because the latter already held two inmates. In the middle of the night, one of the male prisoners yelled for the guard and reported that there was water coming from the high security cell. As that cell had a four-inch sill between its interior and the corridor, the guard was amazed to see water flowing down the hall. He waded up the hallway to look inside the cell and discovered the arsonist sitting on the floor in the back corner, playing in the water. She'd removed the toilet in her cell, ripped the lavatory from the wall and plugged up the drains with her mattress. The sheriff's wife took the situation in hand, and when it was decided that the prisoner needed confinement at the state hospital, Mrs. Sheriff accompanied her to North Warren.

Bootlegging during and after Prohibition involved a lot of women in crime. Edith Weiss' husband, Harry, broke up a lot of bootlegging going on in Holmes County, Ohio, during the first years of his two decades in office between 1935 and 1955. One of his first arrests "netted fifteen or twenty prisoners and half of them were women." Edith's women's jail consisted of one large room that the women shared dormitory-style, with Edith and young Evelyn as their matrons.

Ten years earlier, Mary Lugten of Allegan County, Michigan matroned for two young women, both nineteen years old, one of whom was married to a sixty-year-old bootlegger. Evelyn and Lanny, the May/December couple, were reported to have held parties at their home in the country. After attending one of these, a young man was killed in an auto accident while driving under the influence. This was but one of a string of incidents associated with the bootleg parties at Lanny's place.

The other nineteen-year-old incarcerated with Evelyn was Ardith V who stole $145 from one of the party guests. An older gentleman attended one of Lanny's parties and then went home and killed himself. Sheriff Lugten raided the place and discovered Evelyn smashing jars containing intoxicants. It was reported that she was the one who sold the illegal liquor to the young man who'd died in the accident. The couple surprised everyone by pleading guilty at their trial. The entire community thought they would plead innocent and drag out a trial.

Petty theft and shoplifting were common reasons why women found themselves incarcerated. In 1960s Harvey County, Kansas, Lorna Werner matroned for a pair of shoplifters named Brenda and Ellen. The pair wanted something to do while they served their sentences so Lorna purchased tea towels for them to embroider. The design on the towels was called "Busy Bees" and Lorna's daughter, Karen, recalled how shocked the family was when the towels were finished and turned over for use in the kitchen. "They had embroidered all of the little busy bees in a rainbow of colors. There were turquoise bees, pink bees, purple and so on. For years after that, when we picked up a tea towel to dry dishes, we thought of our time around the kitchen table with Brenda and Ellen."

"Around the kitchen table with Brenda and Ellen" referred to the time that the same inmates informed the sheriff that they needed to get out of the cell in order to iron their hair. "Well, that was a new one on us," Karen reported. "We all sat around the kitchen table while Brenda and Ellen heated up their curling iron on a stove burner. We talked and laughed and listened to their stories. The smell of scorched hair was a little unpleasant, but we sure thought it was fun!"

Many sheriffing families reported they often purchased supplies for inmates to use to pass the time. Inmates paid for supplies unless the item being made was something like the tea towels later used in the jailhouse kitchen. Edith Weiss's daughter, Evelyn, worked in a department store so came to the jail with sewing supplies for one inmate when they were requested. She took the pattern, material, scissors, pins, needles and thread, cut out a dress on the floor of the large cell, and sewed it by hand. Evelyn reported that the dress looked great and the woman was very grateful.

CONVINCING THEM TO MIND

Unlike the industrious inmates above, Eileen Chesbro reported that she had one young female inmate who was very lazy and refused to keep her cell clean in the Oswego County, New York, jail. The same inmate constantly wanted something special, which Eileen refused her since she didn't comply with the jail rules. However, when the girl requested a radio to break the monotony of the silence, Eileen said she'd get her one if she'd clean her cell and kept it clean. When the inmate agreed, Eileen bought an inexpensive transistor radio and presented it to the girl. The next time she came into the women's area, "the radio was blaring and the inmate was dancing with a broom. When she saw me, she happily yelled 'Oh, Ms. Chesbro, dance with me' and just as happily went on dancing with her broom when I declined."

Following the rules had its rewards, and failure to comply had its repercussions. Martha Terrell, in the 1940s at the Garfield County, Colorado jail, discovered she had a female prisoner who refused to bathe. "After a few days of this, the cell was getting rather ripe so mother told the prisoner that she was going to bathe or else," wrote Martha's son, Hal. "The next day, the woman refused again and mother took the situation in hand and bathed the woman herself. After that, there were no cleanliness problems."

In Poweshiek County, Iowa, in the 1950s, Neva Allen found herself with another type of problem. They housed a female prisoner who stripped for people on the other side of the jail wall. Barbara Cook recalled that her mother had a similar problem in Tolland County, Connecticut, the decade before. "There were seven women incarcerated [during World War II] and one was a young girl of limited intelligence whom the others delighted to undress and stand in the window in full view of the busy state road and the town's only store! My mother spent a lot of time on the stairs [to the women's jail] that summer."

Barbara also recalled that many of the women prisoners incarcerated during the war years were arrested for adultery. When men were away at the front, the police seemed to take a special interest in the crime of adultery, and thought it patriotic to make sure women involved in that crime were punished. "There were also those charged with lewd and lascivious conduct, and some petty thieves as well. One, I remember, used a knife on her man. My mother asked her, 'what happened, Jessie, too many boyfriends?' and Jessie replied 'no, ma'am, too many husbands!' which made mother laugh."

Irene Gray "had a gal in a front cell who, one morning, called across to the filling station, using the worst language I had ever heard" in Saguache County, Colorado, in the 1950s. "I had small children so I told her that if she didn't stop, I'd put her in solitaire, meaning one of the cells in the back." The foulmouthed inmate yelled back "where do you think I am?" and Irene gave up.

YOU NEVER KNOW WHO MIGHT SHOW UP

In Park County, Wyoming, after World War II, young Becky Kinkade and her friends secretly exited through the family quarter's bathroom window so they could climb over the roof of the house where it connected to the women's jail. In this manner, they played in the cells when they were empty. In 2003, when Becky and her mother, Martha, sat down to write about their years in the county jail, Becky told her mom about these adventures for the first time. "My mother never knew until I wrote this story," Becky wrote. "She didn't know a lot of my acquaintances were across the wall from our living quarters [in cells]. One school mate passed the door of the kitchen one day and we spoke to each other [as she exited the jail]. When my dad returned home late that night, he told us he had been out looking for an escaped prisoner. Yes, it happened to be her."

While inmate antics proved amusing and inmate stress required time, energy, and heart, those episodes were handled in stride by most sheriffing families. An actual escape, our experienced families reported, was the most difficult to bear as it reflected so poorly on the sheriff. In the following two chapters, families share their stories of escapes discovered after the fact and escapes that involved the families themselves.

—15—

Pa, I Hear Them Sawing Again

> Most of the food received by the jail inmate comes to him through the jail mess. The prisoner is not at liberty to stop for a hamburger and a cup of coffee whenever he is hit by the urge for a between-meal snack. Thus, the food he receives at the regular meal time means a great deal more to him than to a person living in a normal community.
>
> —1961 *Handbook of Jail Food Service*

> July 1878, Russell County, Kansas: delay of Kate Weakley's evening meal led to jail break. Deputy Johnson on duty but called away. Johnson walked to home of Sheriff, who agreed to take watch. Sheriff procrastinated. When asked later, said he was tending to Odd Fellows business. Time got away from him. So did inmate Joseph Gates. Doc Peet walked by jail, heard rustling in bushes, investigated. Doc found Gates on wrong side of jail wall. Gates reported he was tired of waiting for his dinner as he ran for freedom.
>
> —Details taken from *The Advance*,
> Russell City, Kansas, August 3, 1878.

Prisoner escapes provided some of the most exciting and frightening stories imparted during the research of this book. Several Mrs. Sheriffs proved reluctant to talk about escapes even decades after they'd moved from the living quarters. An escape while their husband held office was viewed as a failure to their community; something that could be held against him come election time. As a result, the entire family worked to keep the inmates in their cells.

From time to time, it was inevitable that diligence slipped. Desperate characters will go to any extreme to get out of the predicament in which they find themselves. In the 1970s, Betty Vinson fed three brothers held in the Lyon County, Iowa, jail for killing four young people in the State Park just outside of town. Both the victims and the brothers resided in South Dakota, but the crime took place on the Iowa side of the Sioux River, so Sheriff Vinson held the brothers until they escaped. One managed to pry a chain off the bunk in his cell and whenever possible, pounded it into a wedge. He used that wedge to spring his cell door. Then he got the key to the cells and let his brothers out. They slipped away from the jail by the side door. Betty reported that they "were caught the next day. They were convicted of their crimes and are now serving time in the Iowa Penitentiary."

Some prisoners don't make it that far in their escape attempts. Anyone, including the sheriff's wife or children, might have been responsible for discovering and stopping an escape. That was the case for Sarah Rihle of Ingham County, Michigan.

Sarah and JJ Rihle married in 1867, raised three sons and a daughter, and thirty years after the wedding, they took up sheriffing. One day while Sarah was on duty as JJ rode the county, she discovered a prisoner trying to pry bars from his cell window. She is reported to have quietly gone for her shotgun and returned to the cellblock, surprising the inmate when she said, "You attempt to use that knife and I will shoot you."[1] It was quite effective.

Prying bars from their mortar was but one of several ways in which escapes were effected. Sawing through bars with various pieces of equipment proved easier than it sounds today. The bars were constructed from a softer steel than we are used to seeing. Some jails were constructed with hardened steel in the cells used for high-risk inmates and softer steel in minimum security areas to save on cost.

Escapes also came about when inmates patiently scraped away mortar from between stones in the walls of their cells. The old jail in Schuyler County, Illinois, experienced such an event. One of the inmates played his mouth harp while the other scraped the mortar in time with the tune. Eventually the men were able to slide the block out of the wall and made their exit. If inmates became too musical, many a jailor's suspicions were raised and they looked for signs of digging.

Helen Haugerud's daughter, Renee, walked to school each morning with a friend during their tenure as the sheriffing family in Fillmore County, Minnesota. One morning, the friend dashed into the kitchen to report a big hole in the brick wall of the jail "and one of the inmates was sitting in it, claiming he'd had nothing to do with it."[2] The girls dashed outside to investigate. Helen then told them that an escape had taken place in the night and daddy was out looking for the men.

Neil Haugerud had spent the evening before with his friends, playing a game of poker. Helen heard nothing but the bricks were being removed nonetheless. When the inmates made their way out of the area, "one of the trustees had sent a note down to Helen using the dumbwaiter" and when she got the note, she called her husband. Later, the trustee confessed that he'd been afraid to reveal the escape preparations "for fear that they would hurt him."

Helen alerted every law enforcement branch that she could think of while Neil drove to the jail. She organized the deputies for the manhunt and everyone was on the case by the time Neil walked into his office.

Setting fire to the jail walls was a risk some inmates thought worth taking. They set fire on the inside or their friends set fire on the outside. The object of that game was to try to create an opening large enough to wiggle through without dying of smoke inhalation or being burned to death in the process.

Most, but not all of those who left their cells and ran for it, wanted to do so. Madge Harris in Wilson County, Kansas, told of two prisoners who escaped during the night. When she took in their breakfast, all she found was a note on the bunk that read "2 are gone." Hubert, like most sheriffs, had a good idea where the pair might be and before long he had them back but incarcerated in the women's jail upstairs so they couldn't mingle with the prisoners on the main floor. Madge added that by night, Hubert had the younger of the two back downstairs to sleep. "When they went by the kitchen door, I said 'Hello, Danny, how are you?' and when Danny looked at me, he had tears in his eyes. He was so grateful to be back and away from the older prisoner, whom the others feared."

Another young prisoner in 1886 Jackson County, Missouri, was forced to leave his cell during a jail break when the older prisoners refused to let him stay. They were afraid he would rat them out if he stayed. So the boy ran as far as his mother's house. The next morning, Lydia Potts looked out her kitchen window to see sheets hanging from the second story of the jail, trailing into the water trough. Not long after, she found the young escapee's mother on her porch, son in tow. He thought his mom could explain it better than he could.

WATCHWORKS AND HACKSAW BLADES

Men with little to do and a strong desire to break out of jail, men who have nothing but time on their hands, will find some way to try to gain their freedom. It was not unusual for the "time" in their pockets to be put to such use. Sheriff Sayler in 1887 Miami County, Ohio, proved too savvy to be taken in by the mother of a young man named ET Randolph. Sayler arrested Mrs. Randolph's son for forging postal money orders. She begged that he be allowed to keep his pocket watch on him in his cell. Sayler agreed but kept his eye on the prisoner and soon discovered that "he had taken the works of his watch and made three saws out of the mainspring"[3] to cut through the bars.

Other mothers provided incarcerated sons with hacksaw blades. Mildred Johnson of Allegan County, Michigan, had one such case in the 1940s. Fortunately for the reputation of Sheriff Johnson, the man was discovered sawing at his bars before an escape was made possible.

At the time that Linda Scott's husband served Apache County, Arizona, as sheriff and tax assessor, times were hard and governmental economies were required. One measure that Sheriff Scott did not cut involved providing inmates with jail clothing and slippers. The practicality of this became abundantly clear in April of 1895 when two outlaws, Maupin and Jackson, were brought in from Yuma. Deputy Gonzales inspected the men's shoes after they'd been issued slippers and found "four fine steel saws tacked under the insole of one of the shoes Jackson had relinquished at the door."[4]

The second night of living in the family quarters provided the John Banister family with their first lesson in listening and paying attention to what they heard.

Leona Banister reported "Papa rose hurriedly from his chair. 'I hear those men sawing at their bars,' he said. 'Emma, call Creek [Deputy Brown] to come. I'll turn on the light in their cell and we'll search and move them.' We listened, and became aware of the dull grating sound which was to become so important in our lives for the next three weeks or so."[5] Upstairs, the three hardened criminals on their way to the penitentiary and a juvenile on his way to the reformatory were engrossed in their attempt to break out of the Coleman County, Texas, jail in 1914. The sheriff and the deputy searched the men and moved the prisoners to other cells. They then conducted a thorough search of the cells just vacated and "found fragments of hacksaws in their shoe-soles, in hollow belts and waistbands, pants hems and even in their bushy hair . . . pieces of hacksaws were found everywhere: under rails of the cots, in commode tanks, in the heavy cotton quilts, over the door lintels."[6]

For all that, it was not enough. Over the course of "several nights some of the family would hear the rasping sound of the sawing with the pieces of the saws the deputies had not found."[7] Eventually the foursome sawed their way out of the cells in the center of the jail block and were discovered having at the bars at the windows. The sheriff threw up his hands at that point and from then until the four were transferred, the lawmen took turns sitting up all night in the cell area with the lights on and a shotgun across their laps.

Some prisoners used soap on the blades to reduce the noise. When Jesse Curran served as county marshal in Jackson County, Missouri, in 1922, his prisoners did just that, but to no avail. Their efforts were discovered before they were completed. The marshal also found that the inmates had tied together two blankets to facilitate their drop from the second-floor cells so the discovery had come none too soon. Upon investigation, Jesse learned that six of his guests had prepared to take part in the escape.[8]

Just three years earlier in the same jail, prisoners managed to saw through the steel grating of an upstairs window, bent it up to create nothing more than a 9-by-11-inch opening. It took twenty minutes for each prisoner to work their way through the little opening. Two managed the exercise and ran off. The third wiggled through but broke his leg when he fell to the ground. His cry of pain alerted Marshal HT Hall and prevented the twenty remaining inmates from following their colleagues out the grate.

One December in Natrona County, Wyoming, Emma Ricker's jail emptied of all but one inmate, a trustee who refused to go. Sheriff Ricker had been called away on business. Emma, upon learning of the escape, grabbed a revolver and ran to the front of the jail to fire six shots into the air to alert the town. Emma's trustee revealed that the escapees had hoarded Emma's meals for quite some time in order to have provisions on the trail. Their preparations were complete a week earlier but a blizzard delayed their departure. The men sawed through the bars but the space was so small that each of them had to remove his clothing, drop them out the window, squeeze through the bars, and dress in the snow outside. Because the trustee would not consent to join them, they threatened him, beat him, and restrained him from going anywhere near the pass-through when meals came from Emma's kitchen for fear that he'd get a message to the family.

CEILINGS

What does a prisoner see when laying on his bunk, contemplating his predicament? The ceiling. Prisoners have been quite creative in their use of ceilings to effect an escape.

"I was in bed, reading before going to sleep," Mary Ann Darrow recalled about living in the Powell County, Montana, jail. "I don't recall the title of the book. I do remember it was a historical novel, very graphic in its description of a medieval dungeon with prisoners in chains. I could actually hear the clanking of chained prisoners and the thumping and bumping as they moved about the dungeon. As I continued to read, I began to realize the thumping and bumping sounds were real. My heart was in my throat. I called the night deputy to come up to the apartment. I asked him to listen. Not a sound. Then, there it was again. A thump, thump, and a bump." When the deputy checked on the two boys in the juvenile cell, he discovered the cell had been abandoned.

Two nights before, Mary Ann and Ed had been enjoying a movie at the local theater when the usher tapped Ed on the shoulder with the message that he was needed by his deputy. Ed called in only to be informed that someone had stolen a car. Ed took down the address of the owner and Mary Ann went with him to find out more about the case. "Mary Ann and I began to drive around town in hopes of seeing the stolen car," Ed recalled. Others on the case were Police Chief John Wilson and Cy Timmerman, a Highway Patrolman in the area. They all cruised town, keeping in touch by radio.

Ed spotted the car and "the chase was on. Down alleys and city streets at speed upwards of 80 miles an hour. Mary Ann was terrified. She is very tense in a speeding vehicle." Eventually, the three lawmen cornered the car and everyone was astonished when the occupants emerged. The fourteen-year-old had been driving and his passenger was all of twelve. When the driver confessed that he'd only driven a car once before, everyone "marveled at how well he handled the car during such a high speed chase which lasted well over an hour." The boys were installed in the juvenile cell of the Powell County, Montana, jail for safekeeping . . . until they escaped two nights later.

No one thought that they could escape. The ceiling was twelve feet from the floor. It didn't matter that the trapdoor to the attic was in that ceiling. But boys will be boys and these two found a way. They climbed on the headboard of the steel bunk, and the little one climbed up the bigger one and just managed to get at that trapdoor. Once they got into the attic, which ran the full length of the building, they rummaged around in the dark, trying to find a way out. That was what Mary Ann heard. "They came out covered with dust and dirt," she wrote. "We were relieved when the Butte authorities came for those two boys."

Other juveniles also found ways out of their cells via the ceiling. During World War II in Boulder County, Colorado, Dorothy Everson discovered that one of her juvenile inmates, housed in a rarely used part of their jail, escaped by dismantling a lighting fixture. He wiggled through the hole, out into the hall, and out onto a roof through a window. "From there, he made his escape down five floors using sheets and blankets tied together."

Not just agile youths found ceilings of interest in their escape plans. When there is nothing but time to implement a surreptitious exit, a prisoner can put together a wide variety of plans. One of those reported involved the ceiling at the old Antrim County, Michigan, jail.

Until her death in 1956, Maud Tanner's mother, Donnie Allen, lived in the jail with the family to help Maud tend to inmates. Sheriff Tanner and his friend, Lew Lewellen, caught buck fever on an annual basis and vacationed at Nevins Lake in the Upper Peninsula. One autumn, "Mother and I were left in charge of the jail and four inmates. It was a Sunday" and the women's first day in charge. "We went over town to Mary's Tea Room for a nice chicken dinner. We took our time and were gone an hour or two. Prisoners have a built-in radar system. Besides, the walls in the old jail were thin. While we were out of the building, two of the men, planning an escape, had time to complete some noisy preparations.

"Monday morning a neighbor came in to inform us that some knotted blankets were hanging from a hole in the back wall of the jail. Ben H. and Tom P. were missing. They had pried off the lock from a ventilator that gave access to the attic. With the long common table upended in the bull pen, they could reach that ventilator. In the back of the attic, they were able to smash through the wall. They slid down the blankets to freedom. I called the Sheriff of the county where Ben's family lived" to alert him that the pair might be coming his way. "He told me that they wouldn't come there. I asked him to stake out the house anyway. He didn't bother to do it. Ben and Tom did go to the family house, we found out later. There they stocked up with supplies and took to the woods. Ben was captured in December and Tom was at large until February. The State Police brought him into the office. I said 'welcome home, Tom.'"

Maud also wrote "we were told that the old jail wouldn't hold hay. It didn't always hold prisoners either. Morning would bring the sight of knotted jail blankets hanging down from an attic window, or a break in the side of the jail wall. Sometimes it took several weeks but eventually every escapee was brought back to serve additional time." It was at this time that Sheriff Tanner was forced to begin transporting his prisoners back and forth to Charlevoix, a time-consuming and dangerous endeavor that went on for five years while the new Antrim County jail was built.

When the new jail was built in the 1950s in Leelanau County, Michigan, it included not only a lovely new family quarters but a high ceiling complete with skylight in the cell area. Nothing like a little natural light to keep the prisoners calm. Viola White's daughter recalled how an inmate somehow managed to crawl up to the skylight and dismantled it to get away.

Earlier that same decade, Irene Gray had a prisoner escape through the food pass-through. The inmate didn't stop until he'd broken through the roof of the Saguache County, Colorado, jail to make his bid for freedom.

In Sebastian County, Arkansas, the old jail was built of quarried stone and mortar in 1892. "At least two escapes from the jail are known to have happened. One escape was through the roof. Another time, the prisoner made his escape and ran to his jailor's home. He told the Jailor, 'I just can't stand the snakes any more.'"[9]

WINDOW TO THE WORLD

Only two escapes by females were uncovered during the research for this book: the one mentioned at the end of Chapter 14 and that of a woman who'd became a trustee at the Clarion County, Pennsylvania, jail. She'd been incarcerated long enough to gain the trust of the sheriff and given work in the kitchen to assist with feeding the other prisoners as well as the sheriff's family. Out of the blue, one evening when the trustee returned to her cell, "she opened a window and climbed out onto the fire escape [and ran]. She was apprehended along Route 66."[10]

During the Roaring Twenties, prisoners held in the Jackson County, Missouri, jail worked on the county roads in a chain gang. In April of 1921, County Marshal Jesse Curran searched the cells of the men who were out and discovered two cases of knives with steel blades. He also discovered that someone had been at work on the steel grate on the window in one of the cells and it was loose enough to be taken out.

Lily Serles fed two brothers being held for burglary in 1955 Adams County, Wisconsin. Lily and her husband were relieved of their paramount responsibility of keeping the inmates in when a night jailor came in between 10:00 and 7:00. But the night jailor did not prevent the third brother of the burglars from cutting through the heavy screening on the windows of their cells from the outside. The two young men escaped to Minnesota but were found a week later. Lily then had the privilege of preparing meals for the trio of brothers for the duration of their stay.

GOING DOWN?

In late Victorian times, many jails were built with family quarters plus an upper story that held the jury deliberation room. As mentioned before, some were built with dumbwaiters that were used to hoist food to the jury room or to cell blocks on another floor. "They saved trekking up and down with meals and dirty dishes, and were most appreciated by many a bailiff and Mrs. Sheriff."[11]

Dorothy Rumbaugh recalled a jailbreak involving a dumbwaiter in Jefferson County, Kansas, during her tenure in the 1960s. "I had gone to see a neighbor for a short while and one prisoner pried the bars apart in the dumbwaiter and came down to the kitchen." Then he fled out the door. She went on to describe how the man was captured in California and Dorothy's husband drove halfway across the nation to bring him back. Once again in custody in Kansas, Sheriff Rumbaugh turned the fellow over to authorities at Leavenworth Penitentiary. Dorothy remembered that "the escape was exciting."

A dumbwaiter in the Haugerud jail provided immense entertainment for Helen one quiet Sunday. A few years into their tenure for Fillmore County, Minnesota, Helen Haugerud was privy to the planning and partial execution of an escape attempt involving her dumbwaiter. Neil took the kids with him to the country to look at a farm they owned. The prisoners watched the car leave and mistakenly thought Helen was one of the passengers. But Helen stayed home to attack the clutter in a bedroom closet that just happened to be situated adjacent to the cell area. As she began her work of sorting, she began hearing the inmates' discuss how to break out before the family returned. Helen sat in the closet and listened as they decided that the smallest of them should get into the dumbwaiter and be lowered to the kitchen. From there, he would get into the sheriff's office, grab the keys, come back up and let the rest of them out.

Helen listened as the inmates tried to maneuver the smallest into the dumbwaiter, a feat much easier to contemplate than achieve. Helen recalled that she heard every word the inmates spoke and followed along with their progress at wedging the luckless inmate into the confined space. "I had to restrain myself from laughing out loud as first one body part and then another made its way into the tiny space. By the time that most of the smallest inmate had been wedged in, the look-out reported that the sheriff had returned so the attempt was thwarted and they scrambled to get the inmate back out of the dumbwaiter before the sheriff found them," not realizing that Helen had been their silent observer from the other side of the wall.

JUST UP AND RAN AWAY

In 1774, Timothy Lock found himself flung into the Washington County, Rhode Island, jail for fathering a child with a woman who was not his wife. Sheriff Beriah Brown had assigned the day-to-day care of the inmates to his jailor, Deputy Smith. Abigail Smith, the jailor's wife, ran the facility during the day when the sheriff and her husband were out and about in the county. When Tim Lock just got up and ran away, "it was Abigail who wrote to Sheriff Beriah Brown admitting her error in leaving a prison door open and alerting Brown to Lock's breakout."[12]

The most embarrassing escapes were the result of situations such as Abby Smith found herself. A lack of diligence, or sometimes too much trust, were often the reason. Mary Jahnel was involved in a couple of jailbreaks during her stint with the Mitchell County, Iowa, jail in the 1960s. On one occasion, it was the result of too much trust. Mary's daughter, Dode, recalled the circumstances: "I remember visiting on a hot summer evening and we were all sitting on the porch trying to cool off. We'd let the two prisoners out of the hot cells to join us. One of them said he was going back in to get something but when he didn't return, we checked and he was nowhere around. My infant son was sleeping upstairs and after quickly running up to make sure he was safe, I followed an armed policeman through the many limestone walled rooms in the basement, looking for the escapee. He was returned several months later from Texas."

Dode reported that she didn't think "mom was afraid of being left alone with the prisoners. They would knock on the iron bars if they wanted to summon us as there was only a wall separating our living spaces. One time when answering their call, mother unlocked the first barred door to check on them, not knowing that one [inmate] had fashioned a key from the frame of the radio, gotten out and had hidden in the outer room [bull pen]. The plan was to knock her out and restrain her while he let the others out of their cell, but he double-crossed them." A prisoner reported he had a headache and needed an aspirin. "As she went to fetch an aspirin, leaving the outer door open, he escaped, leaving the rest behind" and Mary Jahnel unscathed.

One of the oddest reports of an escape came from Annis Moore-Littles of Nassau County, Florida. The escape took place prior to her years of service in the 1970s. She recalled a case in which a man, confined to a wheelchair, needed to be incarcerated before he went to trial. Two strong deputies carried the man in his wheelchair up and down the stairs to the men's cells as needed. On the first day of his trial, after the man was carried down the stairs from his cell, wheeled across to the courthouse, and carried up the stairs to his courtroom, "he rose from his wheelchair and literally ran away."[13]

Escapes were rather rare according to sheriffing families. Most of the time, inmates on the wrong side of their cell walls were recaptured to serve additional time for escaping. In the following chapter, escapes that involved interaction with mom and the kids are reported, some quite harrowing.

16

Escape Encounters of the Fourth Kind

> The jail inmate is not in the institution because he wants to be. Rather, he is there against his will and desires. For that reason he is going to be exceptionally critical of everything that happens to him. Chances are that he is going to be most critical of food.
>
> —1961 *Handbook of Jail Food Service*

> In Hamilton County, Florida, "even at the young age of eight, one of Miriam's many chores was to open the small wooden door in the kitchen and pass the food to the prisoners as they scuffled by, one at a time, to get their meal. Likewise, after Grace washed the prisoners dungarees in the old iron clothes pot, Miriam helped her hang the garments out on the clothesline to dry. One summer afternoon while taking the dry clothes down, a frantic prisoner broke loose and went dashing through the yard and the clothesline to escape. While panicking in seeing the prisoner, [eight-year-old Miriam] quickly threw the basket full of clothes down on the prisoner and he immediately tripped, fell into the clothesline and was quickly captured by the Sheriff. Obviously, chores were not boring around the jail."[1]
>
> —About Grace McGhin and daughter who served alongside Sheriff Eddie McGhin, 1941–1949, reported by great-granddaughter Ivy Fransioli.

As noted in the previous chapter, even small children understood the importance of keeping prisoners in their cells. Most children, that is. One of our chief justices of the U.S. Supreme Court was once a four-year-old on a mission. Fred Vinson played around his father's jail in Lawrence County, Kentucky, where he grew up during the 1890s. At the age of four, Fred made friends with one of the inmates and "decided he didn't belong in jail. He hadn't told me he wanted to be out, but I made up my mind I'd help him escape. I got hold of my father's hatchet, and one day when no one was looking, I walked up to his cell and slipped it through the bars to him."[2] One can only imagine what Pa thought when the prisoner called him to the cell and said "here is a little present your boy just gave me. I figured you would like to have it back."[3]

Sixty years later, another four-year-old managed to effect the actual release of an inmate. This time, it was Powell County, Montana, and the preschooler was Coleen Darrow. Ed had arrested a sixteen-year-old boy named Mike for abducting his girlfriend and then burglarizing motels along their route. Being a juvenile, Mike was housed in the women's cell upstairs. Mary Ann, Coleen's mother, home alone with her children, figured it was safe to "step out of the family quarters for just a few minutes" because the kids were napping.

As soon as Mary Ann left the premises, Mike made a commotion in his cell to wake Coleen. "She had been forbidden to go near the heavy steel cell door," Mary Ann wrote, "but she couldn't resist looking into the cell. She couldn't open the door without the key kept hanging above the door casing in our living room, a distance of at least 15 feet from the cell door. Mike, having seen where we kept the key, told Coleen he would give her his box of crayons and the coloring books he had in his cell if she would get a chair and reach the key to the cell and give it to him. The bribe worked. She scooted a chair over from the dining room, somehow reached the key, climbed back down and gave it to him. He unlocked the door to the cell and gave the coloring books and crayons to her."

Upon her return, Mary Ann came upon her daughter happily coloring. When asked where they'd come from, Coleen dutifully reported "a man gave me the coloring books and crayons and then ran through your bedroom and jumped out the window." After letting the undersheriff know that Mike was gone, Mary Ann spent quite some time trying to comfort Coleen who'd become worried. She kept asking "is my daddy mad at me?"

Mike, like most of the escapees unexpectedly absent from the county jail, was soon back in custody. A news report broadcast on the radio informed local citizens of the escape and Mike was spotted by a farmer who took him into custody until Ed could get there.

Some prisoners didn't get that far. Many breaks were stopped in the jailhouse. After Maud and Howard Tanner lived in the jailhouse for five or six years, their son, Howard A., married his sweetheart, Helen, before going off to fight in World War II. Helen stayed with Howard's parents off and on during the war years, helping around the Antrim County, Michigan, jail.

During her interview, Helen elaborated on one escape Maud included in her memoirs: "There were seven doors going into the kitchen. We had a juvenile housed in the women's jail. It was dark and rainy. Maud and I sat alone downstairs as the Sheriff had retired for the night. We were sitting in the living room. I got up to get us some tea. As I came in the kitchen through the dining room door, a juvenile prisoner came through the laundry room door, armed with a gun he'd found in the evidence room. He'd also found the knife in the laundry room as he came through there. It was used to cut the bar of soap for the wash tub."

The burly seventeen-year-old had also donned a raincoat he'd found in the laundry room so he'd put that on, thinking he could find some protection from the weather as he made his way from the jail. Instead, he and Helen came face to face as each entered the kitchen through opposite doorways. Too surprised to be scared, Helen turned on her heel and reported the boy to Maud. Maud leapt up and woke the sheriff.

The escaping juvenile, so unnerved by the surprise encounter with Helen as he emerged from the laundry room, returned to his cell the way he'd come. The sheriff knew the gun in the boy's possession was not loaded as he never kept bullets in the evidence room. Howard asked the boy for both the gun and the knife, which were handed over without incident. Maud noted that the sheriff incarcerated the boy in a more secure adult cell in the men's jail. The youth had gotten out of his cell through the trapdoor to the attic located in the ceiling of the women's jail.

Escapes involving violence were the worst-case scenarios. Nancy Fitzpatrick reported that the only time she was afraid for herself and her children at the Kossuth County Jail in Iowa was during an escape attempt. Deputy Tom, Nancy's husband, patrolled the county at night, so the police alerted Nancy to lock herself and her daughters in because they were bringing in a violent prisoner. The man was high on drugs. At midnight, they got the man situated in his cell and left. As it was a hot summer night, all of the windows in the building stood open. "The man banged on the iron-clad walls of his cell, rattling the sheets of iron and rivets that had come loose over time, and shouted at the tops of his lungs until about 4 a.m. The neighbors called to see if there was anything that could be done to quiet the prisoner since he was keeping them awake too. I called the town police and told them what was going on, and they called the sheriff in from his farm, and he called Tom in from his patrol.

"They decided that they were going to transfer the guy to Fort Dodge right then. The exit from the jail was out the back and into a fenced yard. They handcuffed the fellow and got him out of the jail and into the yard, and got the gate open. At that point, the drugged man escaped from their grasp and lunged through the gate." Nancy watched all of this from the window in her newborn daughter's bedroom. "I was startled to see the man not run off through the yard, but head for my back door. Tom managed a flying tackle and brought the man down before he got to the covered porch. As they wrestled, the other three men piled on. It took all of them to subdue the guy and get him into the car. The sheriff and one of the town police drove away with the prisoner, the other policeman went home, and Tom went back on patrol. I stood and looked at little Sarah, in bed in her flowery little room, and was glad that the night was finally over."

Nancy, herself, had to effect an escape of sorts. The only shower in the old Victorian they called home was located in the basement, not confined by walls. While showering one day, Nancy heard the door to the basement open. In order not to be seen in the nude, Nancy quickly scampered out of the spray of water through the door of the workshop. She closed the door behind her and then watched through a crack while the Culligan man came into the room, pondered the running shower with no one around, turned off the water, and made his delivery.

Clarence Werth learned the hard way what not to say to inmates during the 1960s in Ellis County, Kansas. Anne recalled the time "the sheriff told a prisoner he would be back after supper so the prisoner could call his wife. Bad idea! When he opened the door, he was overpowered and they made their escape. They ran down to the main floor of the courthouse and kicked out the door glass. My eight-year old son and I heard the racket, locked the door of the family quarters and called the local police. The men were later found and apologized to the sheriff."

Maud Tanner matroned for a juvenile offender who had been a handful from the beginning during her service at the Antrim County, Michigan, jail prior to World War II. When Howard brought him from the cell to turn over to the men waiting to transfer him to another facility, he warned them that the boy should be considered a flight risk. The men shrugged, put handcuffs on the boy's wrists, and headed for the door as the sheriff shook his head in disbelief. "As soon as the boy got out the door, he started running, and ran clear through town. Howard and his son, Howard A., leapt in the car and drove after him. At the far end of the main street, the road entered a swamp. The kid made the swamp before Howard could get to him but they drove on in and hopped out of the car. The boy stopped when Howard offered to shoot him and they brought him back to the men still standing in the yard."

Escape attempts can involve a recapture process that takes law enforcement beyond the confines of the county seat. Even before the era of mass transportation, that didn't stop citizens from tagging along after the pursuers to see what was going to happen next.

When she was ten, Zita Singler's widowed mother, Rose, continued to cook for the inmates after her husband died in the line of duty as the sheriff of Jackson County, Oregon. The year was 1915. There were a few automobiles around and many folks still got around in wagons or on horseback. Mr. Basye, noted earlier as the man who shooed the children away when they hung on the bars and talked with the inmates, remained as jailor. Young Zita had gone out to play one day and found herself caught up as a spectator in a jail break. She recalled that she "was just skating back and forth and I hear this moaning and groaning and I thought 'my gosh, what's going on!' I decided to go look. I'd gotten as far as the steps to the jail"[4] when she saw Mr. Basye on the floor with a crushed and bleeding head.

"A lot of people came flying out of the courthouse."[5] The staff shooed Zita away so she wouldn't see what she'd already seen: Mr. Basye dying on the jail floor. A prisoner, on trial for rape, prepared for the day's session by asking Basye to bring him a flat iron to press his clothes. The jailor kindly accommodated the inmate. Unfortunately, Basye turned his back on the prisoner as he left the cell. The inmate brought the pointed end of the iron down on the jailor's head "with great force."[6] The jailor died shortly after Zita discovered him.

Two prisoners escaped that day from the Jackson County jail. The iron-wielding inmate took Basye's gun "and he made this young fellow go with him because he said he didn't know how to drive and he wanted somebody to drive for him."[7] The young man agreed, at gunpoint. They stole a car and off they drove in the direction of Jackson Creek. The National Guard of Medford was called into service and the soldiers caught up with the duo at the Creek. Zita recalled how the townsfolk took off to see what would happen next when word reached them of the confrontation. "Of course, I naturally followed along with them. I had to see everything, you know how kids are curious, so I got behind [one of the local girls] and pulled her skirt out and peeked around. The young man forced to drive had already given himself up. The escaping prisoner killed himself with the jailor's gun rather than be captured."[8] Once again, young Zita was shooed away from the scene, but once again, she'd already seen it all.

NOT JUST THE KIDS

When a lawman found himself in charge of a jail and he was unmarried, he often hired a housekeeper to help. In 1932, Margaret Adams accepted employment as housekeeper for Deputy Bull of Washington County, Rhode Island. When Bull was jumped by three prisoners intent on escaping, she prevented their success by shutting the gate to the cell block with Bull still inside. She quickly alerted the police who calmed the situation down enough to retrieve Deputy Bull from the bull pen.

Another housekeeper did not fare as well during her employment at a county jail. In 1880 Kane County, Illinois, an unnamed housekeeper brought water to the inmates one fine spring evening. The sheriff had been called away from the jail. Knowing this, two inmates overpowered the housekeeper who "made a brave resistance, but threats of throwing her in the cistern"[9] finally took the fight out of her and the men made good their escape.

Mason Knapp hired a housekeeper to assist his wife after Mamie fell and became confined to a wheelchair. When Mason won election as North Dakota's Griggs County sheriff, the housekeeper made the move to the basement of the courthouse with the family. On those frequent occasions when Mason had to be away on business, he left the physical well-being of his family and the jail in the care of the hired woman. Lulu Knapp, seven at the time, recalled that on one such occasion their housekeeper "fed the prisoners early and went to get the keys to lock up and as she was about to close the door, two [inmates] walked right by her and escaped. They had taken a watch spring and sawed two bars and bent the bars over with a table leg. One was recaptured but the other they never found."[10]

In somewhat similar fashion, Mrs. Sheriff Evelyn Robinson entered her cell block one morning in the late 1950s after breakfast to "let the trustees out to work in the garden. Three other inmates shoved her aside and knocked her down to escape. They were caught again" and returned to the Windham County, Vermont, jail.

During the second half of the nineteenth century in Pacific County, Washington, Mae Bullard taught school, met and married a lumberjack named Brown, who then became a deputy sheriff. Many years into her marriage, on a Fourth of July, Mae spread blankets under the trees on the courthouse lawn and prepared for a family picnic. The Bullard children ran around playing until young Floyd "came running from behind the jail yelling 'Papa, Papa, the prisoners are getting away!' "[11] The bars had been cut and the family observed "one prisoner running for the woods while another was squeezing through the gap"[12] in the window. Deputy Brown "pulled his revolver out of his hip pocket"[13] and handed it to Mae, instructing her that "if he tries to get away, shoot him, Mother."[14] He then "left for the nearest tavern to drum up a posse to go after the escapee."[15] Mae's daughter reported that "Mother's hand was shaking and her aim was wandering all over the side of the jail, but her face had an expression of absolute determination."[16] That look was enough to keep the prisoner "half in and half out of the window."[17]

IT STARTED WITH A RUCKUS

Fans of the Old West will be familiar with an outlaw nicknamed Big Nose George. Out in Carbon County, Wyoming, in the 1880s, Rosa Rankin's husband, Robert, served as jailor, splitting the shifts with his brother, James. James took the train to Montana to pick up Big Nose George who was wanted for murder. When the train stopped in Carbon, Jim and Big Nose were overpowered by a mob determined to teach George a lesson. After incapacitating Jim, someone managed to get a noose around George's neck and the crowd dragged him from the train. They strung him up until he confessed to everything he'd done. Then they returned George to Deputy Rankin, rope-burned and badly shaken. He was then put into Rosa's jail and ate her meals while awaiting trial like any other inmate.

George was eventually found guilty and scheduled to hang. He'd had enough of ropes around his neck so he tried to escape. He managed to remove his shackles and, as Rosa's husband brought the latest of her meals to the cell, Robert became the unfortunate recipient of a bludgeoning. Rosa, hearing the commotion, grabbed her pistol, and stopped George in his tracks. She quickly shut and locked the door between Big Nose and freedom. In doing so, she was forced to leave her unconscious husband on the other side.

When word got out that Big Nose had attempted an escape, the townspeople took matters into their own hands. Rosa then had to protect her two children from the lynch mob that stormed the jail. The mob pulled George from his cell and hung him from a telegraph pole, but it took three attempts to get the job done.

One never knew what would happen next at any given jailhouse. At 9:30 in the morning one fine autumn day in 1894 Steuben County, New York, Mrs. Sheriff Sherwood and the cook heard a ruckus in the front hall. Mrs. Sherwood wiped the flour from her hands and stepped into the dining room. She found herself confronted by four escaping prisoners: a forger, two thieves and a con man "confined for false pretenses."[18] The men managed their exit when the jailor brought them fresh water. One of the four, the forger, had blown pepper into the jailor's eyes. With the watery-eyed turnkey in hot pursuit, the men pushed past

Mrs. Sherwood and fled through the kitchen. The cook, quick on her feet, grabbed one of the men and delayed him long enough that the jailor caught up with him in the yard.

As the others fled, a sixteen-year-old local boy observed the escape and followed the two thieves as they made their way to the river, overtook them, and when he stood his ground with a revolver in his hand, one of the escapees surrendered. The other made his getaway. The last of the men hid in a barn and a "lively tussle ensued"[19] when Sheriff Sherwood found him, but the prisoner escaped from Sherwood's grasp, leaving behind his coat, vest, and hat. He leapt into the river and was shot in the leg as he swam across, but that didn't slow him down one iota. When another shot came "uncomfortable close, he succumbed"[20] and was returned to his cell to mend. No doubt, it would have been Mrs. Sherwood who attended to his mending.

Because of the size of the inmate population, some jails required more than one person to distribute meal trays or to make rounds at the end of the day to ensure that all was well. In 1928, Sheriff Sloan held fifteen inmates in the Clarion County, Pennsylvania, jail. His wife always accompanied him as he walked through the jail for lockup. She armed herself before entering the area, just in case, with a "Tear Billy" that discharged tear gas. Prior to their arrival one particular night, someone placed a harmonica above the door between Mrs. Sloan's kitchen and the cell area. It had been carefully placed in such a manner that when the Sloans opened the door, the harmonica lodged between the door and the doorjamb.

Sloan opened the door, the harmonica fell, prisoners rushed, and when Sloan tried to close the door before they got to him, it refused to shut. With her husband clinging desperately to the door to prevent the mob on the other side from opening it any further, "Mrs. Sloan discharged her Tear Billy in the prisoners' faces. Two of them, thinking she had fired a real gun, ran back to their cells. The others were unaffected by the tear gas as there was a strong current of air in that part of the jail."[21]

As her husband was set upon by the remaining prisoners, Mrs. Sloan ran for help. The sheriff was beaten with fists, kicked with feet, and clubbed with whatever was at hand in the kitchen. Sloan managed to get two prisoners down to the floor but a third one hit him over the head and they dragged him into the cell area. With all of their adrenaline pumping, the escaping prisoners forgot about their own harmonica trick and when they tried to shut the door on the sheriff, they couldn't get it closed. With time running out, they left their packed suitcases behind and ran for it. The sheriff recovered and gave chase despite his beating. Mrs. Sloan retrieved the harmonica and slammed the door shut to keep the few remaining prisoners she still had in their cell block. She then called every law enforcement office in the area to alert them to the situation. Every one of the prisoners who made it outside the jail was captured and returned with additional sentences tacked on for the break.

One break of such a violent nature was plenty for any sheriffing family but poor Sophie Bonde endured two. Sophie is remembered by her grandson as an

Sheriff Roy Terrell in his Garfield County, Colorado, office in the late 1930s. Note the leather clubs hanging on the wall to the far left. These were available for use should inmates become unruly or attempt an escape. (Courtesy of Hal Terrell.)

extraordinarily kind and loving person. The first break from the Kandiyohi County jail in Minnesota, in 1911, began with her husband being beaten senseless by two prisoners after one of them threw hoarded pepper in Bonde's eyes when he came in for bed check. The sheriff recovered just as the men got past the lock on the second door to the jail area. He was able to chase after them, firing six shots down the alley. His pursuit was curtailed as he was still too incapacitated by the beating and by his smarting eyes. The newspaper account described Sophie this way: "When she had heard the noise of scuffling in the jail, she rushed to the stairs and saw when the sheriff sank to the floor and the two prisoners opened the door and escaped. She called back to little Harold Bonde, who called the telephone central to give the police alarm, and then she went down and locked the inside jail to keep the remaining prisoner from escaping."[22] The fellow left behind reported later that his life had been threatened if he warned the sheriff. The two escapees were never located.

Ten years later, Sophie suffered an even more horrific escape. She was in charge because the sheriff and his deputy were out of town. Mike, a car thief, was a resourceful and forward-thinking young man. He purchased hacksaw blades before he stole the car for which he was arrested. He hid the blades in his shoes. They came in handy when he wanted to cut through the bolts holding a steel plate over a hole in the jail cell. Mike tunneled under the corridor about four feet and knocked loose one of the cement blocks that made up the floor. This allowed him to crawl up into the corridor, at which point he invited another prisoner, Henry, to join him in an escape.

Adventuresome Henry agreed. His part in the escape ruse was to sit in his cell where Sophie would be able to see him when she looked in before unlocking the door to the cell area. Mike banged on the water pipes to summon Sophie and then hid in the corner. Sophie, seeing Henry securely in his cell, asked him through the door what he needed. He asked if she would shut the window as it was getting a bit chilly. Sophie agreed, unlocked the door, and started for the window. "Suddenly Mike sprang at her, grasped her by the head and chin and in a subdued voice commanded her not to scream. The attacked woman struggled and fought as best she could,"[23] reported the newspaper. Henry joined Mike in the attempt to subdue Sophie, who was still struggling. They gagged her with handkerchiefs, tied her hands behind her with a necktie and carried her into the hallway. "A coat was rolled up for a pillow and placed under her head."[24] Then the men gathered their things and adjusted their clothing to present a more normal appearance in public while Sophie begged them through her gag not to kill her.

Both men told her how sorry they were they had to do this. Mike produced what looked to be a Colt automatic revolver and pointed it at Sophie, but instead of shooting her, he told her that he would use it on anyone who came after them. The men then left, locking the door so no one could enter the house. Sophie, still hysterical, eventually worked her way out of her bindings, stumbled to the phone to call the doctor, and unlocked the front door. When he arrived and heard why she was near collapse, he notified the police and a manhunt was instigated. The men were eventually returned to the jail.

It wasn't always inmates trying to get out that terrified sheriffing couples. In one long frightening saga, Neva Allen and her children experienced jailbreaks of both kinds: breaking out and being broken out.

All hell broke loose in Poweshiek County, Iowa, during Neva Allens' tenure, sometime after 1955. It all started with a big guy named George H. who spent the evening in a tavern in the county and drank too much. One thing led to another and George went berserk, stabbing the woman he was with seven times in the chest. George then took a flyer to avoid arrest for murder.

The woman, with luck and a lot of prayer, survived the stabbing. Eventually, George was discovered in Boston, arrested, and sent back to Poweshiek County. Neva prepared meals for him for quite some time while the lawyers prepared for trial. Once George settled into his new digs, he made a rather good inmate. When not drinking to excess, big George turned out to be a pleasant fellow. As a result,

Max allowed George to keep a hot plate in his cell, for coffee and such, whenever he wanted.

Working at the jail at that time were Neva's father-in-law who served as day jailor and her mother-in-law who served as day matron when there were female inmates. The couple were called in to work when a local gas station reported to Max that they'd been robbed. Detective work led him to arrest three men and two women, one with an infant. The group had driven up from Kansas City for the "easy pickin's" in a rural Iowa county. They hadn't counted on Max.

Neva and Mrs. Allen settled the women and baby in the women's jail. Max's father accommodated the three men in their cells. Everything went along smooth as butter until one day—a day when it happened that one of Neva's two kids stayed home from school because she didn't feel well—everything went awry. Max was out on business, Neva and Mrs. Allen left the family quarters to run errands, an older deputy took one of the trustees to the laundromat to wash the jail bedding.

While the trustee, the deputy, and the laundry were away from the jail along with almost everyone else, one of the Kansas City toughs, Moses, boiled water on George's hot plate; not for coffee, tea, soup or cocoa, but to throw at the deputy when he came back to the bull pen with clean sheets and the trustee. That is exactly what happened, resulting in a terrible scalding of the lawman. A gag was used to keep him quiet.

While the deputy lay incapacitated, Moses gathered the old man's keys, opened the outer door of the men's jail and unlocked the women's jail. Then Moses burst through the kitchen door, a man on a mission. Unfortunately, Debby, Neva's young teen home from school because of illness, happened to be standing in the kitchen at that moment. Moses threw Debby against the wall and proceeded to search frantically through the kitchen drawers looking for keys to the outer doors. In almost no time, he found what he wanted and then some. In the same drawer with the keys, Moses found a loaded gun.

Just then, Debby's grandfather rushed in to grapple with Moses. "Grandpa fought with him and hit him with his ring of keys" while Debby, not one to stand aside with family at risk, grabbed the can of mace to spray in Moses' face. Before she could position herself to spray mace in the correct face during the struggle between grandpa and the escapee, Moses got his hand around the gun in the drawer. "He saw what I had," Debby explained, "and threatened to shoot me if I didn't put it down. I put it down."

Moses knocked out Deb's grandfather with the butt of the pistol instead of shooting him. He then locked Debby upstairs with big George and a female inmate who decided they didn't want to escape with the others. Not being familiar with the workings of the door at the top of the stairs, Moses locked only one of the two locks. The Kansas City men then rummaged through the family quarters and sheriff's office, looking for anything that was of value or that might be useful on the trip they were about to take.

Everything became quiet. Debby and the two prisoners whispered among themselves, trying to determine if they were alone. George picked up a pop bottle and dropped it on the floor upstairs. When it broke, Moses yelled through the door that he would kill everyone if any of them tried anything. Everything went quiet again. "A little while later, George broke another pop bottle and no one said anything, so this is how we knew the gang had gone. George was so big that all he had to do to break through the stairwell door was to run at it with both arms out, and the lock snapped." Had Moses bolted both locks, however, the trio would have been forced to remain upstairs until someone came home.

With the stairwell door broken open, the three former hostages rushed down to the kitchen to offer assistance to Max's father and then to the jail to see about the scalded deputy. Both men survived. Max came back to the jail as soon as he was summoned. He sent word to lawmen between the jail and Kansas City, letting everyone know about the viciousness of the escape. He described the escapees and alerted lawmen that the gang had an infant with them. The escapees were captured and brought back to Neva's jail. "As dad took Moses to his cell, two separate fights broke out, but into his cell he went."

A few days later, someone—probably Kansas City authorities—alerted Neva and Max that they had heard the rumor that friends of Moses were coming up to Poweshiek County to break the gang out of the jail. After talking it over, Max and Neva decided to keep the news from the children, Debby and Bruce. Max, Neva, Grandpa Allen and another deputy devised a plan. Max and Neva armed themselves and arranged an array of firearms and ammunition close at hand. Tension ran high. Other deputies and the Highway Patrol cruised around the jail, prepared to radio in if they spotted the Kansas City caravan. None of them knew exactly who to expect or how many. Neva watched out the front and Max watched out the back, guns and ammo at the ready, prepared to fight off any intruders from their jailhouse fort.

Because the kids didn't know anything about what was going on with the adults in the jailhouse, they got up that morning and proceeded to do what they normally did. Bruce and Debby took the flag out the side door to hoist it up the flag pole before going to the kitchen. They returned through the side door, somehow unnoticed by their nervous parents. As the kids entered the living room, before they noticed the arsenal at their mother's side, "Mom saw the flag fluttering out of the corner of her eye and her nerves got the best of her," Debby reported. "She yelled for dad" and the panic in her voice caught her children off guard. Bruce, still unaware that anything unusual was going on, teased his mom about being afraid of a little flag. Neva, totally out of character, slapped Bruce . . . hard, across the face. The three Allens then stood in shocked silence, looking at each other.

Once she'd regained her composure, Neva explained to the kids that they expected to be under siege at any moment. She sent them upstairs to pack a few things. Not long after, their grandparents whisked the children to safety. Bruce and Debby stayed away from home until the following Sunday night. As unsatisfying as it is, we don't know the end of this story. Neither child was ever told if the gang showed up but it seems unlikely that the shoot-out occurred as the county seat would have been buzzing with the story.

Such events did not happen often during the era of the mom-and-pop jail. After the advent of a drug problem in any given county, the situation intensified and many Mrs. Sheriffs became more fearful. Dorothy Rumbaugh of Jefferson County, Kansas, reported about the time that "Gordon arrested some drug dealers and had found the suitcase of drugs hidden on the school grounds of McLouth. The FBI left the drugs at the jail for several weeks. It was the first time I ever had a loaded shotgun behind the door as you never knew when some of the dope dealers might come and demand the drugs."

For all that there was that could go wrong for families on the premises, most participants in this research reported that they were never afraid, even when they should have been. In the next chapter, additional reasons to feel afraid are explored in more detail.

—— 17 ——

Nerves of Steel—or Not

Powdered eggs have a tendency to clump together during storage and these do not absorb moisture as well. Just before using, regrind the powder by stirring or otherwise breaking up the lumps. Thus, each grain will readily absorb the water.

—1961 *Handbook of Jail Food Service*

I was never really afraid except when a transient would come to the door wanting a place to stay. Some didn't look so good. Actually, as I look back, I should have been afraid all the time!

—From correspondence by Betty Swanson who served alongside Sheriff Wayne Swanson at the Lucas County, Iowa, jail from 1955 to 1981.

Minor worries sometimes grew to full-scale fear but like women everywhere, the wives of sheriffs and jailors did what needed to be done despite what was going on around them. There were times when worries became fears, and occasionally, fear became terror because the normal course of jailhouse routine was interrupted by horrific events. Fortunately, for most sheriffing families, these were few and far between.

Every mother's nightmare came true for Mrs. Sheriff White of Alameda County, California, during the 1880s. Her sons, Charles and Ed, took up the badge to serve as their father's deputies. Word came in July of 1889 that a man had locked himself in the powder magazine at an explosives factory after shooting a coworker over lottery tickets. In the magazine along with the fugitive sat five tons of volatile chemicals. The desperate man remained inside overnight. Ed and Charlie, along with others on the sheriff's staff, arrived on the scene to monitor the situation. Charlie took charge as their father was out of town on business.

Charlie White cautiously approached the building when the fugitive said he wished to surrender. Charlie slowly worked his way to within 300 yards of the magazine with four deputies behind, trying not to spook the nervous culprit. Ed remained vigilant nearby to sound the alarm if anything appeared suspicious. Suddenly, the magazine exploded. Charlie and the other four lawmen died along with the fugitive plus Sadie Hill, a guest staying in a nearby home. Deputy Ed White escaped death but was "painfully wounded"[1] and tenderly cared for by his grieving mother.

FEAR, OR THE LACK THEREOF

Because events such as the loss of a son or the threat of a gang trying to break their friends out of jail were rare, most of the respondents to the questionnaire remarked that they were never fearful. Maureen Elston of Wright County, Iowa, wrote "I can't say I was ever afraid for myself or my children. I think living in a small town had a lot to do with it."

Vernice Cooper, tending to the inmates in the Greenwood County, South Carolina, jail, told her kids that "she was often asked if she was afraid for the children while living adjacent to the jail and she always responded 'no, I wouldn't do it if I were afraid for our safety.' "

Sam, Vernice's son, remembered being afraid only once: "a friend and I took a shortcut while walking home from school one day and it took us through someone's back yard. We were seen and the homeowner came out and yelled at us for trespassing. My friend, not taking kindly to being yelled at, grandly announced that I was the son of Deputy Cooper at the jail. I nearly died. That was never done! We'd been trained early not to flaunt our father's position to get things or to get away with things. As a result, I literally groveled, unashamedly, in hopes that the homeowner wouldn't tell dad what my friend said."

In mid-twentieth century Poweshiek County, Iowa, Neva Allen's husband, Max, feared most that the community would think he played favorites if someone in the family "did something wrong, so they were always arrested and had charges filed against them, even if it was for something that he'd have overlooked in a non-family member." Their son, Bruce, came under arrest by his dad for reckless driving when Bruce wrecked his car. The sheriff "arrested his own mother for the same charge when she wrecked her car."

Sid and Richard Edinger reported "I don't think she [Marian] was ever afraid for herself or children, at least, not because of what any prisoners or the public might do. My mother and dad were very well liked by the public and prisoners. At that time, someone who broke a law generally did not get angry with the officer who arrested him or her, nor hold a grudge because of the arrest." The Edingers were elected sheriff off and on between 1922 and 1942 in McHenry County, Illinois.

Not everything was sweetness and light even during the best of times when one belonged to a family associated with the county jail. Marian Edinger surprised her family at a gathering fifty years after she'd taken up the county apron when the conversation turned to the subject of drugs. It was the 1970s or 1980s, according to Sid, and the younger generation considered Marian much too old to know anything about drugs. She "spoke up with considerable feeling about how bad they were. It seems that when an addict was incarcerated in our jail, they were given a maintenance dosage because there was no facility to handle withdrawal. Mom related that dad would give them a pill that was to be swallowed. He would then have to feel in their mouth to confirm that it had been swallowed. If the prisoner could retrieve it without swallowing, he would likely try to grind it up into a powder, heat it, and inject it, even if the only instrument he had was a nail. This was part of my environment and I was totally unaware."

MAYBE JUST A LITTLE AFRAID

One of the givens for sheriffing couples was that the easiest way to get back at those in authority was through their children. Helen, daughter of Olive Rosenkranz in Washington County, Kansas, reported that her older brothers found it difficult being the sons of Sheriff Rosenkranz during the 1930s. "My father said they needed to be very careful, be only in safe places so no one could set them up as doing something wrong in the eyes of the public. I was young enough this didn't bother me, I was home with my parents anyway."

Twenty years later, Randy Harris recalled that "living in the jail seemed ordinary at the time. I get astonished reactions now when I tell people." He remembers feeling watched by people in the county and held to a higher standard than his peers by virtue of his father's role. When he had turned twenty-two, he "went to a street dance in a small community and was drinking beer with some of the other guys, when someone came up and asked if my dad knew I was drinking that beer. I explained to him that I was 22 now and my dad didn't mind."

Madge Harris, Randy's mom, didn't mind very much that her children were in the public eye, so to speak, as that helped to keep them safe. She reported how she feared for her son when he learned to drive and had a girlfriend who lived in the county. She worried that he was vulnerable to attack while driving alone in the country, especially at night, if someone with revenge in their heart against the sheriff wanted to take it out on their son.

Sheriff's staff often heard threats against their children by those they suspected of walking on the wrong side of the law. There were times that vicious words were overheard by the family as well. Peggy Schumaker, daughter of Ellis County, Kansas, Mrs. Sheriff Agnes Schumaker, recalled the night her father brought in a gang member. The lawman and his prisoner came through the basement and down the hall next to the family quarters on their way to the cell block. The family "peeked out to see who was being brought in, and we overheard the prisoner tell the sheriff that he and his gang were going to kill the sheriff's family for doing this to him." Peggy recalls being scared by that and she thinks her mother must have been also.

Charlotte, daughter of Allamakee County's Martha Bulman in Iowa, remembered that during the Depression the children were kept away from the cells "when there was someone dangerous in jail. Mom wouldn't let us carry the meals to the inmates but would have the deputy sheriff or dad take the meals to them." Thirty years later, in Boone County, Iowa, Glenda Camelin recalled one such dangerous prisoner in her jail. "A fellow had gone on a shooting spree across Iowa. He traveled across the state just killing at random. It was a very anxious time."

SOMETHING TO WORRY ABOUT

Many a sheriff worried for the safety of his family and their visitors when the family lived in the jail. Mary Ann and Ed Darrow of Powell County, Montana, recalled a local man, Fred, who'd gone AWOL from the Army so he could get home to his pregnant wife. The soldier stopped at his parents' home that happened to be situated across from the jail and sheriff's quarters. There he pocketed his father's .38 revolver. Fred "stole a relative's car, and took off when the law was closing in on him. A highway patrolman named Dick found him and brought him back to town but Fred still had his father's gun plus the patrolman's gun and it was pointed at the patrolman. They drove to the hospital where Fred held a nurse at bay with a gun while he saw his wife."

At the same time, Sheriff Darrow and Police Chief Wilson disabled the patrolman's car so Fred and Dick had to remain on foot. Darrow and Wilson then dropped out of sight. Fred and Dick emerged from the hospital, discovered the car would not start so walked the eight blocks back to Fred's parents home across from the jail, "a gun pointed at the patrolman all the way." Fred returned his dad's gun to his father but continued to cover the Highway Patrolman with Dick's own gun while the two of them walked across the street toward the jail so Fred could give himself up.

Prior to Fred's arrival in town, Mary Ann had been entertaining the undersheriff's wife, Bess McGillis, and her teenage daughter. They'd come to see the Darrow's new son, Mark, just home from the hospital. Alerted to the developing situation, the women watched the drama unfold from the dining room window as it played out right under their noses. Ed wrote in their memoirs, "When I saw Fred and Dick coming from the parent's home toward the jail, I ran upstairs and told the women to lie down on the floor until we could resolve the problem. They would have made good targets in the window. Time stood still through this entire episode which lasted a very long three hours."

Other wives had even worse to contend with. Many a lynch mob caused mothers' blood to run cold when their little ones were home. At the Carthage County, Illinois, Jail Museum, they tell the tale of how the jailor was out of town when the mob came for Joseph Smith and his brother Hyram in 1844. Mrs. Jailor and her children were in the family quarters when the shooting started. As the worried mother bent down to pick up one of her children, a stray bullet came through the door, just missing her head. "She grabbed her children and ran out the door to a neighbor's house."[2]

They called Mrs. Sheriff Elvira Brown by the nickname of "Bunch." She and Tobe lived in the Fayette County, Georgia, jail at the turn of the twentieth century, and stayed on long enough to raise their daughters and welcome grandchildren into the world. "Life was a challenge for the wife of a 1900s sheriff but Bunch was a feisty character up to the challenge."[3]

"Tobe frequently had to fend off lynch mobs, including one in 1908 that had formed bent on hanging Jim Bennett for the murder of Buddy McEachern. Bunch hid Bennett in a clothes hamper while Tobe convinced the crowd to go home. Later in the night, Toby concealed Bennett under a lap robe in his buggy and took him to Jonesboro for safekeeping."[4]

In Clarion County, Pennsylvania, a sheriff and his deputy son attempted to arrest a farmer. When they walked up to the house, they saw the wanted man sitting on his front porch. As the sheriff came onto the porch, the man picked up a board studded with nails and hit the sheriff with it and ran to the barn. "The deputy, thinking his father had been killed, said later that he was glad he didn't have a gun as he would have shot the man right then. But as the deputy ran after the fleeing man, he was surprised to find that his father had not only survived but gotten up and joined in the chase." The two lawmen managed to capture the farmer but stopped in a town between the farm and the county seat. While a local doctor stitched the sheriff's wounds, his son bought dad some new duds. "They saw no sense in letting the sheriff's wife see her husband in bloody clothes."

During an interview by Joan Richardson of Fredonia, Kansas, Lenora Spohn recalled her most exciting time as a jailhouse wife. "She and Charlie [husband and sheriff] were driving to Chanute in their own vehicle. He got a call that two men had escaped from a facility—'maybe Leavenworth'—and were headed south. They saw a 'couple of fellas' coming down a road toward them, but probably upon seeing an approaching vehicle, the men went off the road and under a culvert. Charlie became suspicious, but drove on by. He turned around after driving several miles and spotted them again walking down the road. By this time, with the equipment of the day, he was too far from [the Wilson County Jail] to ask for help. He stopped, called to the men saying he had a warrant for their arrests and that if they 'behaved themselves' he'd simply take them to jail. Lenora recalls that Charlie gave her his pistol, had her sit in the back seat, and told her to 'shoot them if they misbehaved.' Both men sat in front with Charlie. Lenora was shaking, holding the gun, in the backseat. But she said both men took Charlie's advice and caused no trouble, perhaps because they were exhausted. She remembers that they still had on leg irons."[5]

Like the Mrs. Sheriffs before them, modern wives worried about husbands when there were prisoners to transfer and they did not accompany him on the trip. Who knew what might happen when the sheriff was out with his prisoner or in a county where no one knew him? Madge Harris at Wilson County, Kansas, in the 1950s recalled being worried about her husband "because he made many, many long trips to pick up prisoners, not to mention all of the late night calls."

Stress was not limited to the sheriff's wife. In Ellis County, Kansas, a decade later, the children of Anne Werth responded in different ways to seeing their father leave home on official business. Linda recalled that she "was afraid only once. I saw my father rush into the house to get his rifle and that he was all keyed up. I found out that a sheriff to the west had been shot and killed by someone and that my father was going out with other law enforcement officers to hunt down the killer. That incident really scared me."

Linda's brother, Mark, became apprehensive whenever his father went out to pick up prisoners on an overnight trip when Anne didn't go with him. "He'd be right at my side," Anne reported. "He often commented that he hoped dad called in soon. He knew Clarence was a good driver but you just don't know who is out there!"

Mary Richart is reported to have "crawled into bed and stayed there until [George] returned when he'd be gone overnight transferring a prisoner. She couldn't function without him."[6] The Richarts lived on top of the Boulder Courthouse in the 1930s. One of their daughters "remembered seeing my father leave the family quarters to go after a man who was holed up in a house with dynamite strapped to his body. When the sheriff came into view, the man yelled out 'if you come near me, I'll set this off.' Officers already on the scene may have moved or the nervous man twitched because the next moment the dynamite went off, blowing up the house and the man, and seriously crippling a policeman. My father was not injured."[7]

Lucille Ingalsbee, niece of Bertha Miller in Allegan County, Michigan, recalled that when she lived in the jail during the 1930s so she could attend high school, a vigil was kept until Fred returned from late calls out in the county. "When my uncle went out on a night call, my aunt would get me up and she would look out one window and I would look out another window, watching for him to return."

Windows and then radios played a large role in the waiting that took place in sheriffs' homes all over the country. In Van Buren County, Iowa, during the late 1950s, Dolores Lee never acted as if she was afraid, reported her son, Larry. "She took most things in stride. The only time I thought she worried at all was when dad had gone out on a call and didn't answer the radio when she checked on him. She worried until he radioed in that he was back in the car."

Jan Jahnel reported that "the most fearful times would be when dad would be called out in the middle of the night and I would see him put his gun on. I would be up to listen to the police radio to assure the event was over or to be ready to call for back-up" in Mitchell County, Iowa, during the 1960s.

Also in Iowa, in Chickasaw County a decade earlier, Paulette Folkers remembered "one evening, quite late, we were all in bed, there was a call . . . robbery in progress . . . that ended up in a high speed chase. We watched dad grab his shotgun, load it and race away in the car with lights and siren going. That was something he didn't do very often. Mom and I waited by the two-way radio for over an hour. Finally dad called in and said things were under control and he was okay. He told mom to go back to bed, but she didn't. She waited until he got home as she always did. Many nights, she'd sit at the kitchen counter and play solitaire."

Edith Weiss' grandson reported being told by his father about a terrifying incident in Holmes County, Ohio. "One night the telephone rang late in the evening.

The caller stated that the state liquor store [down the street] was being burglarized. My Grandfather went to the gun room . . . put a hundred round barrel of ammo on his Thomson 45 machine gun and crept down the alley . . . [the family] watched their father go down the alley. My grandfather told me that the robbers saw his hat badge reflect off the street lamp. They started shooting at him with hand guns. My grandfather opened up on them with the machine gun. He shot out the front window of the store. Across the street was a gasoline station. The bullets went into that building and broke the toilet and some glass. One robber was wounded but they all got away. The culprits dropped off the wounded person at Massion Hospital, paralyzed from his wounds. Each Christmas he would send my grandfather a card."[8]

Betty Burns, daughter of Elma and Francis Sinclair in Hodgeman County, Kansas, told the following story about her mother and fear. "The only time Elma was in fear was during high speed trips. One time, Elma and Francis had gone after fresh eggs in the country. They were on their way back to the Courthouse when Francis got a message on the two-way in the car, asking him to help in the round-up of prisoners who had escaped from the Larned State Hospital, a facility for the insane. Francis took off at high speed." As Elma clung to the bucket of fragile fresh eggs, she asked, "are you going to drive this fast to Larned?" Betty reported that when "Francis replied that he may even go faster, Elma told him to pull over and let her out. She got out with her little bucket of eggs and started to walk back to town" while Francis continued toward Larned. Not too long after her trek began, the undersheriff drove by and picked her up. "Francis must have contacted him to do so, but he never admitted it," Betty laughed.

Elma Sinclair felt that she'd probably saved her life that day during the 1960s by getting out of the speeding sheriff's car. In 1888 Converse County, Wyoming, Priscilla Campbell saved her husband's life . . . by begging for it . . . babe in arms. It all started when three men were tossed off a ranch for being drunk and shooting up the place. Two weeks later, the same men came into town and got drunk again. They decided to return to the ranch and show the owners a thing or two. While they were discussing their plan at the saloon, Sheriff Campbell heard them talking and tried to reason with them, but to no avail. The next thing heard in town was the sound of gunfire coming from the ranch down the road.

One of the drunken trio, a man named Ferry, managed to get back to town but had been mortally wounded by a shot to his abdomen. Ferry was given a bed in the hospital. As Campbell emerged from helping to put Ferry to bed, someone came in to tell him that another of the trio had died at the ranch. He saddled up and rode toward the ranch. He hadn't gotten very far out of town before he saw two of the boys from the ranch riding toward him at a furious pace. Using all of his diplomatic skills, Malcolm talked them out of killing him but nothing he said could dissuade them from coming into town to kill the two who got away, including Ferry.

Malcolm came into town with the enraged ranchers and when they wouldn't swerve from their desire to kill Ferry, he rushed forward to the hospital. With the two irate men hard on his heels, Malcolm "stood in their way and told them not to come a step nearer."[9] Malcolm's wife grabbed their baby, Donald, and "ran out just as the men stopped and dismounted. She saw that both of them were white with rage and determined to do murder at any cost and she begged them not to start a fight"[10] with Malcolm. With his wife and child in the middle of the scene, Malcolm finally got through to the men that Ferry was already dying. They turned over their guns and went to the saloon for a drink.

In 1967 McNairy County, Tennessee, Pauline Pusser worried constantly, with good reason. It was she who discovered that after his first night driving the county, her husband had been shot. He later was shot four times in the face, arm, and abdomen by another man he attempted to arrest. "Pauline grew more fearful for her husband and his attempt to take on the criminals infesting the state line area of Tennessee and Mississippi. She sought consolation from the minister who conducted services for the prisoners. He remembered her saying 'I don't know what in the world I'd do if something happened to Buford. I don't think I could stand it.' "[11]

Women kept their fears from their husbands and children, even when there were very real reasons to be fearful. Not all of the emotions at the jailhouse fell in the realm of fear and worry. In the following chapter, stories revolve around a myriad of emotions.

18

An Unglamorous and Thankless Job

It pays to use a good cook book. More than one for small jails is not recommended. If the amateur cook attempts to use more than one cook book, it will lead to confusion.

—1961 *Handbook of Jail Food Service*

Dorothy Everson used to wake up decades after putting aside her county apron and report to her daughter that she'd had "that nightmare again." Thirty years after leaving the Boulder County, Colorado family quarters, Dorothy would tell Shirley "I had a nightmare last night. I dreamt I was cooking for the prisoners again."

—About Dorothy Everson who served alongside Sheriff Art Everson from 1943 to 1967, reported by daughter, Shirley.

Fear and worry were not the only emotions associated with living in the jailhouse. Dorothy Everson was not alone in reporting her nightmares of having to feed more prisoners. Helen Haugerud confessed that even today she dislikes grocery shopping after eight years of keeping her kitchen stocked. She found that getting groceries was the hardest part of the job. "I always had two heaping large grocery carts by the time I got finished."

Betty Vinson described to the author the family quarters with its sun porch and the long hallway that ended in the door to the jail through which food was delivered to the cells. She went on to describe how a friend of hers, a dietician, helped her to figure out healthy menus for three meals a day. When the author asked if Betty still had any of the menus or recipes, Betty sounded startled and then blurted out, "NO! I was glad to be rid of them!"

BURDENSOME

The burden of summer occurred each year in Fulton County, Indiana. Polly Clark and her sheriffing husband were "always tickled to death to see school start each fall because when school started, your work was cut in two." There wasn't enough for local children to do in the summer and kids got into all types of trouble until classrooms reined them back in again.

In Poweshiek County, Iowa, like many other places, the cells were often empty right after the summer session of court. It was at that time that Neva Allen's kids played in the cells. They were not allowed to sleep in the cells at night in case a prisoner came in unexpectedly, and they were never allowed to bring their friends in to play. Neva's daughter, Debby, recalled the hardship it was for her and her sisters to remember to answer the telephones correctly. "When it was evening and the bedroom phone rang, we had to answer 'sheriff's office' but if the kitchen phone rang, we had to answer 'Jail' which made for some interesting conversations when boys called us for dates. If one of us made a date in person and he asked how to get to our house, we'd ask if he knew where the jail was and he'd be surprised that he was to pick us up there."

Holidays could prove burdensome from more than the perspective of fixing a huge meal for family, visitors, and inmates. Max, Debby's father, worked holidays so his deputies could have the time with their families. That kindness would have been appreciated by Kossuth County, Iowa's Nancy Fitzpatrick who reported on the unhappy Christmas she and her preschooler, Laura, endured the December the family lived in when Tom served as deputy and jailor. "Tom was on call Christmas morning and a report came in of a robbery at a small tavern in the far north end of the county. He didn't get home until after 2 PM so Laura and I had Christmas pretty much without him. It was an unglamorous, thankless job. I wouldn't care to do it again."

WEIGHING IN

Fulton County, Indiana, Sheriff Roy Calvert once mused about the psychological edge one strove for as one emerged from the patrol car. "You had to stand tall. In fact, that's why we made it so important to wear a hat. If you got out of the car, you would tilt your hat back a bit and you stood as tall as you could—you looked about six foot five."[1] In stark contrast, sheriffs' wives were sometimes petite but still had to fill the boots of many a deputy as events dictated. Neil Haugerud wrote: "Helen, all 103 pounds of her, also performed the duties of a full-fledged deputy sheriff when needed—without pay, of course. In emergencies we enlisted her assistance as matron to frisk female prisoners and otherwise serve when transporting females."[2]

Neil and Helen reported on one of the nights when she functioned as deputy/matron. A female prisoner came in after Helen had gone to bed. When

Neil walked the woman into her cell, she tried to stab him with the sharp end of her steel rat-tail comb. Fortunately, the comb struck Neil's large belt buckle instead of his stomach. Realizing that he had a dangerous inmate on his hands despite her gender, Neil went to their bedroom and asked Helen to strip search the woman to make sure she had no other weapons. Helen asked Neil if he'd gone nuts. Did he really want her to strip search a "drunken wild woman who had just tried to stab him?"[3]

Neil did want exactly that, and somehow managed to talk Helen into getting out of bed and coming in to take care of the matter. With Neil just a step or two away, Helen conducted the search. Then she went back to bed. When Neil came in later after everything was secure and the paperwork had been finished, Helen told him never to ask her to do such a thing again.

TEAMWORK SATISFACTION

Under almost all other circumstances, Helen, like other jailhouse wives, saw herself as part of the sheriffing team and pitched in when needed. Deb Wood wrote of the relationship her parents, Don and Dell Gebers, shared: "My parents were a team here in Ida County [Iowa] for 28 years. Mom's life was the Sheriff's job. She could always be counted on to help with whatever, whenever. She made sure dad always looked good and she was never out front for the praise. I was extremely proud of both of them."

Like Deb Wood, Paulette Folkers recalled that her mother, Pauline "never was one to stand up and take a bow or to have someone applaud her. She just did her job and did it the best she knew how." While this described the wife of the sheriff in Chickasaw County, Iowa, it probably could be said of most Mrs. Sheriffs for over two hundred years in this nation with very few exceptions.

Agnes Schumaker's daughter, Peggy, noted that her parents made a great team: "She was a bold woman. He was a good sheriff. The combination of the two of them made him a better sheriff." Peggy reported that her father, Hilly, suffered from a lack of tact while Agnes "had tact to spare, could talk anyone into doing anything." Peggy also recalled how badly her parents felt decades after sheriffing when they learned that what they'd done for alcoholics essentially had enabled their drinking. Someone would come to the door drunk and ask to be put up for the night. Hilly would settle him in a cell and Agnes fixed him a meal. The family took care of the drunk until he could leave the jail on his own.

Annice Webb, daughter of Bart and Annie Gordon Broxson who served in Santa Rosa County, Florida, in the 1950s, recalled that "Mama could have been the general of an army. She directed our lives and our father's life. They both felt that there were 'his' and 'her' jobs. Her job was to take care of him, the house, and anything else that came across her plate. His job was to be the best sheriff, to rest, and to keep himself safe. Mama was often fearful for Daddy as he did not carry a gun. Daddy could not bear to see children hungry. Many times, if he saw a family with children out hitchhiking, he would pick them up, take them to the jail, [Momma would] feed them, he'd get them some money, and get them to their designated place in ways other than hitchhiking."

Husbands and wives formed sheriffing teams but only on rare occasions have both members of the team been celebrated. Maud Tanner's role was lauded by Ken Parker in his unpublished manuscript, *Making the News*. "No one who truly remembers Sheriff Tanner, however, can avoid recalling that his wife Maud was, in effect, elected to office with him, for the sheriff had to be absent a lot to perform his duties, and during those periods she became the voice and personality of the Tanner tenure.... One time I found the sheriff's reception room decorated with some rather striking art work. When I asked about it, Mrs. Tanner said that one of the prisoners had requested art materials, which she had supplied, and he had produced what I saw. She could have kept these works out of sight, but she was really proud of what the young man had done. I have sometimes wondered if her interest and sympathy might have been a turning point for that prisoner, and others, too."[4]

Compassion blended with common sense with most sheriffs' wives. Leila Pedersen's daughter, Marge, recalled the time in which her father brought in a woman who was the head of a chicken-thief operation. The woman's sons had been sent to prison. The judge gave their mother a ninety-day sentence. "She had such a hatred toward dad for wrecking her family business that she put a curse on him. She would not eat because, she said, the curse would not go into effect if she ate. Mother told her that liquids were not food. She lived on soups and juices the rest of the summer. It was a long, hot summer, and mother let her sit on the screen porch and crochet. She made a bedspread for mother."[5]

Teamwork was what made the county jail work. As revealed in previous chapters, it took not only the sheriff/husband and wife plus deputies, but children, parents and many community members to take care of inmates. During the early 1920s in Walworth County, Wisconsin, Ella Banks Wylie and her husband, Hal, served their community as a typical sheriffing team. They employed several deputies of both sexes to care for inmates. It was during 1923 when they all had a hand in the case of *The Poison Widow*. Myrtle Schaude had been caught trying to kill her four children with strychnine. She'd removed the crème centers from chocolates, replaced the centers with strychnine and gave them to her children just as they set out in the car for a ride in the country without her. The driver was Myrtle's oldest son. Anticipating that the chocolates would be gobbled down in one gulp, she'd left nothing to chance. If the poison didn't get them, Myrtle figured, wrecking the car would when her son lost his ability to drive.

As fate would have it, the plan didn't quite work and Sheriff Wylie brought Myrtle to the jail. She is reported to have remained hysterical for ten days. Her condition was described variously as a "stupor, coma, or extreme agitation"[6] depending on which newspaper one read. With the tender ministering of Ella Wylie and deputies Margaret McCarthy and Helen Harrison, two weeks into the ordeal Myrtle made a confession. This one was a humdinger. It was while Margaret was sitting with her that Myrtle began telling everything. Margaret listened and talked Myrtle into telling the entire thing to the sheriff. Myrtle agreed. Helen sat with Myrtle and Hal while the confession came out one more time.

Helen then testified at the trial. The confession started with Myrtle and her husband, their four children and one of their boarders, a young man named Ernst Kafahl. Ernst and Myrtle became lovers. During her confession, Myrtle implicated Ernst in the murder of Edward Schaude, Myrtle's husband. The year before, Edward had died, but no one suspected that it was of strychnine poisoning. Myrtle revealed that the idea had been masterminded by Ernst. Once they got away with that murder, Ernst moved out of the house and allegedly told Myrtle that he wanted her but not her children. She knew just what to do. And she did it.

After telling all of this to Helen and Hal, Myrtle told the authorities to arrest Ernst, and they did. Myrtle remained too fragile to go before the judge so Ella and Margaret nursed her for weeks. As a result, Ernst stood trial first. Ella walked Myrtle across the street on the day she was to testify and sat with Myrtle in the back of the courtroom until it was her turn. Despite all the evidence and testimony, Ernst was found not guilty.

At long last competent to stand trial in February of 1924, Myrtle's children attended and heard in complete detail what their mother had done. Myrtle was found guilty of killing their father and trying to kill them. Afterward, while Myrtle remained in her cell and permanent guardians were found to care for her children, Myrtle collapsed again "telling her woes to her steadfast companion, Mrs. Wylie."[7] When it came time to transfer Myrtle to Waupun to serve her sentence, Ella Wylie made the trip with her. The two women then corresponded. During her years of incarceration, Myrtle could always count on Ella Wylie to visit her when she and Hal brought a prisoner to Waupun.

On the other hand, compassion and friendship are not always the answer. There was another type of teamwork that sometimes proved effective. Ed Darrow reported the following story on his wife in their family memoirs: "Saturday night Mary Ann would often accompany me while I went on patrol in the county. In the event a country dance was scheduled, I would often put in an appearance to make sure all was going well. This particular evening, I had invited Bob and Pat Zaharko to accompany us. As we were riding around, I received a call from the office. The Special Deputy who was working the Hunter's Dance had called in and reported he had a problem. When we arrived at the Dance, I told Mary Ann and Pat to remain in the car. Bob and I went to find the Special Deputy. We found him in the restaurant, and he was quite badly beaten up. He told us there was a group of University students from Missoula causing trouble. He identified the ring leader as a smart aleck, a tough guy, in a body cast.

"Bob and I found the trouble makers. When I went to arrest the kid in the body cast, he took a swing at me. I knocked him down, then cuffed his hands behind his back. I then took him to the car." Ed described the kid as full of fight and spewing foul language. He ignored Ed when he was told to watch his language because there were ladies present. "I had to leave him in the car with Mary Ann and Pat, and he was basically helpless in the body cast and with his hands cuffed behind him. I returned to the restaurant which had been pretty well demolished during the fight before we got there. I had to get the names of those involved in the brawl."

Having accomplished all that he could do for the night, Ed and Bob returned to the car. "We found a much subdued young man speaking politely to Mary Ann." Ed couldn't believe it. He asked Mary Ann what had caused this transformation. Mary Ann replied "This knot head was talking terrible. I told him to shut his mouth. He wouldn't shut up, so I just reached down on the steering column, got your six cell flashlight, and hit him over the head with it. He looked kind of startled. I told him I didn't want to hear any more of that kind of language. He just looked at me and said 'Yes, ma'am.'"

Of course, not everyone on the receiving end of a jailhouse wife's irritation was someone under arrest. Sometimes the sheriff, himself, had the riot act read to him by the little woman while putting her dainty little foot down firmly. There are occasions when the repercussions of that stomp can last for generations. Such is the case of Pearl Boyd Buster of Boulder County, Colorado. Pearl and Sanford began their service to the county in 1912. One year when Sanford's birthday rolled around, Pearl bought him a comfortable chair for his office. Sanford thoughtlessly gave Pearl's gift to a prisoner who complained about the rickety old Windsor chair in his cell. When Pearl heard about the fate of her gift, she hit the roof. Pearl made Sanford use the rickety old Windsor chair at his desk instead of buying a replacement or taking back the comfy chair she'd given him.

That wasn't the end of it though. After serving as sheriff, Sanford went on to serve as assessor and county commissioner. He could have become the king of England for all Pearl cared. If he had, his throne would have been that wired up old chair from the jail cell. He used that rickety chair for the rest of his life.

When Sanford died, the chair was passed on to their oldest son, who used it as his own. The chair and the story were passed along to Louden Buster for use as his personal chair. It remains in the family today, in the possession of Louden's oldest son. It isn't used as much these days, but then again, it was old in 1912 or so. But it remains as a wonderful reminder of one of those "firm but loving" jailhouse wives and what could happen when one of them got riled.

Friends of the sheriffing families found themselves involved in the business of law enforcement from time to time. Martha Kinkade of Park County, Wyoming, reported on the time she and a friend drove to a neighboring state and while they were returning, "we were pulled over by a Highway Patrolman. He told us that they needed a woman prisoner returned to Cody. We thought we were lucky for not getting a speeding ticket. After thinking it over, we rather would have had a speeding ticket.

"My friend, a banker's wife, was very nervous, having never been around prisoners. Our prisoner bad mouthed the county attorney and the sheriff for the first half of the journey. She then asked how we were connected to the sheriff's office. Finding out that I was the sheriff's wife, we rode in silence the rest of the way home. Arriving in Cody, the banker and their four children were lined up waiting to see their mother bring home the prisoner."

WHAT'S IN A TITLE?

After the end of the era in which the sheriff's wife was known as Mrs. Sheriff, and the doctor's wife was no longer known as Mrs. Doctor, Maureen Elston recalled that she, like most other women, still "wasn't called by my name." It was "this is our sheriff's wife" with no name given, which emphasized her role over her individual self. Maureen longed for the time that has finally come in most parts of our country in which she would be introduced as "Maureen Elston, who is married to our sheriff."

Maureen was one of just a few of the participants in this research who attended the state sheriffs' conventions. She reported that "for me, it was a time of socializing with other wives of sheriffs and deputies and finding we all shared the same thoughts and problems. It was also a time of meeting the husbands of these women and seeing how they worked with each other to provide good law enforcement across the state."

A QUESTION OF COMPENSATION

For a hundred and fifty years, it was a rare woman who spoke out when asked to perform all of the responsibilities expected of a sheriff's wife for no pay. Tradition be hanged, grumbling commenced, and a modern era was born.

Madeline Coleman wrote about her term as sheriff's wife in Brown County, Nebraska, between 1975 and 1978: "My life as a sheriff's wife was not easy. I was the unpaid cook, never knowing if I had five or twenty five prisoners to feed. The prisoners ate what we did. We lived across from the jail and I took it over in plates or pots for them to eat. I was informed that this was part of my job and I was expected to do it.

"I would get up at four in the morning and start the day cooking. I made homemade bread and rolls. Long term prisoners told me what their favorite foods were and once a week it was on my menu. Many of our prisoners were younger and liked me for treating them well. I liked working with young people. I got my reserve deputy certification by traveling back and forth to Oneil two nights a week and spending a weekend now and then in physical training. After certification I was called a lot—also by the state patrol. Unpaid!!! Dale [her husband] said that the way it was—because I was his wife, the county wouldn't pay me. I told him I wouldn't do it anymore. After much arguing between us, he asked and they said they would pay me five dollars for one hour or ten [hours, a flat rate of $5 per incident]. Being a deputy, I took care of males and had access to the keys for lock up. Though I was good to the prisoners, they knew I meant business and could handle my own. I patrolled with the other deputies and did what any deputy would be expected to do. . . . "

Glenda Camelin of Boone County, Iowa, believed "it was asking too much for a sheriff's wife to assume all the duties with no pay and very little free time" in 1964. Mary Ann Darrow couldn't have agreed more. When she discovered, ten years earlier, all that she was expected to do for free, she visited the county commissioners. "I felt it was only right that when I had to act as jail matron I should receive the same compensation as a deputy. The Commissioners weren't too agreeable to this, but then they realized they would have to hire someone if the sheriff's wife refused to act in this capacity, they agreed to pay me a wage whenever there was a female or juvenile prisoner in the jail. We didn't pay rent or utilities at the jail and the grocery allowance helped our grocery bill so that was accepted as some compensation for my other duties."

Some sheriffs during the era of the mom-and-pop jail solved the pay-for-work problem by hiring their wives as deputies. WR Maynard in Collier County, Florida, did this in 1923. Collier county was 2,880 square miles and a lot of that fell within the Everglades. He rode the county and she kept the peace at home. In 1925, the Maynards became the proud parents of a bouncing baby boy. Not long after, a fist fight broke out on the streets of the county seat so Mrs. Maynard calmly passed her infant boy to a "startled bystander"[8] and stepped in to break up the fight.

A year later, Mrs. Maynard was again keeping the home fires burning while WR made his rounds. Three prisoners flooded the jail and stole the key during the excitement. All three of them ran off into the mangrove swamp. Because the break had occurred on her watch, Mrs. Maynard "donned her gun and holster, grabbed her toddler son, and took off after the men. At noon the next day, the threesome were spotted. Mrs. Maynard and her guide tracked two of the escapees to Dismal Key, eighteen miles from the jail. She found the third one sleeping on a raft not far away and drew her gun, persuading him to come on back to his cell. Thirty hours after the jailbreak, Mrs. Maynard [with toddler in tow] trotted those boys back to town, all of them hungry and bedraggled."[9]

It was not reported how much Sheriff Maynard paid his deputy wife for her services. As noted previously, there were some women who were paid to take over the work of their husbands when he could no longer hold office due to death or illness. In 1954 Bristol County, Rhode Island, Mary Nunes was named jailor and received a salary of $2,000. In addition, like all those who lived in, she was compensated by receiving light, heat, allowance for food and transportation plus 85 cents per day per prisoner for food. Mary often heard from former inmates who thanked her for her generosity and kindness. "To one sailor thrown into jail she remarked: 'well, the service don't want you and your family don't want you; I guess I'll have to be mother to you.'"[10]

RESPONDING TO THE WINDS OF CHANGE

Dode Jahnel had spent her teens helping her parents tend to inmates in the Mitchell County, Iowa, jail. Theirs was a family where everyone pitched in to feed prisoners and help in the sheriff's office. Dode married William Westendorf and he won election as sheriff of Bremer County, Iowa. By 1973, things were changing at many county jails. Modern professional law enforcement practices were replacing those of the mom-and-pop jails that had been in existence for nearly two hundred years. Dode found this change frustrating. She cooked for the prisoners but did not interact with them. She served as matron when needed and operated the radio after hours from her dining room. Although the family quarters were located in the courthouse, they were situated across the building from the sheriff's office. The jail cells were located above the sheriff's office.

Dode reported that it irked her the first few years of their tenure because her husband did not discuss his work with her. She'd grown up in a sheriffing family where everyone knew what was going on and were trusted to keep all matters confidential. So to suddenly be excluded from what was going on around the jail took some getting used to on Dode's part.

Down in Rogers County, Oklahoma, after World War II, Irene Ward helped her husband in the sheriff's office and was glad to do so. She noted that the jailor's wife "did all the cooking but did not get paid. Like me, she was just helping her husband with his job."[11] After the federal law went into effect "requiring sheriffs to have a jailor or dispatcher on duty all night to check the welfare of the prisoners on a regular basis, managing the jail was one jailor, his wife the matron, and three jailor/dispatchers, all female, who worked the night shift. They could handle the staying awake all night without much to do after midnight better than the men could."[12]

In county jails all over the country, in response to that federal law, the cost of running the place rose at a meteoric rate as trained professionals were paid to do what the sheriffs' families had done since before the American Revolution.

FOND MEMORIES

Gloria Peterka was once approached on the street by a local man who came up and announced that he'd just gotten out of jail. "My eyebrows raised in surprise! He told me 'your mom was so nice to me' and proceeded to sing her praises for all her kindness while he was in his cell." Gloria was so surprised because Christina only saw the prisoners when she took them their meals. But apparently, that was all that was needed for her to make quite an impact on at least one inmate.

Irene Ward recalled that when she and Amos went after their first out-of-state prisoner, they drove from Rogers County, Oklahoma, to Meeker, Colorado, to pick up "an older man with a long history of crime, but nothing violent."[13] The man was put in the backseat behind Irene who "sat sideways so I could see him and talk to him if he turned out to be a good traveling companion."[14] As it turned out, he was. He then stayed in the county jail until he was transferred to the penitentiary at McAlester. Irene went along on that ride also. "He seemed to like that. He said Amos treated him better than any of the many officers he'd come in contact with throughout the years and that we were both a good pair of kids."[15]

Madge Harris loved hearing compliments about her meals. Madge was lucky in that she loved to cook and it showed. She said that the compliments from the prisoners made the hard work worth it. She reported that when the new law enforcement center was built across the street, the jail and sheriff's office moved

Marian Edinger with her huge coffee pot preparing Thanksgiving meals in 1931 for inmates of the McHenry County, Illinois, jail. Sheriff Lester "Doc" Edinger (center) and Sylvester Muldoon stand over the dishes to be filled. (Photo courtesy of the McHenry County Historical Society.)

there. Madge did not cook for the inmates then. "Yes, I missed them. It was a lot of work and long hours, but I'd like to go back and do it all over again!"

Marian Edinger's octogenarian son, Richard, observed, "I imagine that becoming a sheriff's wife was a much greater challenge for my mother than becoming sheriff was for my dad. Most of the time in France during World War I, he'd been acting commander of his infantry company and was used to being in a position of authority. She had been married just over three years when she had to learn to plan menus, order the food and cook for, at one time, over seventy prisoners. Besides, she had a newborn baby and another who was 1½. She was subject to being awakened at any time during the night when dad had to respond to a call. Also, you have to keep in mind that she did not have a refrigerator, although she did have a large icebox, and she did not have an automatic washing machine. I am beginning to appreciate my mother even more than I did. Thanks for making me think about this."

By this time we've explored pretty much every aspect of the mom-and-pop jail except how their service ended. For most, their tenure ended quietly and the family went on with life. For others, it ended in death. In the following two chapters we will see how jailhouse wives lost their lives and how others pinned the badge on their county apron and carried on when their husbands fell.

—19—

'Til Death Do Us Part

Jail Matrons' Memorial[1]
Anna Hart, Matron
Hamilton County, Ohio
Died June 24, 1916
Served for six years
Anna was beaten to death by Reuben Ellis during an escape attempt while he awaited trial for burglary. He was convicted and executed seven months later.

Kassie Mae Chandler, Matron
Dallas County, Texas
Died December 14, 1948
Kassie was beaten by two female inmates in an escape attempt, she died ten hours later. The names of the juvenile perpetrators were not released.

Phyllis M. Myers, Matron
Niagara County, New York
Died June 15, 1970
On her last day of work after a 27-year career, Phyllis was fatally beaten by inmates during an escape. Three women were charged but only one was convicted of first degree manslaughter. She served twelve years and then was paroled.

The matrons listed above were paid professionals who died in the line of duty. They performed the duties of jail matron at the time of their deaths, a job we have identified as a major responsibility of the jailhouse wife wherever there was a mom-and-pop jail. No one expected the jail matron, paid or unpaid, to die while serving.

For most Mrs. Sheriffs and other women of their era, death most often came about due to complications of childbirth or an illness. However, the deaths of the following women came about because they were married to the sheriff, or, in the case of Mary Ramsey, death was hastened by the loss of her sheriffing husband in the line of duty.

PAULINE PUSSER

Perhaps the most well-known case involving the death of a sheriff's wife is that of Pauline Milligan Pusser of McNairy County, Tennessee. Pauline has been identified throughout this book as a woman who worried, with justification, about the safety of her husband as he attempted to clean up his county after decades of corruption. Several books have been written and movies have been made about her husband, Buford.

Because of her fears for Buford's safety, Pauline took the call with him when the phone rang at 4:30 a.m. on August 12, 1967. They were called out to investigate a report of "serious trouble along the state line."[2] With Pauline riding shotgun, they headed for the site.

As local farmers milked their cows and fed their stock, the dawn of a day that Pauline would never see colored the horizon as a car pulled up behind Buford's Plymouth. The car sped up and moved alongside. A bullet shattered the driver's side window. It missed Buford and struck Pauline in the head. Buford stomped hard on the gas pedal to outrun the gunmen. Thinking that the car had not followed, Buford stopped a couple of miles down the road to see what he could do for his wife. Buford assumed incorrectly and the assassins "riddled the car at point-blank range,"[3] seriously injuring the sheriff. The same hail of bullets also found their mark on the far side of the car as another round shattered Pauline's skull. She died immediately.

The assailants assumed both husband and wife were dead and drove away. Buford somehow managed to drive to a gas station to use the phone. He called his father at the jail. The elder Pusser recognized his son's voice, made out only a few syllables of what Buford was trying to say, but it was enough to send help to his son. Pauline's lifeless body was found in the front seat of the family car. Beside her, and barely alive himself, lay Buford.

EILEEN GEWECKE

At 2:00 a.m. on January 8, 1961, in the charming county seat of Holdredge, Nebraska, Frank S. sighted down the barrel of his rifle and squeezed off seven rounds into the front bedroom of the home he believed to be owned by Phelps County Sheriff Wilbur Gewecke. The bullets came in low through the window, plowed through the back of the closet and embedded themselves in the far wall of the hallway. The home did not belong to the Gewecke family but to Jim and Dee Van Marter.

Somehow, Dee found the presence of mind to show her young children how to belly crawl down the hallway to avoid being hit. She followed suit and hid with the children in the basement. Jim, not thinking clearly because bullets were flying through his house, intended to go out the front door and confront the shooter. If he had, Frank would have taken him for the sheriff in the dark and killed him. Fortunately, as he reached for the front door knob, Jim noticed that the family dog was barking at the side door. That diverted him from his plan. By the time Jim got out the side door and around to the front, Frank had gone. Very quickly, Sheriff Gewecke arrived on the scene as he lived next door.

By the following evening evidence had led to the identity of the shooter and his motive. Eileen Gewecke, in a highly nervous state, sat home alone with her three young children. The phone rang. According to Wilbur, "I was out following some leads on the shooting and the man called my wife and informed her that he had killed me, and was coming to our house to kill her and the three kids."[4] When Wilbur returned home, he found Eileen "lying dead of a heart attack in the hallway and the phone torn off the wall."[5] Eileen had not previously suffered from a heart condition. She was only twenty-six years old.

What had brought on such a series of events? They were several months in the making. Maxine, the mother of twin teenage boys, had been living with Frank S., a self-described trapper and construction worker. When Maxine's boys stole a pickup truck and wrecked it, Wilbur donned the hat of social worker and began making weekly visits to check on the boys. For several months, Wilbur told Maxine that Frank was a bad influence on her sons. Unfortunately, all that accomplished was that Frank would leave when he saw Wilbur drive up. Maxine began lying about Frank having moved out but Wilbur found evidence to the contrary. He finally gave Maxine an ultimatum that if she didn't get rid of Frank for the sake of her boys, then he (the sheriff) would have her welfare money discontinued. Nobody messed with Frank's free ride on Maxine's welfare check, so the sheriff needed to be eliminated.

Frank S. was caught because he'd asked around about where the sheriff lived instead of looking him up in the phone book. Someone told him "the corner of Ninth and Tibbals next to the vacant lot." Unfortunately, there were two houses that matched the description. Frank shot up the wrong one and then frightened Eileen Gewecke to death the next evening.

Both Frank and Maxine served time for the shooting, he for actually firing the rifle, and she for aiding and abetting. It was Maxine who cruised the Gewecke's neighborhood in the middle of the night, trying to find Frank to take him home. One of her twins moved away from the area and the other slowly drank himself to death while living in squalor. Ironically, Dee and Jim Van Marter provided him with meals-on-wheels during the last few years of his life. It wasn't until the author interviewed the Van Marters that Dee realized who the recipient of her kindness had been.

PAM JONES

In 1991, as Pam enjoyed the Jones family Christmas party taking place in her home in Moniteau County, Missouri, bullets from a .22 rifle ripped through the front window, spraying those who celebrated the birth of the King of Peace. Sheriff

Jones' wife died in front of her children and in-laws, the victim of five of those rounds. The shooter was soon captured but not before he'd wreaked havoc upon the county seat.

The triggerman turned out to be a local fellow who, after an intense argument with his wife and daughter, indulged in a killing spree. Earlier that day, Deputy Les Roark took the domestic disturbance call at the home of James Johnson. Roark satisfied himself that Mrs. Johnson and her daughter were fine and then started back to his car. James Johnson "stepped outside and shot the deputy twice."[6] Johnson returned to the house, "but when he heard Roark moaning, he went back outside and shot him in the forehead, killing him."[7] Johnson, heavily armed and leaving his terrified family behind, drove to the home of Sheriff Kenny Jones where the Jones family Christmas party was taking place.

During the ensuing chaos after the shootings at the Jones' house, Johnson drove to the home of Deputy Sheriff Russell Borts. Johnson shot Borts four times while he was speaking on the phone. Fortunately, Borts survived. Johnson slipped away again and this time, positioned himself outside of the sheriff's office where law enforcement from several counties were gathering. While they met inside to plan how to capture Johnson while waiting for others to join them, they had no way of knowing that he lay in wait outside for them. That is, until he opened fire on Cooper County Sheriff Charles Smith. Moments later, Miller County Deputy Sandra Wilson arrived and was killed.

Johnson then fled the scene and took a woman hostage for most of the next day while authorities combed the area. That evening, he inexplicably allowed his hostage to attend a Christmas party. She'd managed to convince him that as she was expected, he wouldn't want anyone to come looking for her only to find him. The woman left home and immediately contacted authorities. Surrounding her home, they talked Johnson into surrendering. Johnson was tried, found guilty and executed eight years and one month later.

MARY RAMSEY

On June 7, 1875, Ellis County, Kansas, sheriff, Alexander Ramsey, was killed in a shoot-out in Rook County after trailing horse thieves with his deputy. Although quite ill with consumption, Mary insisted that she be taken to meet her husband's body as it was being brought back to Hays. Dr. O'Brien relented and drove Mary onto the prairie where they did meet the woeful group escorting her husband's body. As a result, the already ill Mary "was driven crazy by the sad death of her husband."[8] Dr. O'Brien determined that there was no hope for improvement of Mary's mental or physical condition so he put her on the train for Leavenworth. There she was taken in by the Sisters of Charity who nursed her until the middle of June, when she died.

The vow that ends with " 'til death do us part" works both ways, and more often than not, when one partner in the sheriffing team died, it was the husband. What then did a widow do to care for her family? The following are stories of how women kept a roof over their family's heads when their husbands died while sheriff.

ELIZABETH HAWLEY

In 1801 Albany County, New York, County Jailor Nathan Hawley died several years into his tenure. His wife and nine children were allowed to continue living in the home provided by the county. Elizabeth ran the house as an inn for five years, turning it into the county hotel. As in other places around the country, lawyers, judges, jurors, and lawmen in town on court business boarded at the Hawley's, enabling Elizabeth to keep her children fed.

MILDRED LUCAS

After Independence Day in 1884, Mildred and her jailor husband, William, tried to hold off a mob hell-bent on a lynching in Daviess County, Kentucky. In the melee that followed, William was killed as he stood fighting alongside his wife and son, and the inmate was lynched. The powers that be then appointed Mildred to serve out the term of her husband. At the next election, Mildred ran for the office in her own right and won by nearly 1,500 votes, all from male citizens as this was the time before women had the right to vote. No sooner had the ballots been counted than the defeated opponent filed a lawsuit. His position stated that since women did not have the right to vote, they did not have the right to hold elected office. Mildred fought the case all the way to the Kentucky Supreme Court where she lost. But the legal wrangling took sixteen months "and Mildred more than adequately fulfilled her responsibilities as County Jailor during that time."[9]

MAYBEL SIMPSON

Maybel Simpson in Lincoln County, Oregon, served alongside her husband near the end of the nineteenth century as his deputy in charge of the tax collection department. He died in office and she was appointed to replace him. With Ted McElwain as her deputy, she served out her husband's term. She was noted as being "thoroughly capable of handling the administrative affairs of the office"[10] and Ted possessed "a cool head in the face of danger."[11]

EMMA RICKER

Charlie Woodward shot and then bludgeoned to death Sheriff Charles Ricker not long after he took up the badge at the beginning of 1902 in Natrona County, Wyoming. The citizens felt a tremendous responsibility toward Emma and her four children because Charles had died in the line of duty. The citizens of the community took up a collection and built his widow and her children a home near the jail. Even after she remarried many years later, Emma continued to live in the house provided by her fellow citizens.

ROSE SINGLER

In stark contrast to the compassion of Emma Ricker's neighbors, there are a couple of stories about murdered sheriffs' families who did not share in such a kindness. The one who lacked compassion toward the dead sheriffs' families was not always just a fellow citizen. In the case of Rose Singler, he was a family member.

August Singler, the man who included all of his children in his election postcard photograph in 1912, was killed four months after taking office. The previous Jackson County, Oregon, sheriff had suffered a pistol whipping by a local tough named Lester Jones, who then fled the county. August heard that the Jones boy had returned and was declaring that he'd never be taken alive. Much like the fearful folks in *High Noon*, the citizens of Jackson County turned their backs on August. He could find no one to form a posse. Not to be deterred, he went after the nineteen-year-old himself. The sheriff "had his gun drawn and was wearing a heavy cotton chest pad for protection."[12] But the vest did no good as Lester shot August from the side as he entered the cabin. "When he fell to the floor, August opened fire on Lester and all six bullets hit their mark." August was found still alive and conscious. He died the following day after preparing a will and telling his wife and eight children good-bye.

August's brother, William, was asked to take over the office of sheriff with the understanding that he would provide for Rose and her children from his county pay. William, not being married, would employ Rose as his cook and matron. William came to Rose with a proposal; literally, a proposal of marriage. She told her children later that she turned him down because she did not love him, but more importantly, because he didn't particularly like children and she had eight ranging in age from thirteen years to eight months. William reneged on the agreement he made with the county. No wedding, no money.

Rose and the kids, however, continued living behind the jail and cooking for the prisoners. Out of a sense of responsibility toward the family after August lost his life, the county paid Rose 35 cents per meal per prisoner and a stipend of $65 each month. After one year, that stipend was withdrawn, leaving times lean for the nine Singlers. The older children worked at whatever jobs they could find, from boxing groceries to picking fruit in the local orchards.

When there were a lot of prisoners to feed, Rose managed pretty well at the standard 35 cents per meal. But when there were only a few, her income dropped to nearly nothing and the family experienced lean times.

To add to Rose's worries, some of the women of the community began a campaign to break up the large family. They thought nothing of coming to see Rose to try to convince her that it was in her children's best interest to be placed with other families as Rose was not going to be able to provide for them. Her daughter, Zita, recalled that her mother "grew to hate the sound of someone at the door, fearing that they had come to take her children. I remember I used to hang under her skirts and peek around when they were talking to her. And she'd be crying so I'd be crying."[13]

By 1919, Rose felt that cooking for even several inmates for 35 cents per meal was inadequate, given the rate of inflation. She approached the county commissioners and requested that the rate per meal be increased to 50 cents. They refused. Six months later, she made her request again. Again they refused. The next day, Rose packed up her household and family and moved back to Medford. She took a job at a local dry-cleaning establishment and worked there for twenty years, having kept her family together.

But this is not quite the end of the Jackson County, Oregon, story. Zita reported that with Rose out of the picture, the county commissioners were unable to find anyone to take over cooking for the jail even when they offered the job at the 50 cents per meal they'd refused to Rose. "Finally, the current sheriff's wife had to and she was mad to think that she had to cook for the prisoners. If she didn't feel like cooking, she would just send bread and water. She sometimes did this twice a day."[14]

EMMA BANISTER

In Coleman County, Texas, in 1916, Emma Banister cared for her husband for two weeks after he was struck over the heart by a blacksmith's fist while trying to break up a fight at a carnival. During that time, Emma "kept the deputies doing the routine chores of the office."[15] Two years later, John suffered a massive heart attack and died. The county fathers appointed Emma to fill out his term.

"Mama ran the office well, sending the deputies out to patrol each night, handling the drunks and the gamblers just as Papa would have done. . . . By day she was in her office, answering mail, directing the deputies and the handling of prisoners, replying to inquiries. At night she sent the deputies where they were needed, and she kept the sheriff's and jail records, made menus for the meals, ran our household."[16]

CLARA CROWELL

Clara Dunham Crowell's husband, George, ran for Lander County sheriff in Nevada but lost in 1908 and again in 1912. In 1916, his campaigning paid off and the Crowells took up their duties at the start of 1917. They swore in Thomas White as their deputy. When the 1918 elections rolled around, George proved successful once again but fell ill. He required medical treatment in California so Clara accompanied him. Deputy White held down the fort. By the end of February, George was dead from his illness. The citizens of the county circulated a petition proposing that Clara take up the badge. On March 6, 1919, Clara was sworn in.

MARY MITTEN

A very similar scenario played out in Pennsylvania just a few years later. A former school teacher, married to a teacher who ran for Bradford County sheriff in

1923, helped her hubby with his duties. Fred and Mary Morrow Mitten served for nearly two full years. In the autumn of 1925, Fred became ill and died. "Hundreds of Bradford Countians signed petitions demanding that Mary be appointed to complete her husband's term of office. Pennsylvania Governor Gifford Pinchot was impressed, and his letter offering her the appointment clinched the deal. Mary Morrow Mitten was sworn in as Bradford County Sheriff on Oct 24, 1925, the first woman sheriff in Bradford County and in Pennsylvania. She was fifty-two years of age. Mary did not wallow in her grief but actively worked to help her fellow citizens and to uphold the law. Although she opted not to run for re-election in 1928, she took over as the County Probation Officer, a position she held for ten years until her death. Mary Morrow Mitten 'equaled, if not exceeded her husband in the hearts and minds of their fellow Bradford Countians.'"[17]

MAUDE COLLINS

When her husband of eleven years was killed in the line of duty on October 8, 1925, Maude Collins buried him and began packing the belongings of her family of five children, preparing to leave the jailhouse for the next couple to fill out Fletcher's term. The commissioners of Vinton County, Ohio, arrived at her door with a commission for sheriff in hand and asked "What's your hurry, Maude?"[18]

The young mother and jail matron accepted the commission and endured the first month of her service while the trial of her husband's killer was held. She filled the remainder of Fletcher's term and proved a capable sheriff. So much so that when election time rolled around and "Sheriff Maude" ran for her own term of office, the voters cast twice as many votes for Maude than her opponent.

Sheriff Maude gained nationwide celebrity when her attention to detail broke a case. Following clues in a murder, Maude realized that the footprints at the site didn't quite sit right with her. The footprints appeared to belong to the murdered man but they didn't appear to be made by a man as heavy as the deceased. Maude put on the shoes and walked beside the existing footprints and it became obvious that someone of her own physical stature had tried to lead suspicion away from herself by making the prints. Maude and her deputy had one suspect who fit that description. The woman confessed the next day and served a life sentence for first degree murder.

When her term of office ended, Maude ran for Clerk of the Courts and won. She was enrolled in the Ohio Women's Hall of Fame in 2000. The newspaper article announcing this honor was appropriately titled "She traded her apron for a badge."[19]

HELENA DOLDER

During Prohibition, Helena Dolder's jail took in some of the excess number of bootleggers that overflowed the Cook County Jail in Chicago. As a result, she always had a full house to provide for as cook and matron. When her husband died in 1928, Helena pinned the badge on her county apron in DeKalb County, Illinois. It is reported that she tended to as many as a hundred prisoners at one time. Her son, Fritz, served as her chief deputy and slept in the jailor's room. To spruce that room up a little, Sheriff Dolder "fashioned lace curtains for his windows which, of course, could be seen from the street. Her jail became known as 'the lace curtain jail.'"[20]

The first night that Helena was on the job, she was tested by that full house of inmates. She served them cornmeal mush and like our friends in Texas who didn't care for boiled mustard greens, the mush caused a riot. She told them to eat or go hungry. That made them even madder. She ordered them back to their cells. They wanted to know who was going to make them go back to their cells. Helena "picked up the fire hose and flattened the prisoners against the wall with the strong water spray."[21] They did not question her authority again and the following evening they were served the same mush, which they ate with no argument. Sheriff Helena Dolder epitomized that double life these families lived: putting up lace curtains and putting down jail riots.

LOLLIE JANE GUM

As we have seen with Rose Singler, not every county was grateful for the sacrifices made by the sheriff and his family, even after he died while performing his duties. Incoming sheriff's have been known to put the grieving widow and her children out of the jailhouse, despite promises to do otherwise. This is exactly what happened to Lollie Jane Gum.

At the same time that Natrona County was building a home for Emma Ricker in Wyoming, the citizens of Bath County, Virginia, welcomed their new sheriff, Charles Gum, who took up his badge and served Bath County well for twenty-seven years. He and his wife, Lollie Jane, tended to the needs of the inmates and of their fellow citizens while raising four children in the family quarters. In December of 1929, Charles was killed while attempting "to arrest a man and his son for beating up a patron of a roadhouse."[22]

Charlie had deputized his son, Warren, and the owner of the roadhouse to help make the arrest in the middle of the night. "They went to the home where the suspects were thought to be holed up and that was where the shoot-out took place. The sheriff shot the older suspect and then was killed by the younger. The deputized roadhouse owner severely wounded the younger suspect."[23]

Lucille Gum, eleven years old when her father died, had been born and raised in the family quarters. "My brother, Warren, went with me to feed the chickens that next morning, and that's when he told me my Daddy was dead. Things were never the same after that, no they were not."[24]

Judge Anderson arranged that Lollie Jane and her children could continue living in the jailhouse for the remainder of Charlie's term. When the judge died shortly thereafter, the deputy who had been appointed to fill Charlie's term "put us out," reported Lucille. There was no hue and cry from the citizens when this took place. Lollie Jane bought a small home for herself and the children with the family savings.

PEARL HOBBS

Pearl Hobbs in Moore County, Tennessee, finished Oliver's term when he passed away from a heart attack on May 29, 1932. Her chief deputy, as with Oliver, was her son, Lacy. He and his family lived in the jailhouse during the term filled by Oliver and then Pearl.

Pearl "had to continue cooking for prisoners and cleaning the jail. As there were not many prisoners in the jail, this was not a daily job, unless there was a prisoner spending the night. When the Circuit Court Judge, RW Smart, was holding quarterly court in town, he usually came for the noon meal but generally, court only lasted for one day so he was not eating at the jail very often."

SARAH JONES

In Christian County, Missouri, Frank and Sarah Tucker Jones took up their county badge and apron on January 1, 1933. On Friday, the 13th of January, four inmates dug their way out of their cells and escaped. This put into effect a chain of events that resulted in the death of Sheriff Jones. On the evening of April 6, Frank and Sarah visited with friends and Frank decided he needed to drive over to the jail just to look in on the current inmates. He felt a bit skittish about not watching them after the recent escape. It was decided that Sarah would continue her visit and Frank would return in a few minutes. "His car slid on loose gravel at a curve and crashed into the end of a culvert. The impact flipped his 1932 Ford Sedan over as it landed in a field."[25] The injuries Frank suffered finally killed him on May 25.

Between the time of the accident and the day he died, Sarah and her daughter, Estia, ran the office and made decisions on Frank's behalf. But this was on an unofficial basis. When it came time to conduct the County Tax Land Sale on May 22, the sheriff was still incapacitated so the Sale was postponed. When Frank died, the county court met the next day to appoint Sarah as the acting sheriff until a special election could be held in a month. The local leaders of the Democrat party did not include Sarah's name on the ballot. As a result, "Estia Jones wrote an open letter in the Christian County Republican" and told the county that "I take this opportunity of making a clear statement as regards the feeling which my family and I have. Personally, either mother or myself would have gladly accepted the Democratic nomination for this office and owing to the unexpected expense of my father's accident and his lingering illness, we personally feel that we were entitled to the same."[26]

FLORENCE THOMPSON

Fifty years after controversial Mildred Lucas accepted the commission of jailor in Daviess County, Kentucky, Florence Thompson took up the sheriff's badge. Flo wasn't even able to bury her husband before taking over his job because Kentucky's law didn't allow deputies to act if there was no sitting sheriff. Everett Thompson had died of pneumonia leaving Flo with four children to raise. Pinning on the star was one way to keep a roof over their heads.

By 1936, unlike the half-century before when Mildred Lucas stirred things up, "it was not confoundedly uncommon for a woman to be asked to fulfill the unexpired political term of her deceased husband. Some observers recall that no one really thought that much about it. After all, the family of a politician had to contribute a great deal of time and energy, and sometimes make financial sacrifices in order for the head of the household to get elected. It was understandable, then, that the elected man's widow should rightfully take over."[27] It is reported that Florence refrained from donning a uniform, but she pinned her badge to her dress. She left arrests to her deputies unless they were all out on business.

JOSIE ROGERS

Like Leona Banister in Texas, Josie Mae Rogers worked beside her father in Evans County, Georgia, twenty years later. In 1940, she "filled the unexpired term of her father, Jessie C. Durrance. It was noted that she carried her Smith & Wesson in her purse and not on her hip because she wasn't interested in dramatics."[28] When her father's term was up, Josie Mae ran for and won election to the office of sheriff in her own right, and became the first elected female sheriff in Georgia.

LASSIE BALDREE

Lassie Baldree learned that her husband was killed in the line of duty in November of 1945 in Sumter County, Florida. Her brother served as interim sheriff until after the funeral when Lassie took up the badge. Like Josie Rogers, Lassie didn't wear a gun in a holster on her hip but carried one when needed. Her mother moved in to help with the children and tend to inmates. At next election for sheriff, Lassie ran and won, serving three additional years.

MARTHA BULMAN

Not every widow was prepared to step in for their husbands. Martha Bulman's daughter reported that "father and mother served terms from 1928 to 1932 [in Allamakee County, Iowa] and again in the 1940s. He was killed on January 9, 1946. Dad was shot by an inebriated man while making an arrest in Postville. Mother was appointed to finish dad's term in office but that evening there was a robbery downtown. My mother had never shot a gun and didn't feel like having to tote a gun so she wrote a resignation thanking them for the consideration."

Death was not the only reason women took up the badge. We will explore various scenarios in which jailhouse wives chose to serve as sheriff. Like their jailhouse sisters above, most pinned the badge on their county apron and continued doing what they'd always done.

20

The Final Chapter

> It pays to garnish food trays with a little parsley, curly kale leaves, or a small amount of colorful salad. Remember that inexpensive food is inexpensive only when it is consumed. The garbage can does not need nourishment but often becomes the best fed inmate of the jail.
>
> —1961 *Handbook of Jail Food Service*

> The summer of 1941, Roy and Erma decided it would be a good thing for him to run for sheriff of Schuyler County, Illinois. They campaigned and when the votes were counted in November, Roy won. He and Erma would move into the Victorian Schuyler County jail family quarters come the first of the year.
>
> On December 7, 1941, the Japanese bombed Pearl Harbor. The entire world changed. Roy enlisted and Erma accepted appointment as sheriff of Schuyler County. She performed all of the duties of both sheriff and sheriff's wife until Roy returned from the service in 1945. He pinned on the badge and filled out his term.
>
> —About Erma Schieferdecker who served alongside and on behalf of Sheriff Roy Schieferdecker, 1942–1946.

In sharp contrast to the women who not only served their counties as matron, cook, etc., but also as sheriff when the situation dictated, there were others who could not tolerate the life, or just got worn down by it.

When Sophie Poe's husband, John, served as sheriff of Lincoln County, New Mexico, in 1883, the territory he patrolled was huge and mostly unpopulated. Nick Aragon, convicted of murder and awaiting transfer to the penitentiary, proved to be an exemplary inmate, so when he volunteered to help with meal preparation, John and the jailor agreed. Nick was kept shackled at all times but he managed to saw through the chain on his shackles and escape. Two months later, one of John's deputies found Nick and in the shoot-out that followed, the deputy was killed and Nick continued running.

In December, John told Sophie that he thought it would be a good idea for her to pack up her things and go for a visit with their old friend, Captain Lea and family at Roswell. John had a lot of work to do and it was almost Christmas, so this way Sophie could start the season pleasantly and he'd join her in time to enjoy Christmas Eve with all of them. It sounded like a good idea, so Sophie did just that.

What Sophie didn't know was that Nick Aragon had been located and John meant to get him or die trying. The sheriff and his deputies developed a plan for taking the murderer and put it into motion. During the fight that ensued, one other deputy lost his life but everyone else, including John, survived. Word reached Captain Lea's home and Sophie learned of her husband's activities at that time. When he rode in to the Lea place, Sophie recorded that "I clung to him frantically, crying on his shoulder and begged him to give up his office of sheriff. John William petted me and promised that he would soon do as I wished."[1]

Some women lobbied to get out of the situation they found themselves in behind the jailhouse door. In Jackson County, Missouri, in 1886, Joe and Lydia Potts moved their sons into the family quarters. For ten years previous, one jailor had served the county. However, after but one year on the job, Lydia talked Joe into quitting. She didn't think it was any place to raise her boys, and she said she was "born and raised in the country and I don't think this is any place for me."[2]

In 1958, Ed Darrow decided not to run for sheriff of Powell County, Montana, again. In their family memoirs, Ed wrote "After much discussion with Mary Ann, we decided we did not want to raise our family in the atmosphere of the jail. Barry would be eight years old in June and Coleen six years in September. They were nearing an impressionable age. Also, we were expecting another baby."

"I was so relieved to be moving out of the jail, I jumped for joy!" Mary Ann added. "This turning point in our lives couldn't have come at a better time. I had begun to really hate the position I was in. The constant ringing of the telephone day and night was hard to live with. Life wasn't normal going for a ride in the car because of the constant squawk of the police radio. I couldn't believe we would soon be living the life of a normal family. We would no longer be living in a glass house. Our life would now be our own and not the business of the entire county. I couldn't wait to live in a real house again. I looked forward to being able to go to a dance and not have the whole room shush because the Sheriff and his wife had just walked in. It was going to be a real treat to have weekends off! I would no longer have to wonder when I got up in the morning if I would have other than my own family or fifteen extra people for which to prepare meals."

In 1966, in Sawyer County, Wisconsin, Delores Lein won election to the office of sheriff to hold the position in the family until her husband, Ernie, could run again. He returned to the office after Delores tried to talk him out of running again. All of their kids were grown and out of the family quarters and Delores "couldn't see continuing as an unpaid jail assistant."[3] She wanted to find a job that paid her for her time and talents. Delores was not as persuasive as Sophie Poe and Mary Ann Darrow, so Ernie ran again. Delores, however, was successful at finding herself a paying job. She went to work for the Chamber of Commerce.

WE ARE RESIGNED TO RESIGNING

Sophie Poe's husband did not wait until the end of his last term to put down the badge. A business opportunity came up in South America that couldn't be ignored, so John sent in his letter of resignation. Another couple of the same era, Jim and Linda Scott of Apache County, Arizona, did likewise. While Jim served as sheriff in the 1890s, Apache County citizens voted to divide their county in two. The new entity became known as Navajo County. In 1896, Jim put his name on the ballot to run for treasurer of Navajo County while still fulfilling his duties as sheriff and tax assessor for Apache County. Jim won that election in November and resigned as sheriff directly afterward.

As their neighbors bid them a fond farewell at the end of the year, the newspaper printed the following: "The society of St. Johns will suffer a severe loss when Lady Linda Scott leaves us. Her pleasant face and congenial spirit always made a visit to the house of Sheriff Scott a delightful remembrance. Wherever her lot may be cast, our best wishes attend her."[4]

SHERIFF JUST UP AND RAN AWAY

Sheriffs who did not resign before leaving office left their wives in a less enviable position in the community. Such was the case of JG and Kate Weakley.[5] In the summer of 1875, when JG was thirty-eight years old, he was approached by the Republican party to run for sheriff. Kate's brother-in-law, George Smyser, agreed to run for county treasurer. Both men won their elections and the sisters packed up their households and moved into Russell City, a town of 400 situated ten miles west of the Weakley homestead. Russell City, like the rest of the county, stood on the verge of an inrushing of emigrants and immigrants from back east, from Russia and Germany.

Kate took up her responsibilities as jail matron, housekeeper, cook, and sheriff's helpmate while she was pregnant with their fifth child, Emma Jane. As JG was both sheriff and town marshal, he supervised two jails, two sets of deputies and three sets of prisoners as his county jail also held those awaiting trial in the federal district court which met in Russell City on a quarterly basis. Kate fed them all and matroned for those who needed it.

In the winter of 1879, a stranger calling himself ML Stanley arrived in Russell and brandished about a check made out for $9,800 drawn on the First National Bank of Leavenworth, Kansas. Stanley talked several merchants into providing him with supplies, promising to pay them as soon as he found time to mosey over to the Russell Bank and have his funds transferred. Then Stanley skipped with the goods.

It was learned however, that slippery Mr. Stanley might be going under the alias of Leon Belmont. In February, word arrived that Stanley alias Belmont was being held in Anthony, Kansas, so JG rode down to get him and brought his man to the Russell jail. Stanley was forced to sit in jail, enjoying Kate's three meals a day, until the next session of the federal district court when it commenced in April. Or not.

On March 18, 1879, JG borrowed a spring buckboard pulled by a team of excellent horses from Hendershot and Fargo's livery stable. Kate packed his belongings for the long trip down to the Indian Territory. JG informed everyone that he was off to collect another wanted man and bid his wife and children farewell.

When Sheriff JG Weakley pulled out of Russell, he had with him the delinquent tax money he'd collected on behalf of the county, fines paid to him by those who lost cases in the federal district court, and ML Stanley alias Leon Belmont, who, it turned out, was a woman dressed as a man.

It took five days for the "eloping" pair to make it as far south as Medicine Lodge. JG introduced himself as the Russell County sheriff. He also introduced Stanley as a Pinkerton Detective. Meanwhile, the unsuspecting Kate waited for her husband at their home in Russell for three weeks, at which time she learned the true story of what had transpired from county officials. She immediately packed up her family of six children, the youngest born the year before, and moved back to the homestead.

JG Weakley wasn't the only cad among sheriffs. Sheriff Richard Hanes, his wife of many years and their numerous children welcomed to the Muskingum County, Ohio, jail a woman named Frankie Wise in 1883. Frankie had been charged with adultery with a married man. While she remained behind bars, Frankie's husband divorced her. Frankie, however, didn't miss him all that much as she served her six-month sentence getting to know Sheriff Hanes—in the biblical sense of the word "know."

A wealthy man of standing in the community, Sheriff Hanes was so smitten with Mrs. Wise that when she was no longer close at hand in his jail, he purchased a home in her name "and lavished a savings of years on her"[6] to fuel the affair. He retired from serving as sheriff and started his own business to try to keep both his family and his mistress fed, clothed, and in the latter's case, bejeweled. Frankie apparently had expensive taste.

By the end of the winter of 1888, Richard Hanes reached the end of his financial tether, faulted on a $30,000 loan, "and the woman dropped him."[7] The stress of losing everything including his mistress of five years drove Richard over the edge within a month. On the night of March 4, 1888, he rode to Frankie's home that he'd purchased, "placed a revolver against her breast and fired. The bullet struck a gold watch, one of his gifts to her, and turned aside, making a bad flesh wound."[8]

Hanes escaped from the home, leaving Frankie with a serious flesh wound from which she was expected to recover at the time of the newspaper report. It is not clear what happened to former Sheriff Hanes after this report.

In an even worse case, they hanged Sheriff George Swearingen for his errant ways. This took place in Maryland in 1829. He was tried and convicted of killing his wife after taking up with another woman. George was another of these sheriffs who just couldn't help himself when it came to his mistress.

George wed Mary Scott five years before his hanging. A year later, the two produced a daughter. While campaigning for the office of sheriff, George met Rachel Cunningham. George won his election, and Rachel won George's heart.

When Mary and the rest of the town found out about the affair, Mary left George, taking their three-year-old daughter with her. George came up with a plan: send Rachel to Virginia and attempt "a reconciliation with his wife. But he later moved his mistress back to Cumberland without telling his wife."[9]

George came up with another plan. On September 8, 1828, the family rode out into the countryside on horseback. At one point, the trio stopped, George "put his daughter on the ground and led his wife, on horseback, up a steep hill and into a thicket of brushwood. It is believed that is where he cut, clubbed and killed her. He then rode after a cattle drover and told him his wife had fallen from her horse. By the time others had arrived, she was dead."[10]

George, ever resourceful, planned his departure with Rachel Cunningham but he was arrested on a Mississippi steamboat and returned for trial. The death warrant was signed on the first anniversary of the murder of Mrs. Sheriff Mary Scott Swearingen. "George Swearingen was hanged in Cumberland, Allegany County, Maryland on October 2, 1829."[11]

NO GOLD WATCH

Most jailhouse teams ended their careers on a much higher note than the Weakleys, the Hanes, and the Swearingens. In Chippewa County, Iowa, after sheriffing from 1927 to 1954, Leila Pedersen and her husband retired. Leila said, "No prisoner meals to get; no washing of dishes for jail inmates; no admittance of wrong-doers in the wee hours of the morning; and no more having to be on the job tied down like a farmer with a dairy herd."[12]

Malcolm and Priscilla Campbell celebrated his 92nd birthday together. They'd survived the settling of the Old West and the Johnson County Range War. In 1931, at the age of ninety-two, Malcolm wrote, "I find myself at peace with all people. Mrs. Campbell is beside me, and we are surrounded by our children and grand-children. There are flowers heaped upon the tables and telegrams, letters, and post-cards from all of my friends of the old days when I was doing my small part in bringing law to the frontier as Malcolm Campbell, Sheriff."[13]

This book began with a letter by Mrs. Sheriff Jennie Krider and it seems appropriate to end it the same way. In the same letter, Jennie reported that "the first day of January we will have to move. We do not know where yet. Will be glad when the times comes."

Personal belongings of Mary Lugten, who served with Sheriff Benjamin Lugten in Allegan County, Michigan, between 1925 and 1928. Included is her Defender 89 pistol that she always carried in her apron pocket when serving meals to prisoners. (Photo courtesy of Mary Drenten.)

Appendix 1

Jailhouse Family Members Who Provided Information

Contact Date	Last Name	First Name	Method	Regarding	Era
5/14/2003	Bonde	Thomas	C	Sophie Bonde	1906
5/9/2005	Bunnell	Rod	C	Mae Brown	1895
10/6/2003	Burns	Betty	Q, C, I	Elma Sinclair	1960
8/8/2003	Camelin	Glenda	Q	Glenda Camelin	1964
7/3/2003	Chambers	Jeanette	C	Violet Joss	1923
8/24/2003	Chesbro	Eileen	Q, I	Eileen Chesbro	1973
2/14/2004	Coleman	Madeline	C	Madeline Coleman	1975
11/15/2003	Cooksey	Bernice	Q	Bernice Cooksey	1961
10/5/2003	Cooper	Sam	I	Vernice Cooper	1965
8/28/2003	Darrow	Mary Ann	Q, C	Mary Ann Darrow	1954
8/24/2003	Draper	Peggy	I	Agnes Schumaker	1965
7/26/2003	Drenten	Mary	C	Mary Lugten	1925
6/13/2003	Drury	Burton	Q, C	Philomena Drury	1932
6/7/2003	Edinger	Lester	C	Marian Edinger	1923
6/3/2003	Edinger	Richard	Q, C	Marian Edinger	1923
5/27/2003	Edinger	Sid	C	Marian Edinger	1923
5/12/2003	Eifert	Evelyn	C	Erma Schieferdecker	1942
9/8/2003	Elston	Maureen	Q	Maureen Elston	1977
11/30/2003	Fiquet	Kathleen Nancy	Q, I	Bessie Kelly	1924

(*continued*)

Contact Date	Last Name	First Name	Method	Regarding	Era
7/3/2003	Fitzpatrick	Fitzpatrick Layton	I, Q, C	Nancy Fitzpatrick	1971
9/3/2003	Fulton	Candace	C	Bernice Cooksey	1961
6/4/2004	Gerber	Evelyn	C	Edith Weiss	1935
7/16/2003	Gooding	Florine	I, C, Q	Mildred Johnson	1941
8/17/2003	Harris	Madge	Q, C, I	Madge Harris	1963
8/17/2003	Harris	Randy	I	Madge Harris	1963
9/21/2003	Haugerud	Helen	Q, I, C	Helen Haugerud	1956
9/3/2003	Hobbs	James	C	Pearl Hobbs	1928
9/3/2003	Hobbs	Billy	C	Pearl Hobbs	1928
7/7/2003	Ingalsbee	Lucille	Q	Bertha Miller	1933
11/5/2003	Jernigan	Frances	C	Mildred Lucas	1882
6/30/2003	Kinkade	Martha	Q, C	Martha Kinkade	1959
6/30/2003	Kinkade	Becky	C	Martha Kinkade	1959
7/16/2003	Ledford	Jeanne	Q, I	Vernice Cooper	1965
11/20/2003	Lee	Larry	Q, I	Dolores Lee	1956
9/21/2003	LeLonde	Joyce White	I	Viola White	1948
12/7/2003	Matthews	Helen	Q, C	Alice Ketchum	1900
9/19/2003	McGovern	Shirley	I, Q	Geraldine Spielman	1958
7/15/2003	Miller	Marguerite	Q, C	Bertha Miller	1933
6/3/2003	Nondorf	Gloria	Q, C, I	Christina Peterka	1950
10/13/2003	Nosbisch	Paulette	Q, C	Pauline Folkers	1952
8/15/2003	Pace	Patsy	I	Mrs Clarence Pace	1930
8/20/2003	Pannbacker	Helen	C, Q	Olive Rosenkranz	1931
9/15/2003	Price	Marjorie	Q, I	Marjorie Price	1969
10/22/2003	Reeder	Charlotte	Q, C	Martha Bulman	1928
10/14/2003	Robinson	Larry	Q	Evelyn Robinson	1957
6/23/2003	Rumbaugh	Dorothy	Q	Dorothy Rumbaugh	1960
8/3/2003	Serles	Lily	Q, I	Lily Serles	1955
6/3/2003	Skirvin	Peggy	Q	Bessie Voorhees	1938
8/11/2003	Stanford	Debby	Q, I	Neva Allen	1968
8/18/2003	Swanson	Betty	C, Q	Betty Swanson	1955
7/20/2003	Tanner	Howard A.	Q, C, I, M	Maud Tanner	1937
7/20/2003	Tanner	Helen	I	Maud Tanner	1937
11/22/2003	Taylor	Martha	C	Mrs Howard	1877
8/29/2003	Vinson	Betty	Q, I	Betty Vinson	1969
6/26/2003	Walker	Diana	Q, I, C	Rose Singler	1913
5/30/2003	Wall	Karen	Q	Lorna Werner	1962
12/7/2003	Ward	Irene	Q, I, C	Irene Ward	1949

Contact Date	Last Name	First Name	Method	Regarding	Era
6/30/2003	Wendel	Theda Jo	C	Florence Whelan	1945
5/30/2003	Werner	Mary	Q	Lorna Werner	1962
9/1/2003	Werth	Anne	C, Q, I	Anne Werth	1957
9/3/2003	Westendorf	Dode	Q, C	Dode Westendorf	1973
9/3/2003	Westendorf	Dode	Q, C, I	Mary Jahnel	1964
9/15/2003	White	Bill	I	Viola White	1948
8/4/2003	White	Nora	Q	Ella White	1941
6/25/2003	Wood	Deb	Q	Dell Gebers	1959

Note: C = correspondence, I = interview, M = memoir, Q = questionnaire.

Appendix 2

Alphabetical Listing of Jailhouse Wives

State	Last Name	First Name	County	Date
RI	Adams	Margaret	Washington	1932
MO	Allen	Mrs. Jesse	Jackson	1918
IA	Allen	Neva	Poweshiek	1968–1978
IN	Bailey	Essie Myers	Fulton	1902–1906
FL	Baldree	Lassie	Sumter	1945
MD	Baldridge	Dorothy	St. Mary's	1637
MD	Baldridge	Grace	St. Mary's	1639
TX	Banister	Emma Daugherty	Coleman	1914–1917
TN	Bean	Mrs. Alva	Moore	1922
MN	Bonde	Sophie	Kandiyohi	1906–1926
WI	Bridenhagen	Gloria	Door	1960s
MD	Brosenne	Katherine	Howard	1920–1923
GA	Brown	Elvira	Fayette	1904–1918
WA	Brown	Mae Bullard	Pacific	1895–1900
FL	Broxson	Annie Gordon	Santa Rosa	1956–1959
IA	Bulman	Martha Jane Barthell	Allamakee	1928–1932, 1940–1946
NM	Burleson	Mary E.	Colfax	1878
CO	Buster	Pearl	Boulder	1912–1916
IA	Camelin	Glenda J.	Boone	1964–1970
ID	Campbell	Mattie	Logan	1890–1892
ID	Campbell	Mattie	Ada	1899–1901
WY	Campbell	Priscilla	Converse	1888
NY	Chesbro	Eileen	Oswego	1973–1977
RI	Church	Mrs. Charles	Bristol	1720s
IN	Clark	Polly	Fulton	1959–1966

State	Last Name	First Name	County	Date
NE	Coleman	Madeline	Brown	1975–1978
OH	Collins	Maude	Vinton	1914–1925
CT	Cook	Mabel F.	Tolland	1943–1947
TX	Cooksey	Bernice Mills	Terrell	1961–1972
SC	Cooper	Vernice Yates	Greenwood	1965–1967
MI	Corbett	Mrs. Silas	Ontonagon	1897
NE	Crandall	Mary	Knox	1898–1902
NV	Crowell	Clara Dunham	Lander	1916
MO	Curran	Jennie	Jackson	1921
MT	Darrow	Mary Ann	Powell	1954–1958
TX	Denman	Mrs. Mose	Brown	1899–1903, 1909–1911, 1927–1929
MA	Doan	Myrtle	Franklin	1930
IL	Dolder	Helena	DeKalb	1920s
MO	Drury	Philomena C.	St. Genevieve	1932–1936
IL	Edinger	Marian	McHenry	1923–1927, 1931–1935, 1939–1943
IL	Edmondson	Sarah Barbee	Schuyler	1860s
TX	Ellis	Mrs. Ivan	Brown	Unknown
IA	Elston	Maureen	Wright	1977–1989
CO	Everson	Dorothy	Boulder	1943–1967
TX	Fenton	Loretta	Coleman	1948
IA	Fitzpatrick Layton	Nancy	Kossuth	1971
CO	Fling	Goldie Pundt	Boulder	1950–1975
IA	Folkers	Pauline	Chickasaw	1952–1980
AZ	Fryer	Pauline	Pinal	1887–1890
IA	Gebers	Dell	Ida	1959–1987
NE	Gewecke	Eileen	Phelps	1960
TX	Goodson	Mrs.	Lee	1947
CO	Gray	Irene	Saguache	1951–1959
VA	Gum	Lollie Jane	Bath	1902–1929
OR	Hamilton	Mrs.	Union	1890
OH	Hanes	Mrs. Richard A.	Muskingum	1880s
KS	Harris	Madge	Wilson	1963–1980
MN	Haugerud	Helen	Fillmore	1959–1967
NY	Hawley	Elizabeth Sears	Albany	1800–1810
TN	Hobbs	Pearl Leona Ervin	Moore	1928–1932
TX	Hoskins	Mrs.	Bastrop	1950
KS	Howard	Mrs.	Miami	1877
MO	Hulse	Mama (Mrs. Mel)	Jackson	1906

(*continued*)

State	Last Name	First Name	County	Date
FL	Hunter	Ethel	Hamilton	1929–1937
MT	Irvine	Mary Flynn	Custer	1890s
WI	Jacobson	Mary	Barron	1920s
IA	Jahnel	Mary C.	Mitchell	1962–1984
MI	Johnson	Mildred Barrett	Allegan	1941–1954
MO	Jones	Pam	Moniteau	1991
MO	Jones	Sarah Tucker	Christian	1933
WY	Joss	Violet	Niobrara	1919–1926
HI	Kahanamoku	Nadine	Honolulu	1934–1960
MO	Kelly	Bessie M.	Texas	1924–1932
WV	Ketchum	Alice Adkins	Wayne	1900s
WY	Kinkade	Martha	Park	1959–1973
ND	Knapp	Mamie	Griggs	1907–1910
OH	Krider	Jennie	Stark	1890–1893
IA	Latty	Mollie E.	Des Moines	1870
IA	Lee	Dolores M.	Van Buren	1956–1979
WI	Lein	Delores	Sawyer	1960s
RI	Lillibridge	Nabby	Washington	Unknown
NJ	Lindsley	Phebe	Morris	1827
KY	Lucas	Mildred	Daviess	1882–1884
MI	Lugten	Mary Brower	Allegan	1925–1928
TX	Masters	Mrs. Ray	Brown	1955
FL	Maynard	Mrs. WR	Collier	1923–1927
FL	McGhin	Grace	Hamilton	1941–1949
PA	McKinley	Mrs. Mervin O.	Clarion	Unknown
MI	Miller	Bertha Punches	Allegan	1933–1940
PA	Mitten	Mary Morrow	Bradford	1924–1925
FL	Moore-Littles	Annis	Nassau	1969–1977
CO	Mumford	Anna	Summit	1940
IN	Norris	Marguerite	Fulton	1947–1959
MS	Pace	Mrs. Clarence	Tishomingo	1930–1950
MN	Pedersen	Leila	Chippewa	1927–1954
KS	Peterka	Christina	Republic	1950–1959
NM	Poe	Sophie Alberding	Lincoln	1883
FL	Polhill	Laura	Hamilton	1892–1899
MO	Potts	Lydia	Jackson	1886
MO	Price	Marjorie	Randolph	1969–1985
TN	Pusser	Pauline Mullins	McNairy	1964
KS	Ramsey	Mary	Ellis	1875
WY	Rankin	Rosa	Carbon	1870
CO	Richart	Mildred Mathias	Boulder	1932–1942
WY	Ricker	Emma	Natrona	1901–1902
TX	Riddell	Essie	Burnet	1950
MI	Rihle	Sarah	Ingham	1897

State	Last Name	First Name	County	Date
VT	Robinson	Evelyn	Windham	1957–1969
KS	Rosenkranz	Olive	Washington	1931–1933
MO	Ross	Ella Thomas	Jackson	1887
KS	Rumbaugh	Dorothy	Jefferson	1960–1962
IL	Schieferdecker	Erma	Schuyler	1942–1946
KS	Schumaker	Agnes Pfeifer	Ellis	1965–1968
AZ	Scott	Linda	Apache	1895–1896
WI	Serles	Lily M	Adams	1955–1969
IN	Sheets	Mrs. Lewis	Fulton	1911–1913, 1917–1919
NY	Sherwood	Mrs.	Steuben	1879
OH	Simpson	Maybel	Lincoln	Unknown
KS	Sinclair	Elma	Hodgeman	1960–1969
OR	Singler	Rose Probst	Jackson	1913
PA	Sloan	Mrs.	Clarion	Unknown
RI	Smith	Abigail	Washington	1774
RI	Smith	Evelyn G.	Kent	1880
IA	Spielman	Geraldine	Dubuque	1958–1964
KS	Spohn	Lenora	Wilson	1953–1958
IA	Swanson	Betty	Lucas	1955–1959, 1965–1973
MD	Swearingen	Mary Scott	Allegany	1827–1828
MI	Tanner	Maud Marie	Antrim	1937–1960
CO	Terrell	Martha	Garfield	1936–1960
KY	Thompson	Florence	Daviess	1934–1936
IA	Vinson	Betty	Lyon	1969–1981
KY	Vinson	Virginia	Lawrence	1885
IN	Voorhees	Bess Baldwin	Fulton	1938–1942
OK	Ward	Irene I.	Rogers	1949–1982
KS	Weakley	Kate	Russell	1875–1879
OH	Weiss	Edith	Holmes	1935–1966
KS	Werner	Lorna	Harvey	1962–1966
KS	Werth	Anne	Ellis	1957–1964, 1969–1974
IA	Westendorf	Dode	Bremer	1973–2001
KS	Whelan	Florence	Barton	1945–1949
SC	White	Ella Mae	Greenwood	1941–1964
CA	White	Mrs. Sheriff	Alameda	1898
MI	White	Viola Miser	Leelanau	1948–1964
TN	Wiseman	Margaret	Moore	1936–1942, 1944–1958
TN	Woodard	Mrs. Gil	Moore	1898–1902
TX	Wright	Mrs. Harlan	Wilson	1903
WI	Wylie	Ella Banks	Walworth	1923
NM	Wynn	Mrs. JC	San Juan	1921

Appendix 3

Jailhouse Wives by State and County

State	Last Name	First Name	County	Date
AZ	Scott	Linda	Apache	1895–1896
AZ	Fryer	Pauline	Pinal	1887–1890
CA	White	Mrs. Sheriff	Alameda	1898
CO	Richart	Mildred Mathias	Boulder	1932–1942
CO	Gray	Irene	Saguache	1951–1959
CO	Terrell	Martha	Garfield	1936–1960
CO	Everson	Dorothy	Boulder	1943–1967
CO	Mumford	Anna	Summit	1940
CO	Fling	Goldie Pundt	Boulder	1950–1975
CO	Buster	Pearl	Boulder	1912–1916
CT	Cook	Mabel F.	Tolland	1943–1947
FL	Baldree	Lassie	Sumter	1945
FL	Maynard	Mrs. WR	Collier	1923–1927
FL	Hunter	Ethel	Hamilton	1929–1937
FL	Moore-Littles	Annis	Nassau	1969–1977
FL	Broxson	Annie Gordon	Santa Rosa	1956–1959
FL	Polhill	Laura	Hamilton	1892–1899
FL	McGhin	Grace	Hamilton	1941–1949
GA	Brown	Elvira	Fayette	1904–1918
HI	Kahanamoku	Nadine	Honolulu	1934–1960
IA	Allen	Neva	Poweshiek	1968–1978
IA	Camelin	Glenda J.	Boone	1964–1970
IA	Swanson	Betty	Lucas	1955–1959, 1965–1973
IA	Vinson	Betty	Lyon	1969–1981
IA	Jahnel	Mary C.	Mitchell	1962–1984

State	Last Name	First Name	County	Date
IA	Spielman	Geraldine	Dubuque	1958–1964
IA	Latty	Mollie E.	Des Moines	1870
IA	Westendorf	Dode	Bremer	1973–2001
IA	Gebers	Dell	Ida	1959–1987
IA	Bulman	Martha Jane Barthell	Allamakee	1928–1932, 1940–1946
IA	Fitzpatrick Layton	Nancy	Kossuth	1971
IA	Elston	Maureen	Wright	1977–1989
IA	Folkers	Pauline	Chickasaw	1952–1980
IA	Lee	Dolores M.	Van Buren	1956–1979
ID	Campbell	Mattie	Logan	1890–1892
ID	Campbell	Mattie	Ada	1899–1901
IL	Schieferdecker	Erma	Schuyler	1942–1946
IL	Edinger	Marian	McHenry	1923–1927, 1931–1935, 1939–1943
IL	Dolder	Helena	DeKalb	1920s
IL	Edmondson	Sarah Barbee	Schuyler	1860s
IN	Sheets	Mrs. Lewis	Fulton	1911–1913, 1917–1919
IN	Norris	Marguerite	Fulton	1947–1959
IN	Voorhees	Bess Baldwin	Fulton	1938–1942
IN	Bailey	Essie Myers	Fulton	1902–1906
IN	Clark	Polly	Fulton	1959–1966
KS	Sinclair	Elma	Hodgeman	1960–1969
KS	Peterka	Christina	Republic	1950–1959
KS	Werth	Anne	Ellis	1957–1964, 1969–74
KS	Howard	Mrs.	Miami	1877
KS	Weakley	Kate	Russell	1875–1879
KS	Werner	Lorna	Harvey	1962–1966
KS	Rumbaugh	Dorothy	Jefferson	1960–1962
KS	Spohn	Lenora	Wilson	1953–1958
KS	Whelan	Florence	Barton	1945–1949
KS	Schumaker	Agnes Pfeifer	Ellis	1965–1968
KS	Rosenkranz	Olive	Washington	1931–1933
KS	Harris	Madge	Wilson	1963–1980
KS	Ramsey	Mary	Ellis	1875
KY	Thompson	Florence	Daviess	1934–1936
KY	Vinson	Virginia	Lawrence	1885
KY	Lucas	Mildred	Daviess	1882–1884
MA	Doan	Myrtle	Franklin	1930

(*continued*)

State	Last Name	First Name	County	Date
MD	Swearingen	Mary Scott	Allegany	1827–1828
MD	Baldridge	Grace	St. Mary's	1639
MD	Baldridge	Dorothy	St. Mary's	1637
MD	Brosenne	Katherine	Howard	1920–1923
MI	Rihle	Sarah	Ingham	1897
MI	Tanner	Maud Marie	Antrim	1937–1960
MI	White	Viola Miser	Leelanau	1948–1964
MI	Johnson	Mildred Barrett	Allegan	1941–1954
MI	Corbett	Mrs. Silas	Ontonagon	1897
MI	Miller	Bertha Punches	Allegan	1933–1940
MI	Lugten	Mary Brower	Allegan	1925–1928
MN	Bonde	Sophie	Kandiyohi	1906–1926
MN	Haugerud	Helen	Fillmore	1959–1967
MN	Pedersen	Leila	Chippewa	1927–1954
MO	Jones	Sarah Tucker	Christian	1933
MO	Kelly	Bessie M.	Texas	1924–1932
MO	Curran	Jennie	Jackson	1921
MO	Drury	Philomena C.	St. Genevieve	1932–1936
MO	Allen	Mrs. Jesse	Jackson	1918
MO	Ross	Ella Thomas	Jackson	1887
MO	Potts	Lydia	Jackson	1886
MO	Hulse	Mama (Mrs. Mel)	Jackson	1906
MO	Jones	Pam	Moniteau	1991
MO	Price	Marjorie	Randolph	1969–1985
MS	Pace	Mrs. Clarence	Tishomingo	1930–1950
MT	Irvine	Mary Flynn	Custer	1890s
MT	Darrow	Mary Ann	Powell	1954–1958
ND	Knapp	Mamie	Griggs	1907–1910
NE	Coleman	Madeline	Brown	1975–1978
NE	Crandall	Mary	Knox	1898–1902
NE	Gewecke	Eileen	Phelps	1960
NJ	Lindsley	Phebe	Morris	1827
NM	Wynn	Mrs. JC	San Juan	1921
NM	Poe	Sophie Alberding	Lincoln	1883
NM	Burleson	Mary E.	Colfax	1878
NV	Crowell	Clara Dunham	Lander	1916
NY	Chesbro	Eileen	Oswego	1973–1977
NY	Hawley	Elizabeth Sears	Albany	1800–1810
NY	Sherwood	Mrs.	Steuben	1879
OH	Weiss	Edith	Holmes	1935–1966
OH	Simpson	Maybel	Lincoln	Unknown
OH	Krider	Jennie	Stark	1890–1893
OH	Collins	Maude	Vinton	1914–1925
OH	Hanes	Mrs. Richard A.	Muskingum	1880s
OK	Ward	Irene I.	Rogers	1949–1982

State	Last Name	First Name	County	Date
OR	Hamilton	Mrs.	Union	1890
OR	Singler	Rose Probst	Jackson	1913
PA	Sloan	Mrs.	Clarion	Unknown
PA	McKinley	Mrs. Mervin O.	Clarion	Unknown
PA	Mitten	Mary Morrow	Bradford	1924–1925
RI	Adams	Margaret	Washington	1932
RI	Smith	Evelyn G.	Kent	1880
RI	Lillibridge	Nabby	Washington	Unknown
RI	Smith	Abigail	Washington	1774
RI	Church	Mrs. Charles	Bristol	1720s
SC	Cooper	Vernice Yates	Greenwood	1965–1967
SC	White	Ella Mae	Greenwood	1941–1964
TN	Pusser	Pauline Mullins	McNairy	1964
TN	Woodard	Mrs. Gil	Moore	1898–1902
TN	Bean	Mrs. Alva	Moore	1922
TN	Hobbs	Pearl Leona Ervin	Moore	1928–1932
TN	Wiseman	Margaret	Moore	1936–1942, 1944–1958
TX	Cooksey	Bernice Mills	Terrell	1961–1972
TX	Banister	Emma Daugherty	Coleman	1914–1917
TX	Ellis	Mrs. Ivan	Brown	Unknown
TX	Fenton	Loretta	Coleman	1948
TX	Goodson	Mrs.	Lee	1947
TX	Hoskins	Mrs.	Bastrop	1950
TX	Masters	Mrs. Ray	Brown	1955
TX	Wright	Mrs. Harlan	Wilson	1903
TX	Riddell	Essie	Burnet	1950
TX	Denman	Mrs. Mose	Brown	1899–1903, 1909–1911, 1927–1929
VA	Gum	Lollie Jane	Bath	1902–1929
VT	Robinson	Evelyn	Windham	1957–1969
WA	Brown	Mae Bullard	Pacific	1895–1900
WI	Bridenhagen	Gloria	Door	1960s
WI	Jacobson	Mary	Barron	1920s
WI	Wylie	Ella Banks	Walworth	1923
WI	Serles	Lily M.	Adams	1955–1969
WI	Lein	Delores	Sawyer	1960s
WV	Ketchum	Alice Adkins	Wayne	1900s
WY	Campbell	Priscilla	Converse	1888
WY	Ricker	Emma	Natrona	1901–1902
WY	Rankin	Rosa	Carbon	1870
WY	Kinkade	Martha	Park	1959–1973
WY	Joss	Violet	Niobrara	1919–1926

Notes

INTRODUCTION

1. Hughes, *The Guardian*.

CHAPTER 1: WHAT'S A NICE GIRL LIKE YOU . . . ?

1. *Handbook of Jail Food Service*, Bureau of Prisons, Leavenworth, KS, 1961.
2. Hall and Ambrose, *Memories of Duke*, ix.
3. Poe, *Buckboard Days*, 170–171.
4. Ibid.
5. Barbara Cook, correspondence, Tolland County (CT) Historical Society, August 30, 2003.
6. Farrar, *Reluctant Servant*, 12.
7. Morris, *The Twelfth of August*, 131.
8. James D. Drees, correspondence, March 9, 2004.

CHAPTER 2: FIRST DAYS ON DUTY

1. Bruce, *Four Years in the Coleman Jail*, 1.
2. Quick, Lulu Knapp, Downstairs at the Court House, www.webfamilytree.com/downstairs_at_the_court_house.htm.
3. Willard, *Fulton County Folks*, Fulton County (IN) Historical Society, 56.
4. Haugerud, *Jailhouse Stories*, 26.
5. Morris, *The Twelfth of August*, 164–165.

CHAPTER 3: HOME SWEET HOME

1. Poe, *Buckboard Days*, 205–206.
2. Ibid.
3. Oral history interview, Zita Singler Maddox, Tape 178, January 23, 1981, Southern Oregon Historical Society.

4. Research for this book revealed that 75% of the families included in these chapters lived in. That does not imply, however, that 75% of all sheriff's families lived in during the era of the mom-and-pop jail.

5. Louise Milton interview by James Denham, courtesy of Denham, August 21, 1998.

6. Williamson County (IL) Old Jail Web site, http://thewchs.com/wchs_tour5.htm.

7. McKeown, *Montevideo American-News.*

8. Pettem, *Daily Camera*, November 30, 1999.

CHAPTER 4: BEHIND THE SCENES

1. *St. Johns (AZ) Herald*, 1896.

2. Eifert, Evelyn correspondence, May 12, 2003, and Schuyler County (IL) Historical Jail Museum, www.rootsweb.com/~ilschuyl/OldJail.html.

3. Ross, *Jackson County (MO) Historical Society Journal,* Summer 1969.

4. McKeown, *Montevideo American-News.*

5. Clarion County (PA) Historical Society, *Jail Tales.*

6. Schuyler County jail Web site.

CHAPTER 5: MRS. SHERIFF'S HAT TREE

1. Bickford, *Crime, Punishment, and the Washington County (RI) Jail*, 28.

2. Ibid.

3. Bristol County (MA) Summons 1722.

4. San Diego Sheriff's Museum Web site, http://www.sdsheriff.net/history/1st_lady.html.

5. Ibid.

6. Sitton, *Texas High Sheriffs*, 157.

7. Ward, *The Life and Times of Sheriff Amos G. Ward*, 13.

8. Ibid.

9. Bickford, *Crime, Punishment, and the Washington County (RI) Jail*, 29.

10. McCarthy, Lincoln County, Oregon: A History of Oregon Sheriffs 1811 to 1991, http://gesswhoto.com/sheriff-lincoln.html.

11. Bruce, *Four Years in the Coleman Jail*, 21.

12. San Diego County Sheriff's Museum Web site.

13. Moore-Littles and Moore, Oral History Interview.

14. Weiss, David, A Jail and a Home Web site, www.geocities.com/oldjail_holmescounty/jailandhome.html.

15. Schulz and Houghton, "Married to the Job" *Wisconsin Magazine of History,* Spring 2003.

16. Zita Singler Maddox oral history.

17. McKeown, *Montevideo America-News.*

18. Sitton, *Texas Sheriffs*, 81.

19. Ibid.

CHAPTER 6: WITH A LITTLE HELP FROM MY TRUSTEES

1. Quick, Downstairs at the Court House, 21.

2. Ibid.

3. Seal, *Seize The Time,* 309.

4. Ibid.
5. Ibid.
6. Ibid.
7. Ibid., 311–313.
8. Moore-Littles and Moore, Oral History Interview.
9. Ibid.
10. Bruce, *Four Years in the Coleman Jail*, 21–22.
11. Ibid.
12. Mary Kate Durham, Hood County [TX] Old Jail former Web site, now defunct.
13. Clarion County Historical Society, *Jail Tales*, 31.
14. Sitton, *The Texas Sheriff*, 81.
15. Clarion County Historical Society, *Jail Tales*, 30.
16. Moore-Littles and Moore, Oral History Interview.
17. Oral History Interview, Roy Fling, Maria Rogers Oral History Program Collection, Carnegie Branch Library for Local History, Boulder, CO.

CHAPTER 7: IT TAKES A COUNTY

1. Bruce, *Four Years In The Coleman Jail*, 50–51.
2. Ibid.
3. Sitton, *Texas High Sheriffs*, 163.
4. Sisters of Mercy Archives, Omaha, Ne.
5. Ibid.
6. Ibid.
7. *St. Johns [AZ] Herald*, 1896.
8. Oral History Interview, Mary E. Burleson, American Life Histories: Manuscripts from the Federal Writers' Project, 1936–1940, Manuscript Division, Library of Congress.
9. Thomas H. Irvine, diaries, Montana Historical Society Library and Archives.

CHAPTER 8: WEDDING BANDS AND BADGES

1. McKeown, *Montevideo America-News*.
2. Pettem, *Daily Camera*.

CHAPTER 9: WITH A LITTLE HELP FROM MY YOUNG'UNS

1. Weiss Web site.
2. Ibid.
3. Clarion County Historical Society, *Jail Tales*.
4. Davis, *Independence Examiner*, 1956.
5. Wallowa County AGHP, Notes on Alice Henrietta Balter Oliver and Royal Irwin Oliver, www.usgennet.org/usa/or/county/wallowa/memories/balter.htm.
6. Bruce, *Four Years in the Coleman Jail*, 65–69.
7. Ibid.
8. Ibid., 21.
9. Ibid., 71.
10. Ibid.
11. Jail Stories Web site for Brownwood, Brown County, TX.
12. Sitton, *The Texas Sheriff*, 81.

13. Willard Clark Smith interview, Rochester Sentinel, February 5, 2001.
14. Ibid.
15. Moore-Littles and Moore, Oral History Interview.
16. Ibid.
17. Sitton, *The Texas Sheriff*, 80.
18. Oral History Interview, Mize Peters, March 3, 1963, Truman Library Archives.
19. Ibid.
20. Ibid.
21. McKeown, *Montevideo America-News.*
22. Ibid.
23. Ibid.
24. *The Pittsburg (KS) Daily Headlight*, November 1887.
25. Ibid.
26. Ibid.
27. Ibid.

CHAPTER 10: WITH A PISTOL IN HER (APRON) POCKET

1. Clarion County Historical Society, *Jail Tales.*
2. Godfrey, *The Poison Widow*, 88.
3. McKeown, *Montevideo American News.*
4. Ibid.
5. Pettem, *Daily Camera.*
6. Wheeler, *Concord: Climate for Freedom*, 172.
7. Old Lincoln County Jail Web site, http://lincoln.midcoast.com/~wps/cyberfair/jail.html.
8. Brown County Old Jail, www.browncountyhistory.org/jailstories.html.
9. Ibid.
10. Hamilton County (FL) Old Jail archives.
11. Ibid.
12. Fentenet, *Daily Advertiser*, May 18, 1958.
13. Susan Donaldson, Summit's Courthouse, 61–62.
14. Moore-Littles and Moore, Oral History, Interview.

CHAPTER 11: HERE'S THE GROCERY BILL, HONEY

1. Loretta Fenton Interview by Thad Sitton.
2. Sitton, *The Texas Sheriff*, 84.
3. Ibid.
4. Bruce, *Four Years in the Coleman County Jail*, 21.
5. Ibid., 7.
6. Davis, *Independence Examiner*, 1956.
7. Ibid.
8. Diane Walker family papers, and Southern Oregon Historical Society.

CHAPTER 12: LOAVES AND FISHES

1. St. Clair and Gugin, *Chief Justice Fred M. Vinson of Kentucky*, 5.
2. Fulton County Historical Society files.

CHAPTER 13: BOOTLEGGING BABYSITTERS, STRAIGHT PINS, AND WHIRLIGIGS

1. David, *Malcolm Campbell, Sheriff*, 79.
2. Ibid.
3. Marty Jill Sheets, family archives.
4. Ibid.
5. Zita Singler Maddox Oral History.
6. Clarion County Historical Society, *Jail Tales,* 23.
7. St. Clair and Gugin, *Chief Justice Fred M. Vinson of Kentucky*, 5.
8. Ibid.
9. Charles Ross correspondence to John T. Barker, November 16, 1949. John T. Barker Papers, Western Manuscripts Collection, University of Missouri.
10. Weiss Web site.
11. Quick, Downstairs at the Court House, 21.
12. Haugerud, *Jailhouse Stories,* 136.
13. Margaret Bailey Shafer and Byron Bailey Oral History, *Fulton County Folks,* Vol. 1, 55–57.
14. Hamilton County [FL] Historical Society Archives.
15. Bruce, *Four Years in the Coleman Jail*, 52–56.
16. McKeown, *Montevideo American-News.*
17. Ibid.
18. Ibid.
19. Ibid.

CHAPTER 14: GUESTS OF THE COUNTY

1. Johanson, Murder and Mayhem in This Land, The Ontonagon, www.ontonagonherald.com/books/murder.shtml.
2. Ibid.
3. Hanson, *The Hawk Eye*, www.thehawkeye.com/columns/hansen/2000/cha72300.html.
4. Ibid.
5. Bruce, *Four Years in the Coleman Jail*, 58–59.
6. Ibid., 17.
7. Ibid., 124.
8. Ibid., 124.
9. Ibid., 124.
10. Rising, Sarah Kingsbury, correspondence, Martha Taylor, November 22, 2003.
11. Ibid.
12. Ibid.
13. Ibid.
14. Ibid.
15. St. Johns (AZ) Herald, 1896.
16. Ibid.
17. Ibid.
18. Bruce, *Four Years in the Coleman Jail*, 38.

19. Chavez and Faverino, A History, Sheriffs of San Juan County Web site, www.sjcso.com/OfInterest/AgencyHistory/history.pdf.

20. Clarion County Historical Society, *Jail Tales,* 25–26.

CHAPTER 15: PA, I HEAR THEM SAWING AGAIN

1. Ingham County Sheriff's Office Web site, ingham.org/sh/historical_page.htm.
2. Haugerud, *Jailhouse Stories*, 97.
3. *The Pittsburg (KS) Headlight*, November 1887.
4. *St. Johns (AZ) Herald*, April 18, 1895.
5. Bruce, *Four Years in the Coleman Jail*, 10.
6. Ibid.
7. Ibid., 11.
8. Jackson County (MO) Old Jail Museum archives.
9. Luan Hearn Moore (Sebastian County) Old Jail Museum, Greenwood AR Web site, http://www.greenwoodarkansas.com/localhistory/jail.html.
10. Clarion County Historical Society, *Jail Tales*, 30.
11. Alderman, "The Story of Mrs. Sheriff," *American Western Magazine*.
12. Bickford, *Crime, Punishment, and the Washington County (RI) Jail*, 28.
13. Moore-Littles and Moore, Oral History Interview.

CHAPTER 16: ESCAPE ENCOUNTERS OF THE FOURTH KIND

1. Fransioli,"Lights Out in Two Minutes," The Story Project, Georgia Perimeter College, Decatur Campus Web site.
2. St. Clair and Gugin, *Chief Justice Fred M. Vinson of Kentucky*, 6.
3. Ibid.
4. Zita Singler Maddox Oral History.
5. Ibid.
6. Ibid.
7. Ibid.
8. Ibid.
9. Medicine Lodge Cresset, May 7, 1880.
10. Quick, Downstairs at the Court House, 21.
11. Rod Bunnell correspondence, part of which appeared in the Sou'Wester, a publication of the Pacific County Historical Society, June, 2003.
12. Ibid.
13. Ibid.
14. ibid
15. Ibid.
16. Ibid.
17. Ibid.
18. *The Steuben Advocate*, October 8, 1879.
19. Ibid.
20. Ibid.
21. Clarion County Historical Society, *Jail Tales*, 28.
22. *Wilmar Tribune*, August 2, 1911.
23. Ibid., March 9, 1921.
24. Ibid.

CHAPTER 17: NERVES OF STEEL—OR NOT

1. CA Peace Officers' Memorial Web site, Sacramento, CA. http://www.camemorial.org/.
2. Charlotte M. Meyer, correspondence, June 20, 2003.
3. Sheriff's granddaughter becomes a Fayetteville Flapper, *The Citizen*, October 8, 2003.
4. Ibid.
5. Joan Richardson, "Lenora Spohn Remembers Life as a Sheriff's Wife," Wilson County (KS) Historical Society and Old Jail Museum.
6. Oral History Interview, Mary Richart Nelson Hall, OH0400, July 20, 1988, Maria Rogers Oral History Program Collection, Carnegie Branch Library for Local History, Boulder, CO.
7. Ibid.
8. Weiss Web site.
9. David, *Malcolm Campbell, Sheriff*, 118.
10. Ibid.
11. Morris, *The Twelfth of August*, 165.

CHAPTER 18: AN UNGLAMOROUS AND THANKLESS JOB

1. Smith, Veteran Sheriffs Recollect, Rochester Sentinel, February 5, 2001.
2. Haugerud, *Jailhouse Stories*, 170–172.
3. Ibid., and Helen Haugerud interview.
4. Ken Parker, unpublished manuscript, Chapter XXI: Sheriff Tanner.
5. McKeown, *Montevideo American-News*.
6. Godfrey, *The Poison Widow,* 70.
7. Ibid.
8. The Founding Days: Sheriff's Bride, as Chief Deputy, Used Her Grit to Help Bring Law and Order to County, *Naples Daily News*, January 1, 2000.
9. Ibid.
10. Bickford, *Crime, Punishment, and the Washington County (RI) Jail*, 30.
11. Ibid.
12. Ibid.
13. Ibid., 12–17.
14. Ibid.
15. Ibid.

CHAPTER 19: 'TIL DEATH DO US PART

1. San Diego Sheriff's Museum Web site.
2. Morris, *The Twelfth of August*, 173–177.
3. Ibid.
4. Phelps County Sheriff Web site, History section, http://www.phelpso.org/.
5. Ibid.
6. Capital Punishment in Missouri Web site, State of Missouri v. James Johnson. http://www.missourinet.com/CapitalPunishment/Case_notes/johnson_james.htm.
7. Ibid.
8. Looking . . . Backward 1875, *The Hays Republican*, August 31, 1907.

9. Jernigan and Jernigan, family biography of Mildred Catherine Summers Lucas.
10. McCarthy, *A History of Oregon Sheriffs 1841 to 1991*, Lincoln County Web site.
11. Ibid.
12. Diane Walker family records.
13. Maddox oral history.
14. Ibid.
15. Bruce, *Four Years in the Coleman Jail*, 80.
16. Ibid., 136–137.
17. Pennsylvania and Bradford County's First Woman Sheriff Web site, http://www.geocities.com/vbenson_2000/mary.htm.
18. John C. Sheaffer, The First Lady Sheriff? Maude Collins of Vinton County, http://www.geocities.com/Athens/Olympus/5870/mc.html.
19. Cross, *The Athens Messenger*, October 15, 2000.
20. Nancy Beasley, The Lace Curtain Jail, DeKalb County History Web site, http://www.dekalbcounty-il.com/dolder.html.
21. Ibid.
22. Margo Oxendine, Sheriff Charles Gum Memorial Scheduled for Sunday in Bath, Bath County [VA] Historical Society, 1999.
23. Ibid.
24. Ibid.
25. Fortner, Frank Jones: Christian County's First Democrat Sheriff, http://www.rootsweb.com/~mochrist/frank.htm.
26. Ibid.
27. Ryan, The Last Public Execution in America, http://www.geocities.com/lastpublichang/Chapter2.htm.
28. History of Evans County, GA Web site, http://www.claxtonevanschamber.com/history.htm.

CHAPTER 20: THE FINAL CHAPTER

1. Poe, *Buckboard Days*, 240–242.
2. Jackson County (MO) Old Jail archive files.
3. Schulz and Houghton, *Wisconsin Magazine of History*, 30.
4. *St. Johns (AZ) Herald*, September 26, 1896.
5. Elements of this research funded by the Tihen Research Grant, Kansas State Historical Society.
6. *The Pittsburg (KS) Headlight*, March 7, 1888.
7. Ibid.
8. Ibid.
9. Carroll E. Keller, A History of the Washington County [MD] Sheriff's Office, http://www.washcosheriff.com/swearingen.html.
10. Ibid.
11. Ibid.
12. McKeown, *Montevideo-American News*.
13. David, *Malcolm Campbell, Sheriff*, 361.

Bibliography and Recommended Reading

"After 28 Years as County Cook, Mrs. Pedersen Earned Her Rest," *Montevideo American-News*, 1954.

Alderman, BJ. "The Story of Mrs. Sheriff," *American Western Magazine* (online), May 2003.

Annis Moore-Littles and Cindy Moore. Oral History Interview, November 4, 1999, Amelia Island (FL) Museum of History.

Babcock, Charlotte. *Shot Down! Capital Crimes of Casper*. High Plains Press, Casper, WY, 2000.

Ball, Larry D. *Desert Lawmen: The High Sheriffs of New Mexico and Arizona 1846–1912*. University of New Mexico Press, Albuquerque, NM, 1996.

Beasley, Nancy. "The Lace Curtain Jail," DeKalb County History Web site, http://www.dekalbcounty-il.com/dolder.html.

Bickford, Christopher. *Crime, Punishment, and the Washington County (RI) Jail*. Pettaquamscutt Historical Society, Kingston, RI, 2002.

Brown County Old Jail Web site, www.browncountyhistory.org/jailstories.html.

Bruce, Leona. *Four Years in the Coleman Jail*. Eakin Press, Austin, TX, 1982.

Bureau of Prisons. *Handbook of Jail Food Service*. U.S. Department of Justice, Washington, DC, 1961.

California Peace Officers' Memorial Web site, Sacramento, CA, http://www.camemorial.org/.

Capital Punishment in Missouri Web site, State of Missouri v. James Johnson. http://www.missourinet.com/CapitalPunishment/Case_notes/johnson_james.htm.

Chavez and Faverino, A History, Sheriffs of San Juan County Web site, www.sjcso.com/OfInterest/AgencyHistory/history.pdf.

Clarion County Historical Society, *Jail Tales*, Shippenville, PA, 2001.

Colonial legal document, Bristol County (MA) Summons, 1722.

Cross, Roy. "She Traded Her Apron for a Badge," *Athens Messenger*, Athens, OH, October 15, 2000.

David, Robert. *Malcolm Campbell, Sheriff*. Wyomingana, Inc., Casper, WY, 1932.

Diane Walker family archives and correspondence, July 25, 2003.

Donaldson, Susan. *Summit's Courthouse—Its Past, Pictures and People*. Summit Historical Society, Breckenridge, CO, June 2000.

Dooley, Eugene T. *The Sheriffs of Suffolk County (NY)*. New York Department of General Resources, Albany, NY, 1989.

Eifert, Evelyn. Board Chairman of Schuyler County Historical Museum, correspondence, May 12, 2003.

Farrar, Ronald. *Reluctant Servant*. University of Missouri Press, Columbia, MO, 1969.

Fentenet, Mary Allee. "Cook at City Jail Is Expert on Stew, Beans and Rice, Cooked French Style," *Daily Advertiser*, Lafayette, LA, May 18, 1958.

Fortner, Roger. "Frank Jones: Christian County's First Democrat Sheriff," http://www.rootsweb.com/~mochrist/frank.htm.

Fransioli, Ivy. "Lights Out in Two Minutes," The Story Project, Georgia Perimeter College, Decatur Campus Web site, www.gpc.edu/~heritage/indexChildhood.htm.

Godfrey, Linda. *The Poison Widow*. Prairie Oak Press, Black Earth, WI, 2003.

Gorzalka, Ann. *Wyoming's Territorial Sheriffs*. High Plains Press, Casper, WY, 1998.

Griffith, Diane L. *America's First Woman Sheriff Captures Kentucky's Barefoot Desperado*. Turner Publishing, Paducah, KY, 2000.

Groft, Tammis K. and Mary Alice Mackay. *Albany Institute of History & Art: 200 Years of Collecting*. Hudson Hills Press, New York, 1998.

Hall, Sandra Kimberley and Greg Ambrose. *Memories of Duke: The Legend Comes Alive*. The Bess Press, Honolulu, HI, 1995.

Hanson, Robert. Burlington [IA] Hawk Eye, www.thehawkeye.com/columns/hansen/2000/cha72300.html.

Haugerud, Neil. *Jailhouse Stories*. University of Minnesota Press, MN, 1999.

Hinton, C. "History of the Old Jail, Hamilton County, Florida, 1893–1993," Old Jail archives, courtesy of Shirley Smith.

History of Evans County, GA Web site, http://www.claxtonevanschamber.com/history.htm.

Holmes, Lynn. Correspondence and archival material from the Sisters of Mercy archives, Omaha, NE, February 5, 2004.

Hughes, Kathryn. "The People That Time Forgot," *The Guardian*, London, Saturday, December 11, 2004.

Ingham County Sheriff's Office Web site, ingham.org/sh/historical_page.htm.

Jail Stories Web site for Brownwood, Brown County, TX. http://www.browncountyhistory.org/jailstories.html.

Jernigan and Jernigan, unpublished family biography of Mildred Catherine Summers Lucas.

Johanson, Bruce H. "Murder and Mayhem in This Land, The Ontonagon," www.ontonagonherald.com/books/murder.shtml.

Jordan, Bruce. *Death Unexpected: The Violent Deaths of Fayette*. Midtown Publishing, Atlanta, GA, 1997.

Karraker, Cyrus H. *The Seventeenth-Century Sheriff: A Comparative Study of the Sheriff in England and the Chesapeake Colonies 1607–89*. University of North Carolina Press, 1930.

Keller, Carroll E. *A History of the Washington County [MD] Sheriff's Office*, http://www.washcosheriff.com/swearingen.html.

"Looking . . . Backward 1875," *The Hays Republican*, August 31, 1907.

Mary E. Burleson Oral History Interview, American Life Histories: Manuscripts from the Federal Writers' Project, 1936–1940, Manuscript Division, Library of Congress.

Mary Kate Durham, Hood County [TX] Old Jail Web site, now defunct.

Mary Richart Nelson Hall Oral History Interview, OH0400, July 20, 1988, Maria Rogers Oral History Program Collection, Carnegie Branch Library for Local History, Boulder, CO.

Medicine Lodge Cresset, untitled article, May 7, 1880.

McCarthy, Linda. "Lincoln County, Oregon: A History of Oregon Sheriffs 1811 to 1991," http://gesswhoto.com/sheriff-lincoln.html.

McKeown, Jane. "There Were the Bootleggers, the Bonrud Gang and the Chicken Thieves . . . ," *Montevideo American-News* (late 1990s).

Mize Peters Oral History Interview by James R. Fuchs, March 3, 1963, Truman Library Archives.

Moore, Luan Hearn (Sebastian County) Old Jail Museum, Greenwood AR Web site, http://www.greenwoodarkansas.com/localhistory/jail.html.

Morris, W.R. *The Twelfth of August*. Aurora Publishers, Nashville, TN, 1971.

Newman, Harry Wright. *The Flowering of the Maryland Palatinate*. Published by the author, 1961.

Old Lincoln County Jail Web site, http://lincoln.midcoast.com/~wps/cyberfair/jail.html.

Oxendine, Margo. "Sheriff Charles Gum Memorial Scheduled for Sunday in Bath," *The Recorder*, 1999.

Pennsylvania and Bradford County's First Woman Sheriff Web site, http://www.geocities.com/vbenson_2000/mary.htm.

Pettem, Silvia. "Sheiff Everson's Family Made the Courthouse Their Home," *Daily Camera*, November 30, 1999.

Phelps County Sheriff Web site, History section, http://www.phelpso.org/.

Pittsburg (KS) Daily Headlight, untitled article, November 1887.

Poe, Sophie. *Buckboard Days*. Caxton, Caldwell, ID, 1936.

Quick, Lulu Knapp. Downstairs at the Court House, www.webfamilytree.com/downstairs_at_the_court_house.htm.

Richardson, Joan. "Lenora Spohn Remembers Life as a Sheriff's Wife," Wilson County (KS) Historical Society and Old Jail Museum.

Ross, Helen and Louise Ross. "Jackson County (MO)," *Historical Society Journal*, Summer 1969.

Roy Fling Oral History Interview, Maria Rogers Oral History Program Collection, Carnegie Branch Library for Local History, Boulder, CO.

Ruetti, Oretha. *It Happened Here: Stories of Marshall County, Kansas*. Marshall County Historical Society, 1981.

Ryan, Perry T. The Last Public Execution in America, http://www.geocities.com/lastpublichang/, 1992.

San Diego Sheriff's Museum Web site, http://www.sdsheriff.net/history/1st_lady.html.

Sarah Kingsbury Rising correspondence, from the personal collection of Martha Chase Taylor, descendant of Josiah W. Kingsbury, brother of Sarah Kingsbury Rising.

Schulz, Dorothy and Larry Houghton, "Married to the Job," *Wisconsin Magazine of History*, Spring 2003.

Schuyler County (IL) Historical Jail Museum, www.rootsweb.com/~ilschuyl/OldJail.html.

Seal, Bobby. *Seize the Time: The Story of the Black Panther Party and Huey P. Newton*. Vintage New York, 1970.

Sheaffer, John C. The First Lady Sheriff? Maude Collins of Vinton County, http://www.geocities.com/Athens/Olympus/5870/mc.html.

Sheets, Marty Jill. family stories on file in the Fulton County (IN) Historical Society archives courtesy of Shirley Willard, date unknown.

"Sheriff's Granddaughter Becomes a Fayetteville Flapper," *The Citizen*, October 8, 2003.

Sitton, Thad. *Texas High Sheriffs*. Texas Monthly Press, Austin, TX, 1988.

Sitton, Thad. *The Texas Sheriff: Lord of the County Line*. University of Oklahoma Press, Norman, OK, 2000.

Smith, Phil. "Veteran Sheriffs Recollect," *Rochester Sentinel*, February 5, 2001.

St. Clair, James and Linda Gugin. *Chief Justice Fred M. Vinson of Kentucky*. University of Kentucky Press, Lexington, KY, 2002.

St. Johns (AZ) Herald, various articles between 1895 and end of 1896.

"The Founding Days: Sheriff's Bride, as Chief Deputy, Used Her Grit to Help Bring Law and Order to County," *Naples Daily News*, January 1, 2000.

Thomas H. Irvine diaries, Montana Historical Society Library and Archives.

Visit to Old Jail Brings Back a Flood of Memories for Her, Independence [MO] Examiner, 1956.

Wallowa County AGHP, Notes on Alice Henrietta Balter Oliver and Royal Irwin Oliver, www.usgennet.org/usa/or/county/wallowa/memories/balter.htm.

Ward, Irene. *The Life and Times of Sheriff Amos G. Ward*. Published by the author, Wyandotte, OK, 2001.

Weiss, David. A Jail and a home Web site, www.geocities.com/oldjail_holmescounty/jailandhome.html.

Wheeler, Ruth. *Concord: Climate for Freedom*. Concord Antiquarian Society, Concord, MA, 1967.

Willard Clark Smith interview, Rochester Sentinel, February 5, 2001.

Willard, Shirley. *Fulton County Folks*. 2 vols. Fulton County Historical Society, 1974/1981.

Williamson County (IL) Old Jail Web site, http://thewchs.com/wchs_tour5.htm.

Zita Singler Maddox Oral History, Southern Oregon Historical Society archives courtesy of Carol Harbison-Samuelson.

Index

Ada County, ID, 44
Adams County, WI, 26, 56, 89, 115, 117–18, 138
Alameda County, CA, 153–54
Albany County, NY, 176
Albany County, WY, 6
Allamakee County, IA, 36, 49, 57, 59, 67, 80, 95, 155–56, 182–83
Allegan County, MI, 24, 33, 40, 55, 57, 65, 72, 85, 86, 87, 89, 108, 109, 111, 120, 124–25, 126–27, 129, 136, 158
Allegany County, MD, 188
Allen, Mrs. Jessie, 35
Allen, Neva, 48, 65, 77, 87, 94, 123–24, 130, 149–51, 154, 162
Antrim County, MI, 8, 13, 17, 24, 36–37, 45, 64, 73–74, 80, 89, 97, 105, 124, 137, 142–43, 144, 164
Apache County, AZ, 20, 28, 68, 126, 134, 186

Bailey, Essie, 15, 115
Baldree, Lassie, 23–24, 182
Baldridge, Dorothy, 5
Baldridge, Grace, 5
Banister, Emma, 9, 13, 14, 44, 57, 62–63, 65, 78–79, 100–1, 116, 125, 126, 134–35, 178
Barron County WI, 51
Barton County, KS, 118
Bastrop County, TX, 115
Bath County, VA, 97, 180–81
Bean, Mrs. Alva, 63
Berkley County, SC, 83
Big Nose George, 146
Billy The Kid, 6, 19
Bonde, Sophie, 147–49
Boone County, IA, 48, 167–68
Boulder County, CO, 9, 12–13, 19, 26, 29, 60–61, 74, 86, 88, 89, 98, 112–13, 136–37, 158, 161, 166
Bradford County, PA, 178–79
Bremer County, IA, 60, 67, 74–75, 168–69
Bridenhagen, Gloria, 48, 72, 82
Bristol County, MA, 63
Bristol County, RI, 41, 168
Brosenne, Katherine, 42–43
Brown County, NE, 127–28, 167
Brown County, TX, 36, 79, 90, 124
Brown, Elvira, 156–57
Brown, Mae, 3, 145–46
Broxson, Annie, 163–64
Buckler, Mary Agnes, 35–36
Bulman, Martha, 36, 49, 57, 59, 67, 80, 95, 155–56, 182–83
Burleson, Mary, 68

Burnet County, TX, 44–45, 50–51, 59, 79, 98
Buster, Pearl, 29, 166

Camelin, Glenda, 48, 167–68
Campbell, Mattie, 44
Campbell, Priscilla, 6, 109, 159–60, 188
Carbon County, WY, 146
Chambers, Olive, 43
Chesbro, Eileen, 1, 57–58, 63, 101, 107–8, 124, 128, 130
Chickasaw County, IA, 34–35, 36, 50, 108, 115–16, 120–21, 158, 163
Chippewa County, MN, 24, 28–29, 41, 50, 57, 73, 82, 85, 87, 117, 188
Christian County, MO, 181–82
Church, Mrs. Charles, 41
Clarion County, PA, 23, 34, 58, 59, 77, 85–86, 108, 110, 128, 138, 147, 157
Clark, Polly, 162
Coleman County, TX, 9, 13, 14, 43, 44, 57, 62–63, 64–65, 78–79, 98, 100–1, 113, 116, 125, 126, 134–35
Coleman, Madeline, 127–28, 167
Colfax County, NM, 68
Collier County, FL, 168
Collins, Maude, 179
Converse County, WY, 6, 109, 159–60
Cook, Mabel, 12, 97–98, 102–3, 117, 130–31
Cooksey, Bernice, 50
Cooper, Vernice, 7, 58–59, 76, 77, 99, 114, 154
Corbett, Mrs., 121
Cormier, Olivia, 91
Crandall, Mary, 95
Crowell, Clara, 178
Curran, Jennie, 135, 138
Custer County, MT, 69

Darrow, Mary Ann, 6, 9, 17, 25, 47, 55, 94, 98, 100, 114, 116, 136, 142, 156, 165–66, 185
Daviess County, KY, 176, 182
DeKalb County, IL, 179–80
Denman, Mrs. Mose, 102
Des Moines County, IA, 65, 122–23
Doan, Myrtle, 122
Dolder, Helena, 179–80
Door County, WI, 48, 72, 82
Drury, Philomena, 95
Dubuque County, IA, 9, 71, 93

Edinger, Marian, 8, 25, 27, 29–30, 33, 60, 67–68, 77, 81–82, 86, 103, 112, 117, 154–55, 170, 171
Edmondson, Sarah, 36, 38
Ellis County, KS, 10–11, 37, 41–42, 48, 51, 54–55, 67, 80, 82, 96, 100, 104–5, 113, 117, 120, 144, 155, 157–58, 163, 175–76
Ellis, Mrs. Ivan, 79
Elston, Maureen, 49, 82, 85, 86, 154, 167
Evans County, GA, 182
Everson, Dorothy, 9, 26, 74, 85, 88, 89, 98, 112–13, 136–37, 161

Fayette County, GA, 156–57
Fenton, Loretta, 43, 64–65, 98, 113
Fillmore County, MN, 13, 16, 37–38, 64, 65, 85, 88, 103, 114–15, 117, 133, 139, 162–63
Fitzpatrick Layton, Nancy, 30–31, 49, 53, 99, 105, 143–44, 162
Fling, Goldie, 60–61
Folkers, Pauline, 34–35, 36, 50, 108, 115–16, 120–21, 158, 163
Franklin County, MA, 122
Fryer, Pauline, 21
Fulton County, IN, 15, 79, 103, 109–10, 115, 162

Garfield County, CO, 42, 56, 66, 104, 109, 113, 115, 130, 148
Garrett, Pat, 3
Gebers, Dell, 43, 47–48, 88, 108, 163
Gewecke, Eileen, 173–74
Goodson, Mrs., 80
Gray, Irene, 33, 49, 54, 67, 104, 131, 137
Greenwood County, SC, 7, 31, 58–59, 76, 77, 99, 114, 154
Griggs County, ND, 14, 53–54, 113–14, 145
Gum, Lollie, 97

Hamilton County, FL, 77–78, 90–91, 94–95, 115, 141
Hanes, Mrs., 187
Harris, Madge, 24, 34, 56, 59, 90, 92, 118, 134, 155, 157, 169–70
Harvey County, KS, 32–33, 57, 118, 124, 129–30
Haugerud, Helen, 13, 16, 37–38, 64, 65, 85, 88, 100, 103, 114–15, 117, 133, 139, 161, 162–63
Hawley, Elizabeth, 176
Hobbs, Pearl, 27–28, 29, 70, 114, 181
Hodgeman County, KS, 7, 14–15, 35, 49, 51–52, 71, 96, 105, 115, 159
Holmes County, OH, 15, 25, 45, 47, 56, 73, 76, 88–89, 94, 97, 100, 107, 113, 114, 121, 127, 129, 130, 159–59
Honolulu County, HI, 3, 68–69
Hood County, TX, 57
Hoskins, Mrs., 115
Howard County, MD, 42–43
Howard, Mrs., 125–26
Hulse, "Mama", 77, 101
Hunter, Ethel, 115

Ida County, IA, 43, 47–48, 88, 108, 163
Ingham County, MI, 133
Irvine, Mary, 69

Jackson County, MO, 6, 28, 35, 49, 77, 82, 101, 103, 116, 128, 134, 135, 138, 185
Jackson County, OR, 5, 9, 10, 22, 50, 101, 110, 144–45, 177–78
Jacobson, Mary, 51
Jahnel, Mary, 22–23, 25, 30, 31, 41, 48, 50, 56–57, 60, 74, 77, 81, 98, 99, 118, 139–40, 158, 168
Jefferson County, KS, 42, 138–39, 152
Jerome, Mother Mary, 65–66
Johnson, Mildred, 24, 40, 55, 65, 72–73, 89, 108, 126–27, 134
Jones, Pam, 174–75
Jones, Sarah, 181–82
Joss, Violet, 42

Kahanamoku, Nadine, 3, 68–69
Kandiyohi County, MN, 147–49
Kelly, Bessie, 9, 20–21, 22, 59
Ketchum, Alice, 6, 110, 112
Kinkade, Martha, 39, 131, 166
Knapp, Mamie, 14, 53–54, 113–14, 145
Knowles, Mrs., 94
Knox County, NE, 95
Kossuth County, IA, 30–31, 49, 53, 99, 105, 143–44, 162
Krider, Jennie, 1–2, 67, 188

Lander County, NV, 178
Latty, Mollie, 65, 122–23
Lawrence County, KY, 103, 112, 141–42
Lee County, TX, 80
Lee, Dolores, 8, 10, 25, 38, 41, 66, 71–72, 81, 105, 117, 158
Leelanau County, MI, 21–22, 33, 56, 70, 98, 118, 137
Lein, Delores, 52, 185–86
Lillibridge, Nabby, 44
Lincoln County, ME, 90
Lincoln County, NM, 3, 5–6, 19–20, 184–85, 186
Lincoln County, OR, 44, 176
Lindsley, Phebe, 7, 36
Logan County, ID, 44
Lucas County, IA, 16–17, 35, 60, 95, 116–17, 123, 153
Lucas, Mildred, 176
Lugten, Mary, 85, 111, 120, 129
Lyon County, IA, 14, 26, 32, 34, 46, 64, 75, 87, 132–33

Martin County, MN, 102
Masters, Mrs Ray, 124
Maynard, Mrs. W.R., 168
McGhin, Grace, 90–91, 141
McHenry County, IL, 8, 25, 27, 29–30, 33, 60, 67–68, 77, 81–82, 86, 103, 112, 117, 154–55, 170, 171
McKinley, Mrs. Mervin, 110
McNairy County, TN, 7, 17, 160, 173
Miami County, KS, 125–26
Middlesex County, MA, 89–90
Miller, Bertha, 33, 57, 87, 109, 158

Mitchell County, IA, 22–23, 25, 30, 31, 41, 48, 50, 56–57, 60, 74–75, 77–81, 98, 118, 139–40, 158, 168
Mitten, Mary, 178–79
Moniteau County, MO, 174–75
Moore County, TN, 27, 29, 35, 63, 70, 114, 181
Moore, Harriet, 89–90
Moore–Littles, Annis, 19, 46–47, 56, 60, 80, 91–92, 99–100, 140
Morris County, NJ, 7, 36
Mumford, Anna, 91
Muskingum County, OH, 187

Nassau County, FL, 19, 46–47, 56, 60, 80, 91–92, 99–100, 140
Natrona County, WY, 135, 176
Niobrara County, WY, 42
Norris, Marguerite, 79, 103

Ontonagon County, MI, 121
Oswego County, NY, 1, 57–58, 63, 101, 107–8, 124, 128, 130
Otter Tail County, MN, 32

Pace, Mrs. Clarence, 118
Pacific County, WA, 3, 145–46
Park County, WY, 39, 131, 166
Pedersen, Leila, 24, 28–29, 41, 50, 57, 73, 82, 85, 87, 117, 164, 188
Peterka, Christina, 42, 49–50, 75, 103, 108–9, 113
Phelps County, NE, 173–74
Pinal County, AZ, 21
Poe, Sophie, 3, 5, 19, 184–85, 186
Polhill, Laura, 94–95
Potts, Lydia, 128, 134, 185
Powell County, MT, 6, 9, 17, 25, 47, 55, 94, 98, 114, 116, 136, 142, 156, 185
Poweshiek County, IA, 48, 65, 77, 94, 123–24, 130, 149–51, 154, 162
Price, Marjorie, 14, 16, 88, 98
Pusser, Pauline, 7, 17, 160, 173

Ramsey, Mary, 10–11, 175–76
Randolph County, MO, 14, 16, 88, 98
Rankin, Rosa, 146
Ravalli County, MT, 69
Republic County, KS, 42, 49–50, 75, 103, 108–9, 113
Richart, Mildred, 12–13, 19, 74, 158
Ricker, Emma, 135, 176
Riddell, Essie, 44–45, 50–51, 59, 79, 98
Rihle, Sarah, 133
Robinson, Evelyn, 48–49, 104, 145
Rogers County, OK, 8, 43, 47, 169
Rogers, Josie, 182
Rosenkranz, Olive, 33, 155
Ross, Ella, 6, 28, 82, 103, 112, 116
Rumbaugh, Dorothy, 42, 138–39, 152
Russell County, KS, 8, 22, 67, 79–80, 93–94, 132, 186–87

Saguache County, CO, 33, 49, 54, 67, 104, 131, 137
San Diego County, CA, 43, 46, 62, 94
San Juan County, NM, 127
Santa Barbara County, CA, 121–22
Santa Rosa County, FL, 163–64
Sawyer County, WI, 52, 185–86
Schieferdecker, Erma, 184
Schumaker, Agnes, 80, 96, 104, 113, 117, 120, 155, 163
Schuyler County, IL, 28, 36, 38, 184
Scott, Linda, 20, 28, 68, 126, 134, 186
Seale, Bobby, 54–55
Serles, Lily, 26, 56, 89, 115, 117–18, 138
Sheets, Mrs., 109–10
Sherwood, Mrs., 146–47
Simpson, Maybel, 44, 176
Sinclair, Elma, 7, 14–15, 35, 49, 51–52, 71, 96, 105, 115, 159
Singler, Rose, 5, 9, 10, 22, 49, 101, 110, 144–45, 177–78
Sloan, Mrs., 147
Smith, Abigail, 139
Smith, Evelyn, 42
Spielman, Geraldine, 9, 71, 93
Spohn, Lenora, 157
St. Genevieve County, MO, 95
St. Mary's County, MD, 5, 35–36
Stark County, OH, 1–2, 67

Steuben County, NY, 146–47
Summit County, CO, 91
Sumter County, FL, 23–24, 182
Swanson, Betty, 16–17, 35, 60, 95, 116–17, 123, 153
Swearingen, Mary, 188

Tanner, Maud, 8, 13, 17, 24, 36–37, 45, 64, 73–74, 80, 89, 97, 105, 124, 137, 142–43, 144, 148, 164
Tarrant County TX, 84
Terrell County, TX, 50
Terrell, Martha, 42, 56, 66, 104, 109, 113, 115, 130
Texas County, MO, 9, 20–21, 22, 59
Thompson, Florence, 182
Tishomingo County, MS, 118
Tolland County, CT, 4, 10, 97–98, 102–3, 117, 130–31
Tompkins County, NY, 31
Truman, Harry S., 28, 103, 112

Union County, OR, 77–78

Van Buren County, IA, 8, 10, 25, 38, 41, 66, 71–72, 81, 105, 117, 158
Vinson, Betty, 14, 26, 32, 33, 46, 64, 75, 87, 132–33, 161
Vinson, Virginia, 103, 112, 141–42
Vinton County, OH, 179
Voorhees, Bess, 15, 16

Walworth County, WI, 87, 164–65
Ward, Irene, 8, 43, 47, 169
Washington County, KS, 33, 155
Washington County, RI, 41, 44, 139, 145
Wayne County, WV, 6, 110, 112
Weakley, Kate, 8, 22, 67, 79–80, 93–94, 131, 186–87
Weiss, Edith, 15, 25, 45, 47, 56, 73, 76, 88–89, 94, 97, 100, 107, 113, 114, 121, 127, 129, 130, 158–59
Werner, Lorna, 32–33, 57, 118, 124, 129–30
Werth, Anne, 37, 41–42, 48, 51, 54–55, 82, 88, 96, 100, 104–5, 113, 144, 157–58
Westendorf, Dode, 60, 67, 74–75, 168–69
Whelan, Florence, 118–19
White, Ella, 7, 31
White, Mrs., 153–54
White, Viola, 21–22, 33, 56, 70, 86, 98, 118, 137
Williamson County, IL, 24
Wilson County, KS, 24, 34, 56, 59, 90, 92, 118, 134, 155, 157, 169–71
Wilson County, TX, 63, 81
Windham County, VT, 48–49, 104, 145
Woodard, Mrs., 35
Wright, Mrs. Harlan, 84
Wright, Mrs. Will, 63, 84
Wright County, IA, 49, 82, 85, 86, 154
Wylie, Ella, 87, 164–65
Wynn, Mrs. JC, 127

About the Author

BJ ALDERMAN has published articles in several popular magazines, including *Chronicle of the Old West* and *American Western Magazine*.